ALSO EDITED BY WILLIAM COLE

The Best Cartoons from *Punch*
The Best Humor from *Punch*
A Big Bowl of *Punch*

THE Punch LINE

*Presenting
Today's Top Twenty-five Cartoon Artists
from England's Famous
Humo(u)r Magazine*

EDITED BY WILLIAM COLE

Simon and Schuster
New York

All rights reserved
including the right of reproduction
in whole or in part in any form
Copyright © 1964, 1965, 1966, 1967, 1968 by *Punch* magazine
Copyright © 1969 by William Cole
Published by Simon and Schuster
Rockefeller Center, 630 Fifth Avenue
New York, New York 10020

FIRST PRINTING

SBN 671-20373-8
Library of Congress Catalog Card Number: 75-92186
Manufactured in the United States of America

CONTENTS

Introduction 7

The Artists in Line

Bill Tidy 9
Handelsman 17
Ed Fisher 26
Thelwell 32
Don Roberts 38
ffolkes 41
Atchison 50
Larry 54
J. W. Taylor 65
Hargreaves 68
Eric Burgin 72
Graham 75
Edward McLachlan 80
Starke 87
Hitchins 92
Arnold Wiles 97

Hector Breeze 102
McKee 104
Mahood 106
Raymonde 108
W. Scully 110
Heath 113
Smilby 118
Anton 121
S. McMurtry 123

INTRODUCTION

The main difference between America's humor and England's humour is that they overspell it. As was once wisely remarked, fun's fun. Contrary to popular belief, there is nothing obscure about English humor. Many English cartoons, of course, refer to things that an American won't always twig: cricket, Guy Fawkes Day, the Common Market and transitory political aberrations; but except for that, most of the cartoons in this collection could just as easily have appeared in *The New Yorker* as in *Punch*. Except—and this is really a surprise—many of them are too sexy for *The New Yorker*! The two magazines even share many of the same cartoonists; the English artists study the physical details of American life, and are thus enabled to sell to such relatively high-paying markets as *The New Yorker* and *Playboy*. "It's easy to make people look American," says the English cartoonist Smilby; "you draw them fat."

The two outstanding contemporary *Punch* cartoonists are Bill Tidy and Bernard Handelsman. For the past six or seven years each has been appearing in the magazine with accelerating frequency. Neither is particularly an innovator, but each is fecund and funny. Tidy is self-taught, and his drawing is deceptively corny. There is a great deal of artfulness in his use of black solids, and his dumpy figures have surprising grace. Obviously, like two other fine contemporary cartoonists, André François and Tomi Ungerer, he knows anatomy cold. His Lily Marlene cartoon—the first in the book—is certainly a classic, and I don't think you have to know that London has ex-servicemen's street bands to appreciate its humor. Handelsman is an American who has chosen to live in England. His drawing is more—what is that terrible word?—elegant; more sophisticated; and it is a pleasure to contemplate.

But it is unfair to single out two cartoonists from these gifted twenty-five. One could go on about what a superb idea man the other American, Ed Fisher, is; or discuss that fine stylist, McLachlan, or say how lovable Larry is, or talk about how the New School of cartooning is represented by McKee and Heath. But I hope that my method of presentation—giving each cartoonist his own portfolio—will point out such things to the reader, and show him where the individuality of each artist, in line and laughter, lies.

WILLIAM COLE

BILL TIDY

Bill Tidy was born in Tranmere, Cheshire, in 1933. He lives with his Italian wife and two children near Liverpool. Self-taught, he has been a free-lance artist since 1958. His cartoons appear frequently in *Private Eye* and, in the United States, in *Cavalier*.

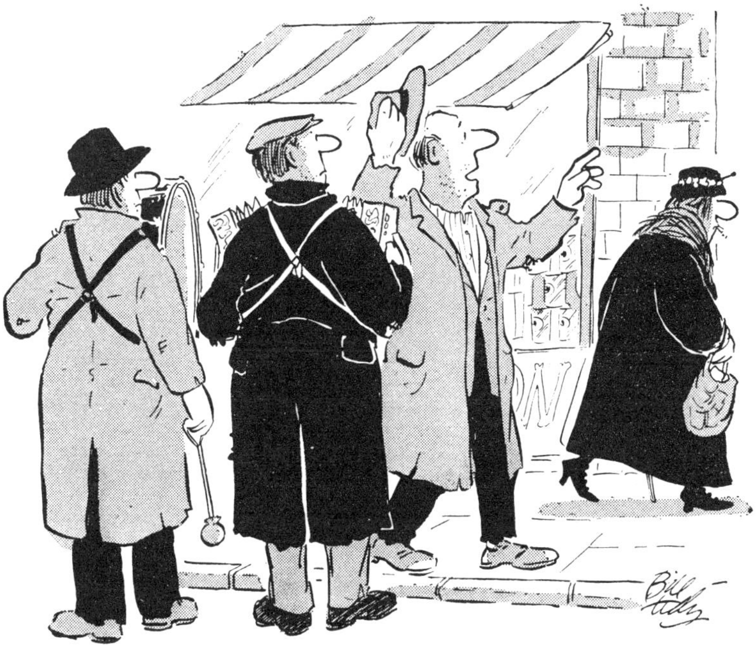

"Lily! Lily Marlene!"

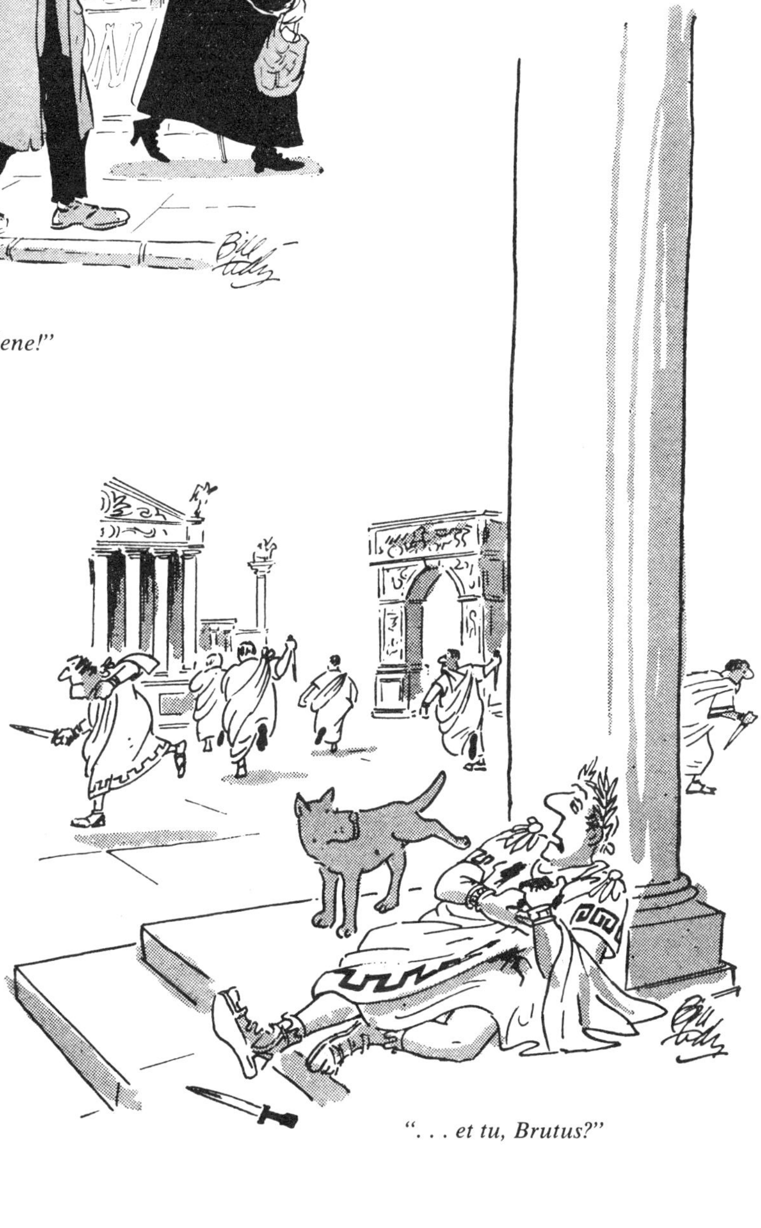

". . . et tu, Brutus?"

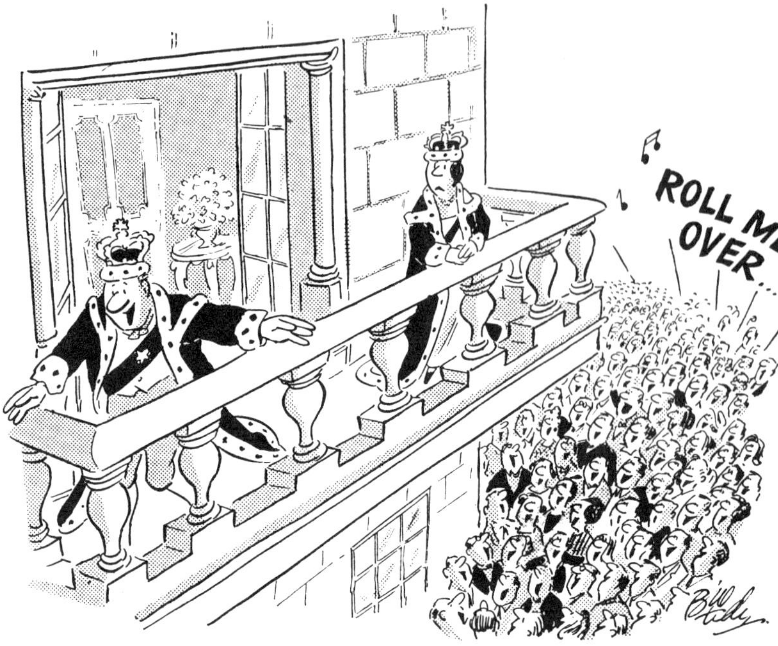
ROLL ME OVER...

". . . and everyone on my right, sing the National Anthem."

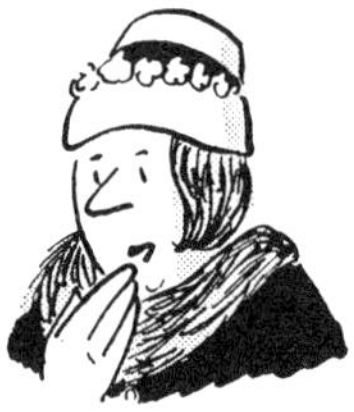

*"It's so difficult!
They all look so
shining white!"*

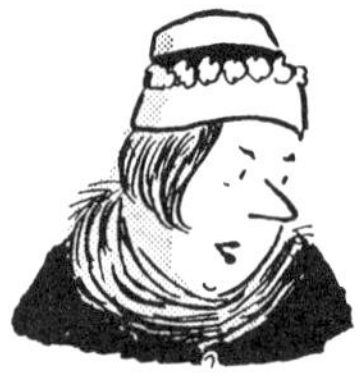

*"No! This sheet here!
There's a definite whiteness
bonus . . .*

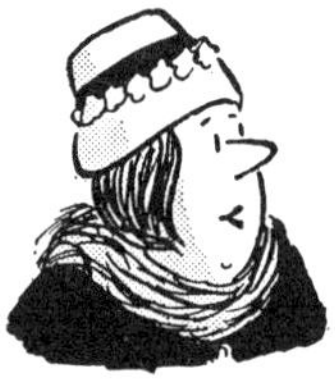

*. . . I'd say that this
is the one washed
in Super Tide."*

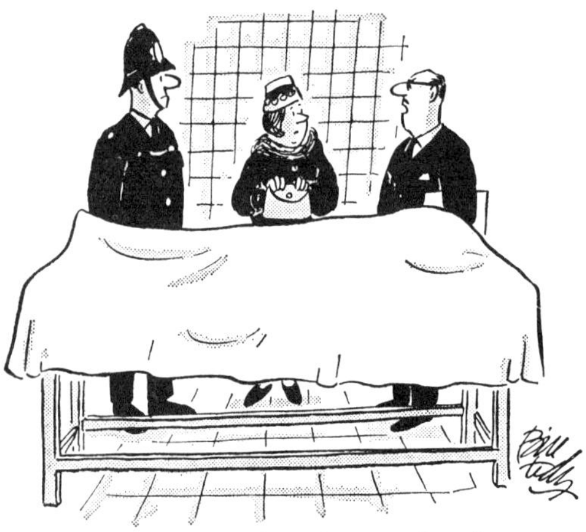

*"You may be right, Mrs. Beesley, but
that's not what you're here for."*

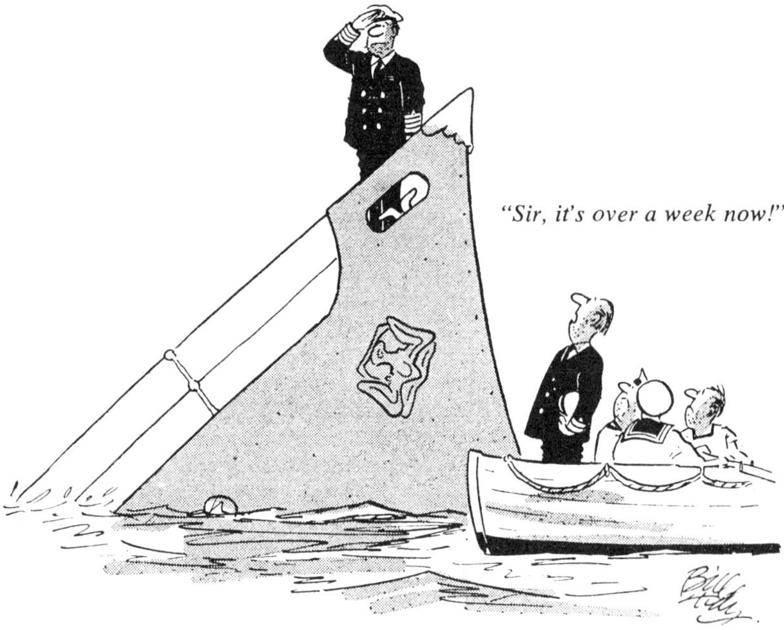

"Sir, it's over a week now!"

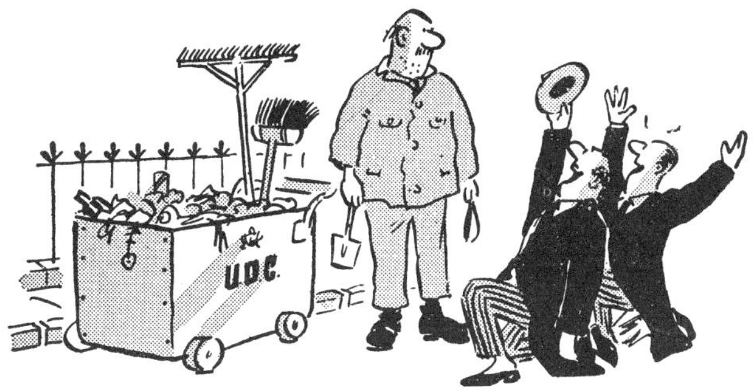
U.D.C.

*"The Monarchy has been restored, Sire.
God save the King!"*

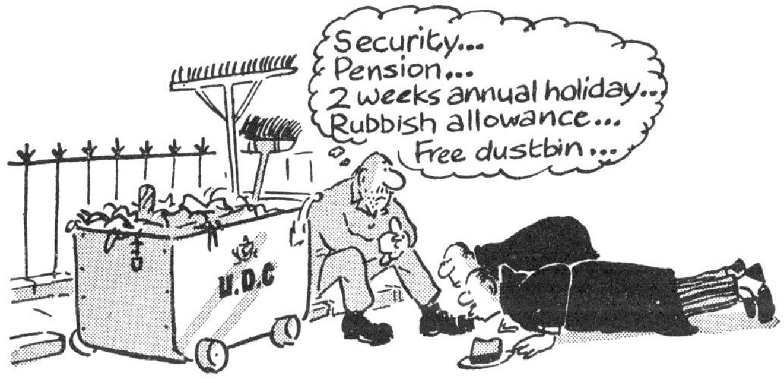
Security...
Pension...
2 weeks annual holiday...
Rubbish allowance...
Free dustbin...
U.D.C

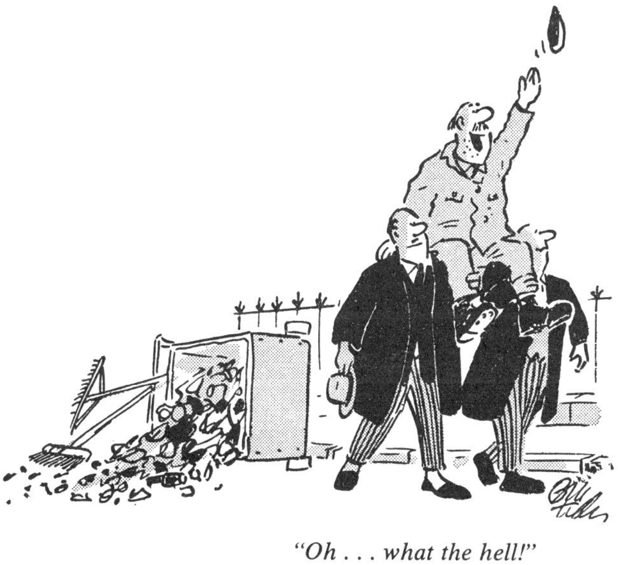

"Oh . . . what the hell!"

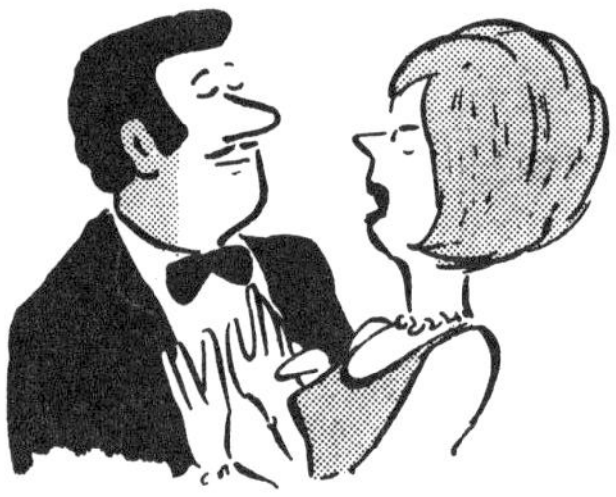

"I've heard all about your little black book . . .

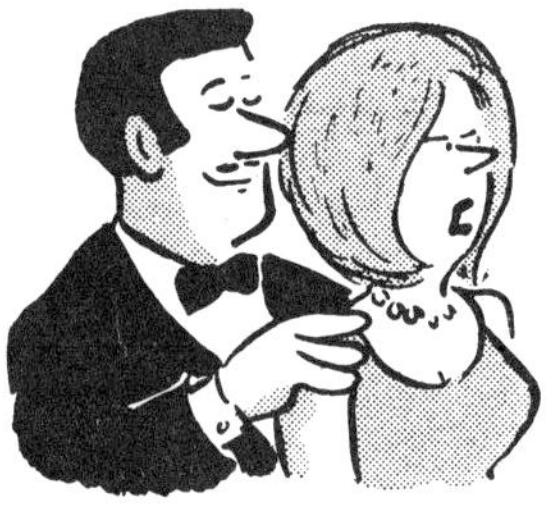

Intimate details of all the girls you've . . . you've . . .

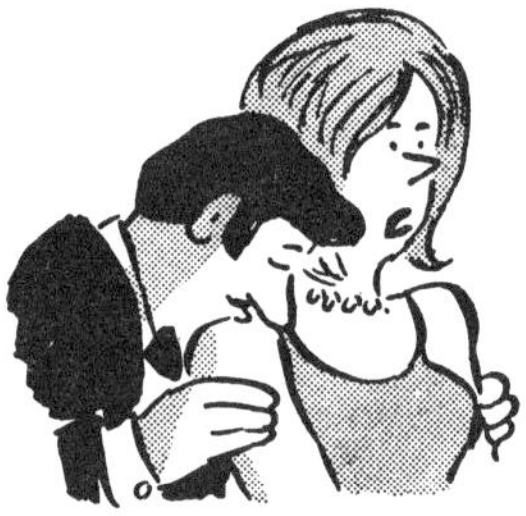

You're not getting me in there . . ."

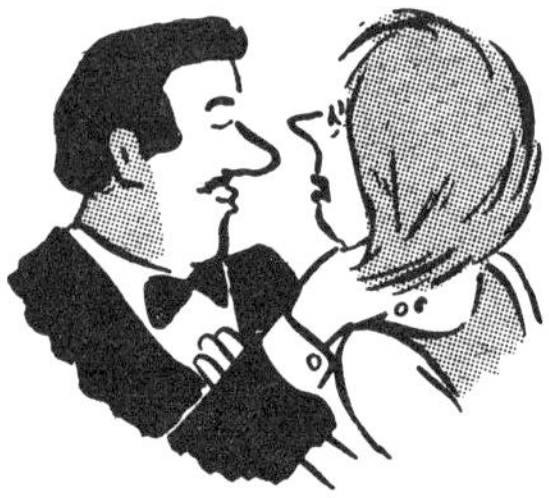

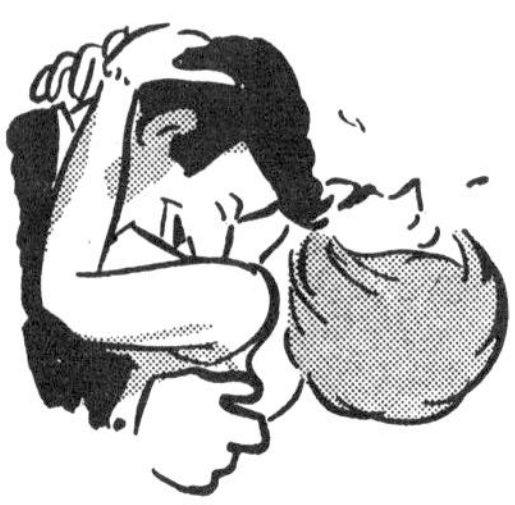

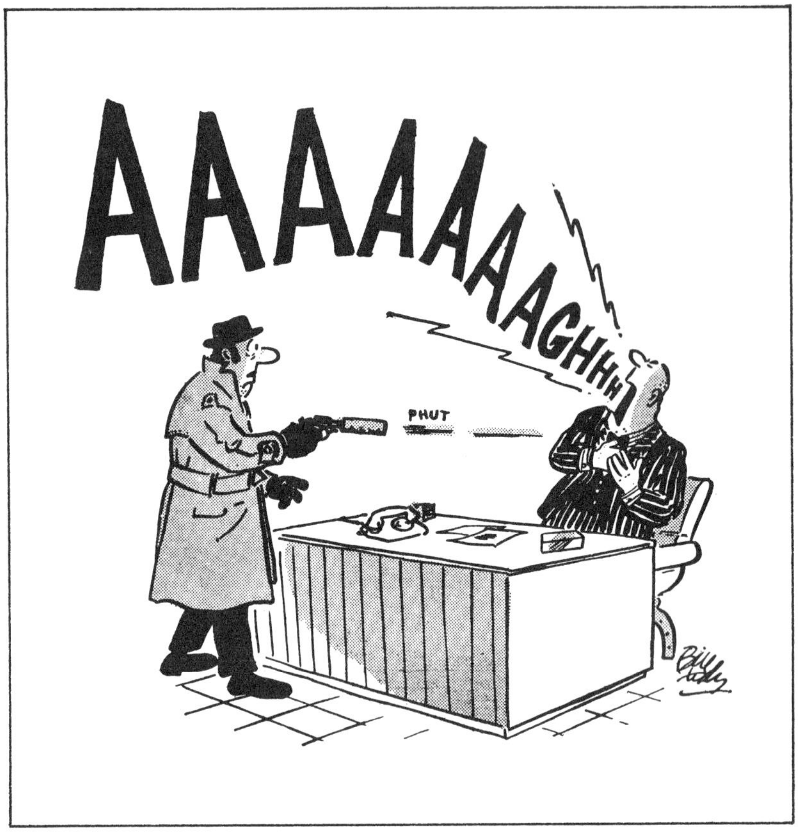
AAAAAAAGHHH
PHUT

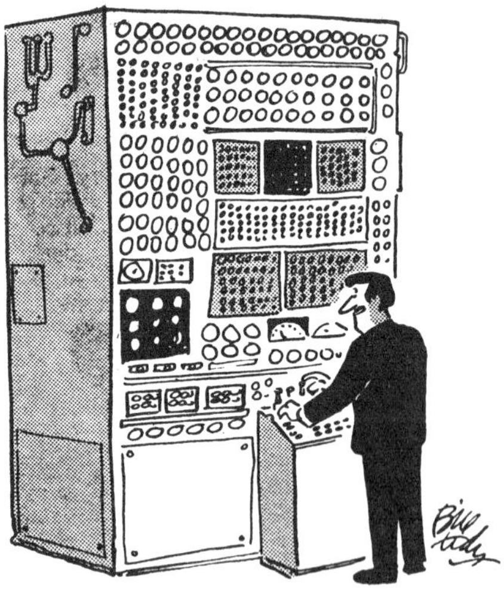

"Laura Wyngarde . . . red hair . . . twenty-five . . ."

"... highly organised ring ... we need one more flywheel and we'll have a complete wristwatch."

"... and over here, we have the ruined Abbot of Lindisfarne."

"Gentlemen . . . isolated units of the enemy have broken through."

"Your eighteenth Command Performance!"

"Fetch the stage manager— he's passed out."

"My God, he's really loaded this time. Get gallons of black coffee . . . he's got to be ready for curtain-up."

"Bomb scare, sir . . . we had to evacuate the building."

"He's coming round . . . drink this . . ."

"Where the hell have you been?"

"We stand here craning our necks for hours— and what for?

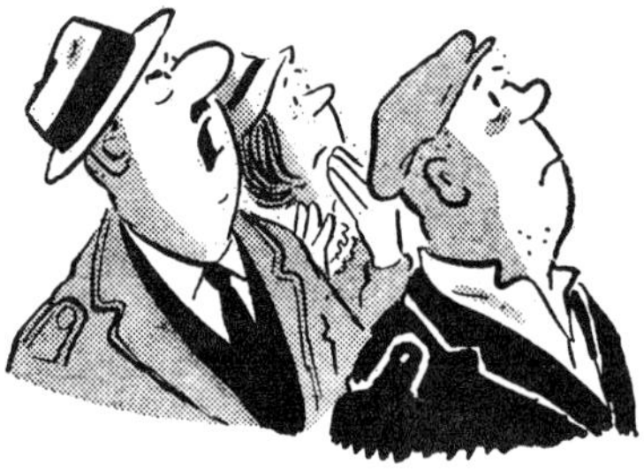

He's not going to jump . . . they never do!

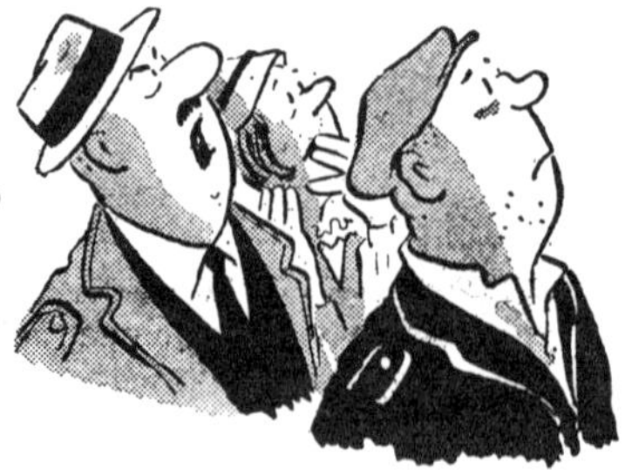

What did I tell you!

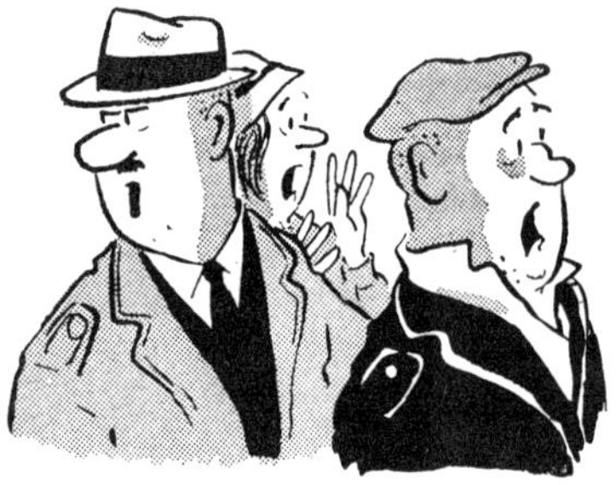

Let me through— I'm a doctor!"

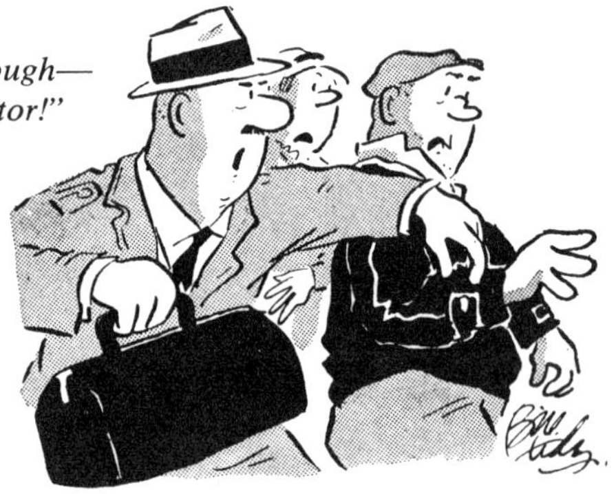

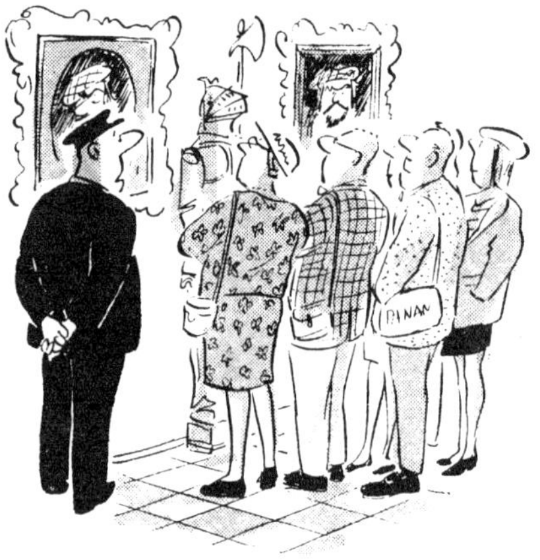

"Portraits of the ill-fated McDoon family, and if we're lucky, we might catch the laird himself walking in the gardens."

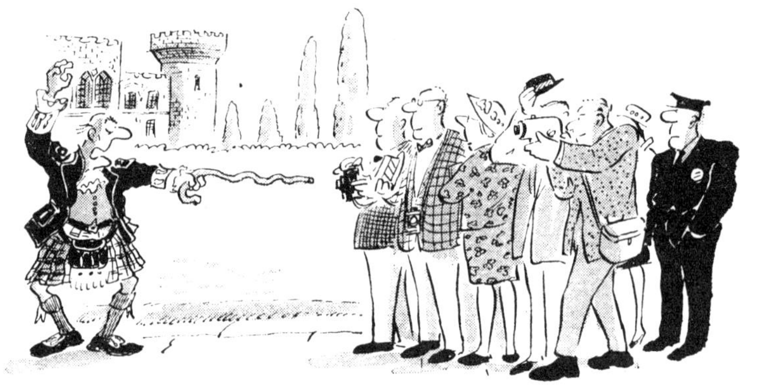

"The curse of the last of the McDoons be on ye!"

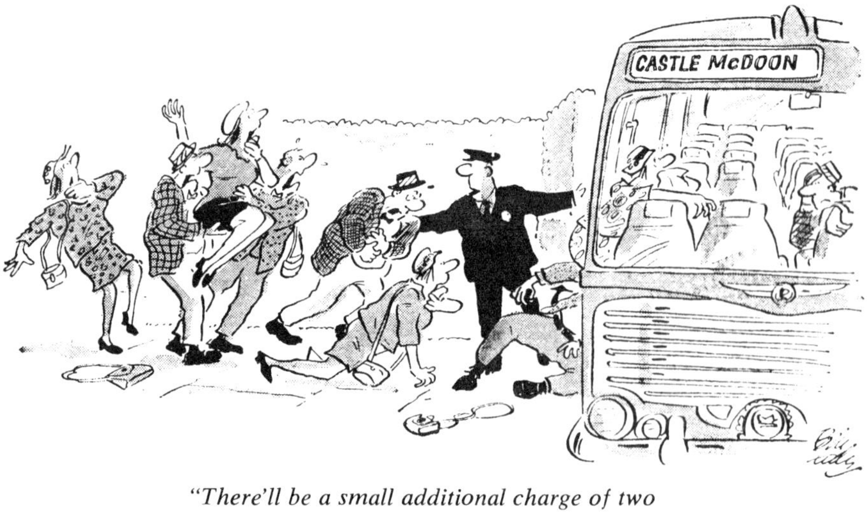
CASTLE McDOON

"There'll be a small additional charge of two shillings and sixpence."

HANDELSMAN

Bernard Handelsman was born in New York City in 1922. He studied engineering at New York University and art at the Art Students League and worked as a commercial artist and typographical designer. He moved to England with his wife and three children in 1963. His cartoons appear frequently in *The New Yorker, Playboy* and many other magazines.

"And how are we today?"

"You've certainly held this marriage together, haven't you, boy?"

"Doctor! I think we're dead!"

18 HANDELSMAN

"What's a transvestite, mom?"

"Catherine, don't talk with your mouth full. Robert, get your elbows off the table. Edwin, stop selling yourself."

"Pray don't be alarmed. We've had a little coup back home, and I'm the new Ambassador."

Transatlantic

Americans take a look at their Britain.

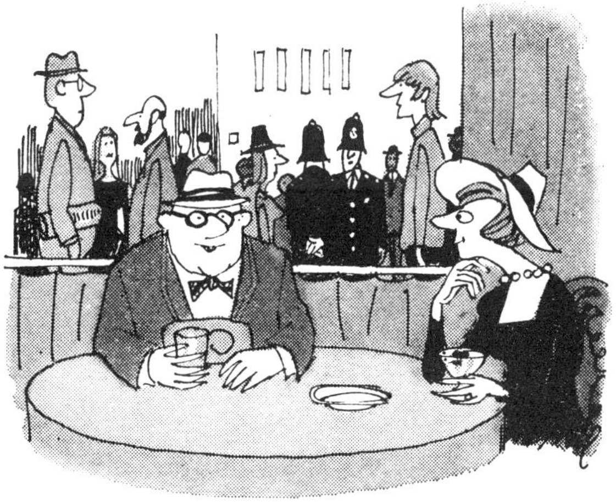

"And if it turns out that I am Lord Greystoke, it figures that you'll be Lady Greystoke."

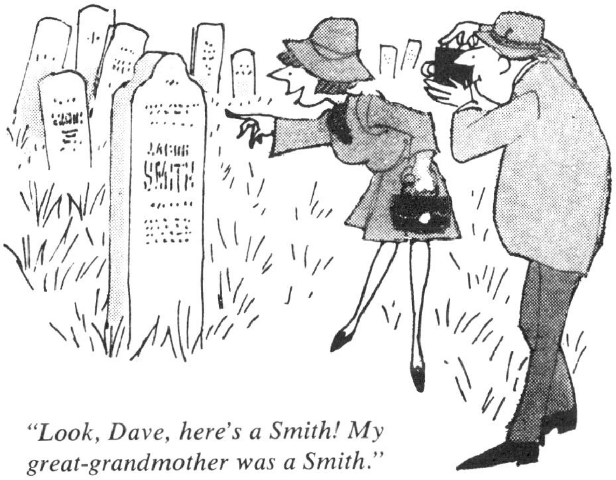
SMITH

"Look, Dave, here's a Smith! My great-grandmother was a Smith."

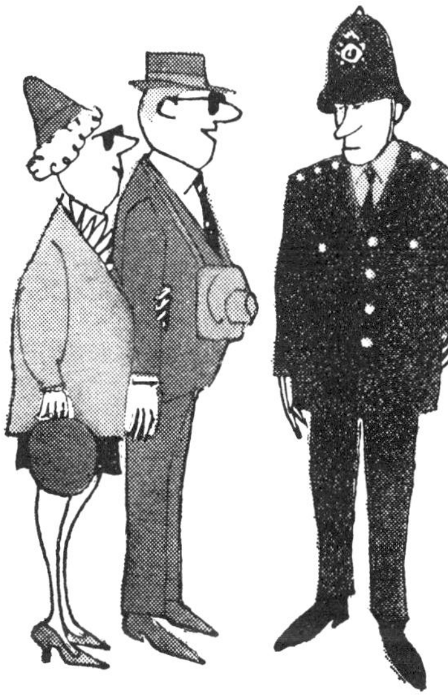

"Is there a bureau where people can find out whether they might be the Duke and Duchess of Northumberland?"

"If there ever were any MacHandelsmans—which seems doubtful—some other clan must have disposed of them rather quickly."

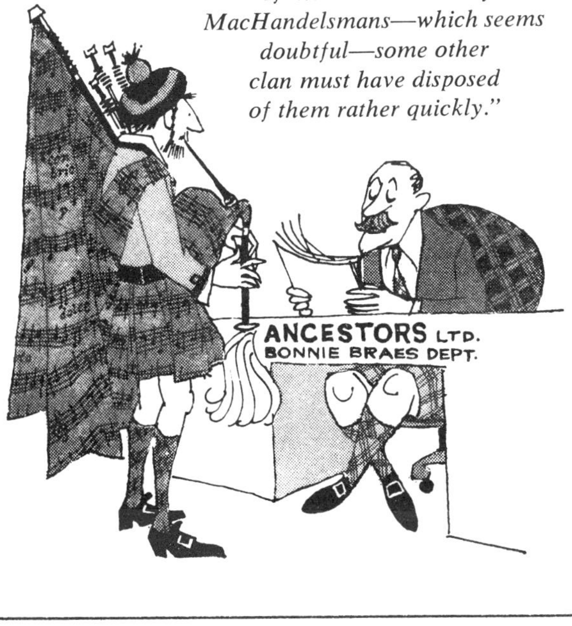
ANCESTORS LTD.
BONNIE BRAES DEPT.

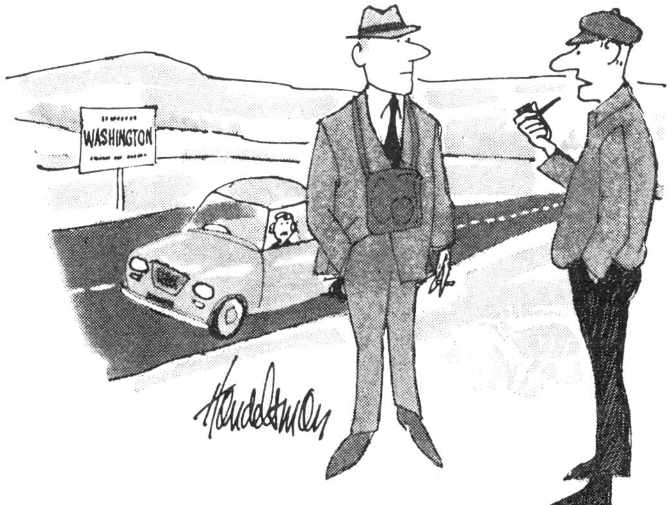
WASHINGTON
Handelsman

"There might have been a Washington family here once, but they're all gone now. Don't know where they went."

"Now, woodwinds!"

"First of all, we'll discontinue the pills."

"Good God! It's gone Commie!"

"Do the Mad Scene from 'Lucia.'"

"And believe me, baby, when you can make a publisher blush you've got something."

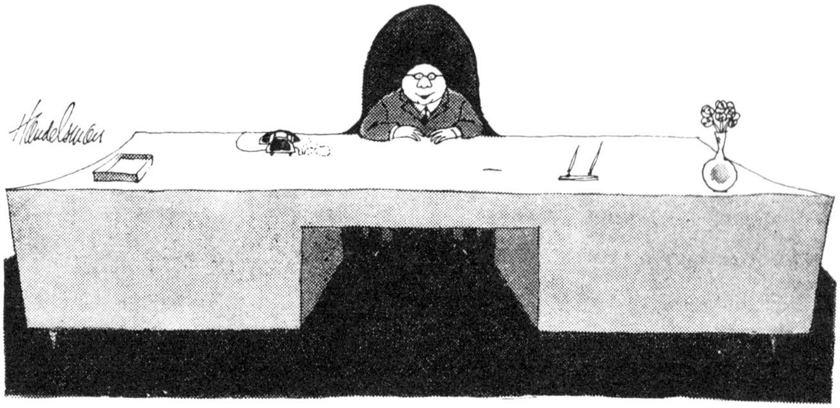
Handelsman

"Power! It corrupts! I can feel it!"

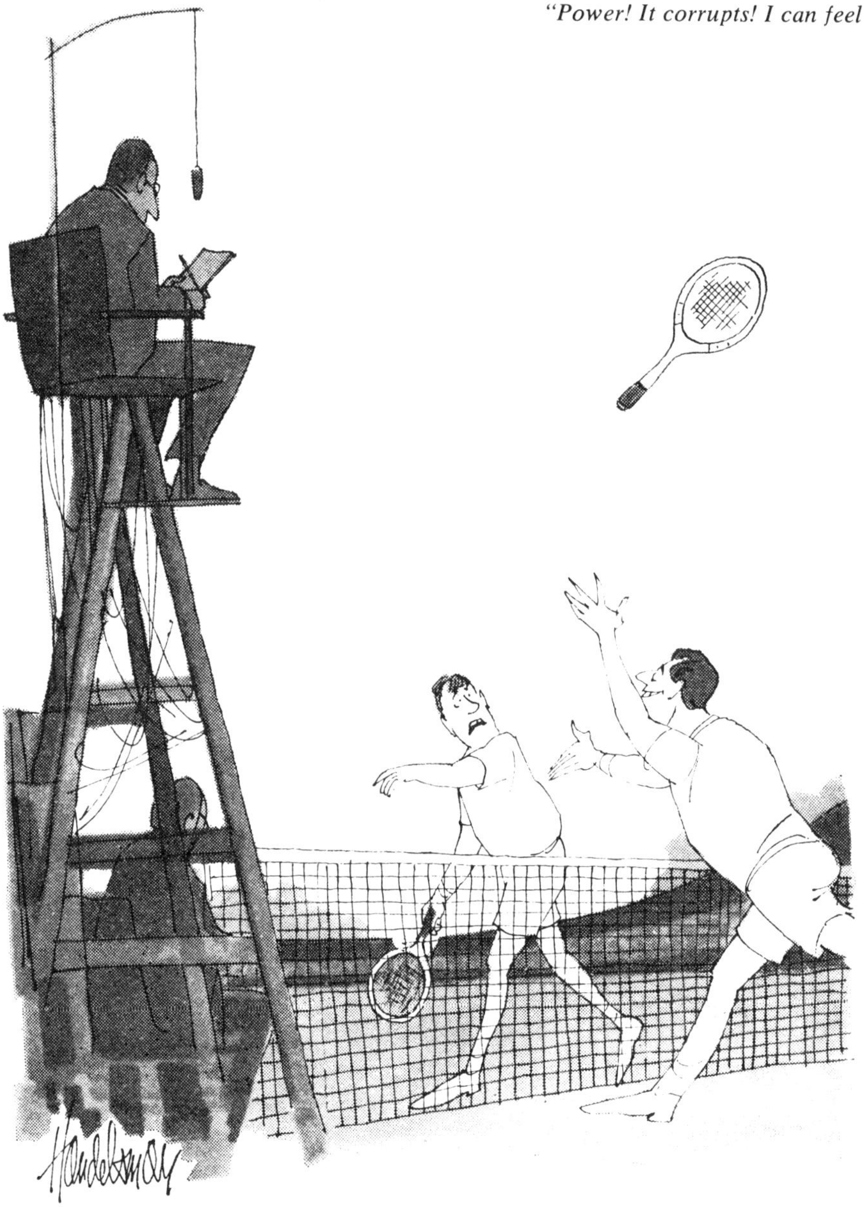
Handelsman

"Please! The International Lawn Tennis Federation hasn't ruled on amateurs shaking hands with professionals."

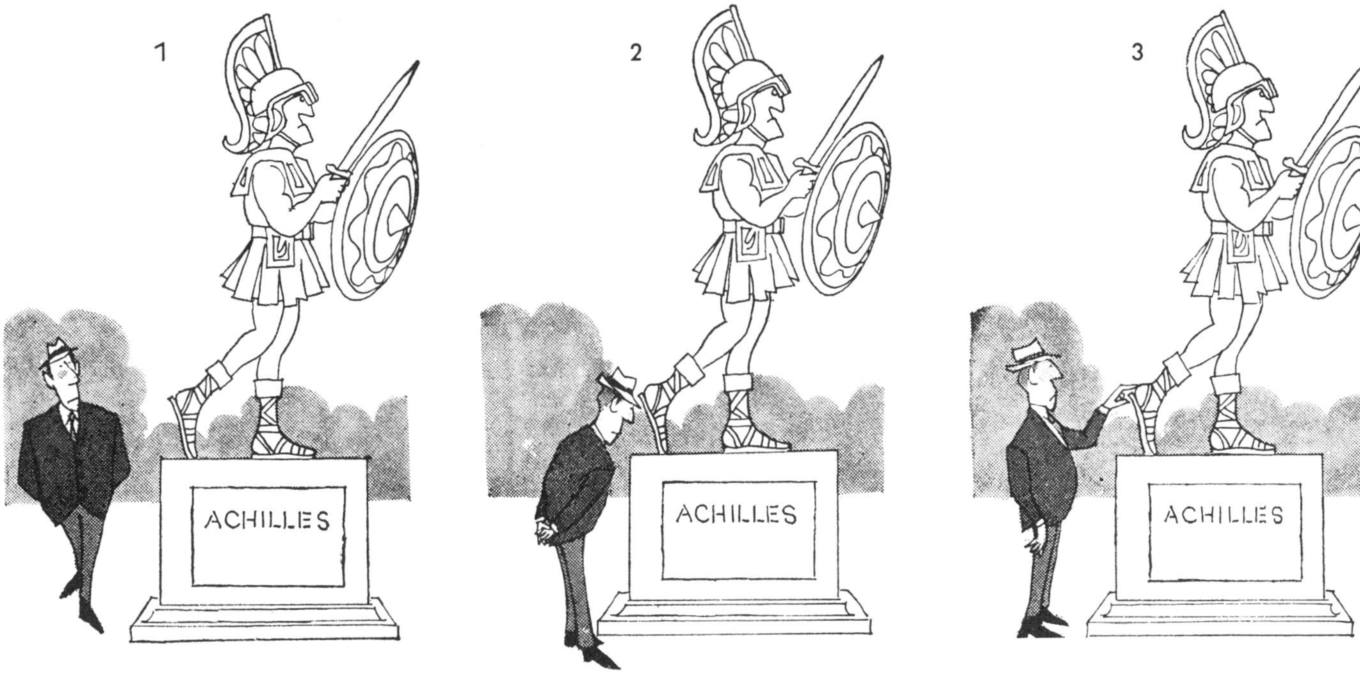
1
ACHILLES
2
ACHILLES
3
ACHILLES

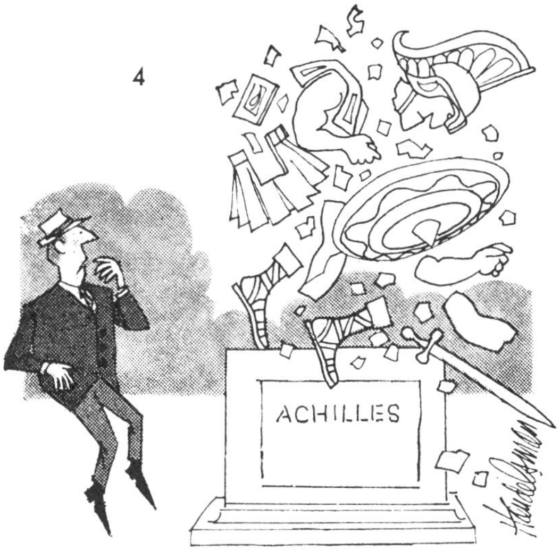
4
ACHILLES

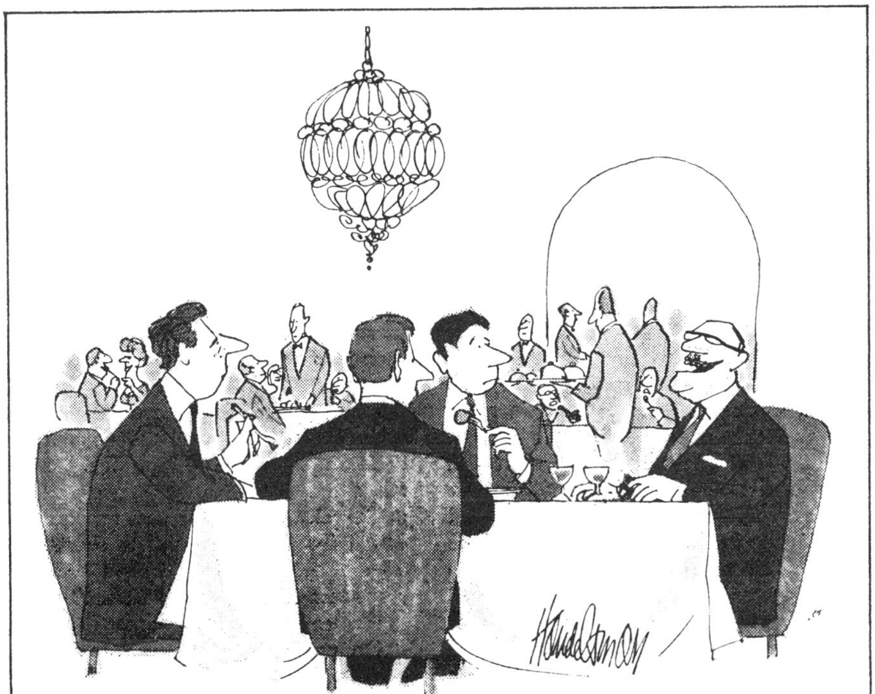

"You talk about boredom! Young fellows nowadays don't know what boredom is. I've had some incredibly boring experiences. Back in the summer of 1923 . . ."

Atlantic Alliance

An American couple is invited to meet the English at home.

"I'd like you to meet an American couple, but they're very nice."

"I can never remember whether Americans are offended at being taken for Canadians, or the other way round."

"Of course, by the time you fellows came along, we already had the Jerries on the run."

"You're in favour of Vietnam? But most of us are against it!"

"Yes. A marvellous sort of innocence. A marvellous sort of childlike enthusiasm."

"You ought to visit the Norfolk Broads."

"As I see it, there are two options open to you British. You could be Sweden. Now, if I were in your shoes, I'd be Athens."

"I'd like to punch one of them on the nose. Any one of them."

ED FISHER

Ed Fisher is an American cartoonist, living in New York City. He has had one novel published and is currently working on a second.

"*Dad, can I join the Jehovah's Witnesses?*"

"*We're crashing!*"

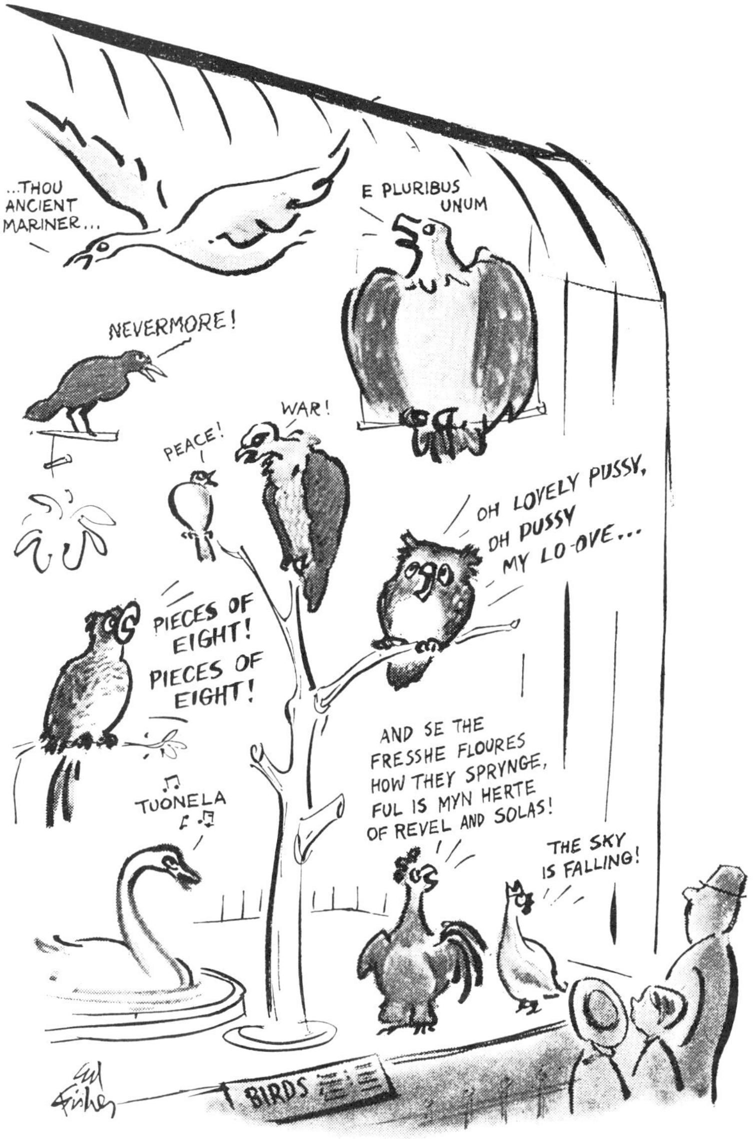
...THOU
ANCIENT
MARINER...
E PLURIBUS
UNUM
NEVERMORE!
WAR!
PEACE!
OH LOVELY PUSSY,
OH PUSSY
MY LO-OVE...
PIECES OF
EIGHT!
PIECES OF
EIGHT!
AND SE THE
FRESSHE FLOURES
HOW THEY SPRYNGE,
FUL IS MYN HERTE
OF REVEL AND SOLAS!
TUONELA
THE SKY
IS FALLING!
BIRDS

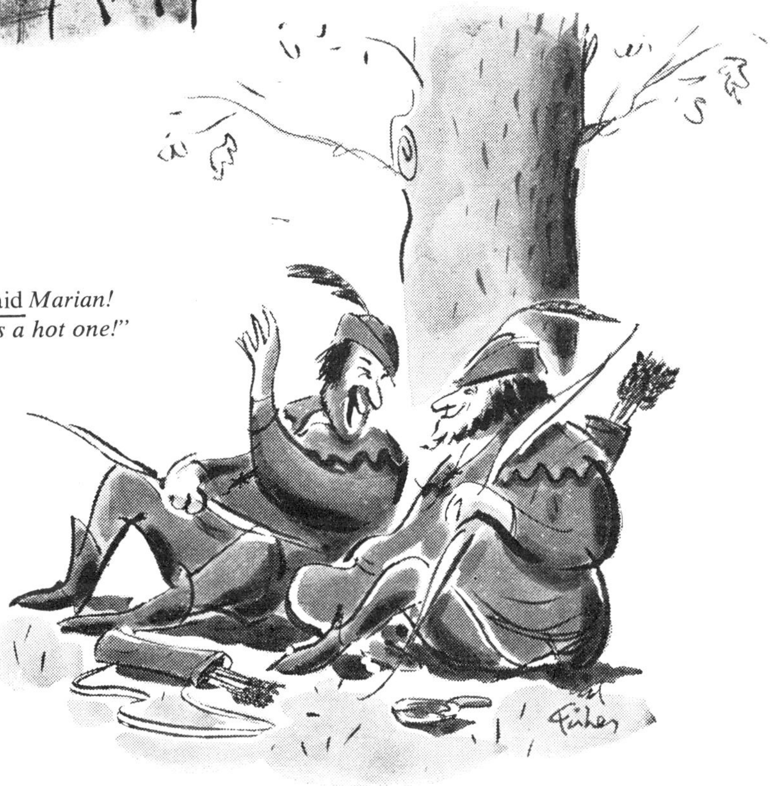

"Maid *Marian!*
That's a hot one!"

28 ED FISHER

1

"... Yes, I'm fine; instruments working perfectly; the Earth looks like a big green ball from up here..."

2

"... starting my descent. Retrorockets fired. Everything A-OK..."

3

"...'Chute open; approaching water; waves look a bit big, but everything normal descentwise..."

4

"... Waiting to be picked up. Launch from carrier approaching..."

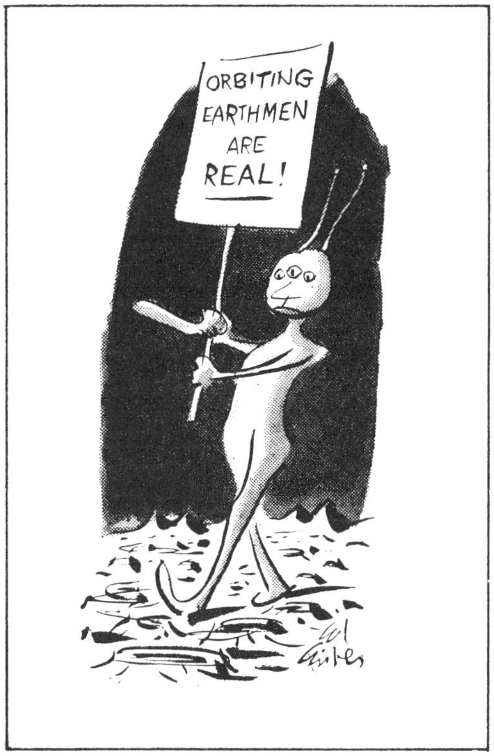
ORBITING
EARTHMEN
ARE
REAL!

5

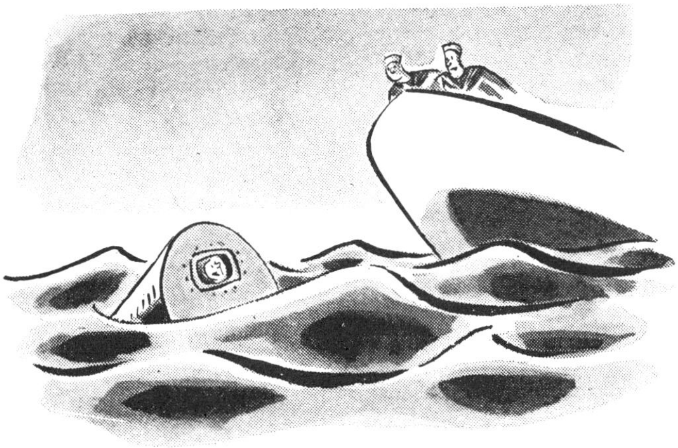

"Looks like a routine, text-book flight . . ."

6

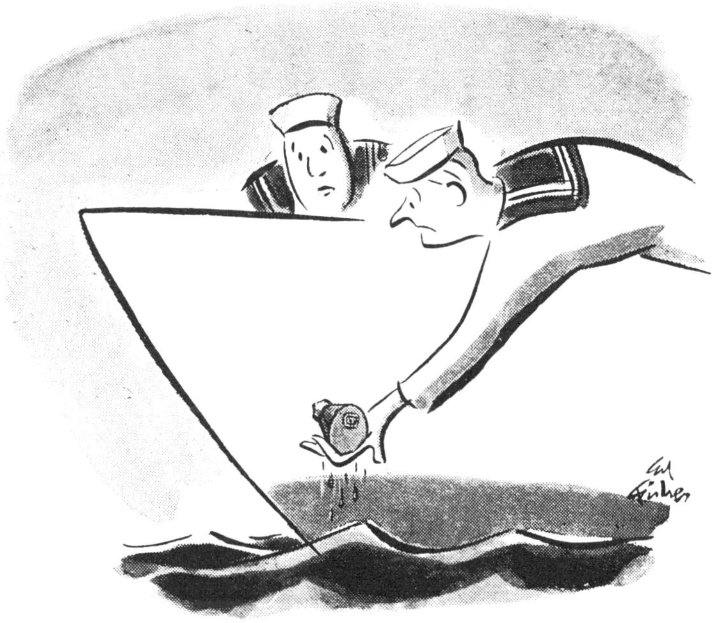

". . . am being picked up now . . ."

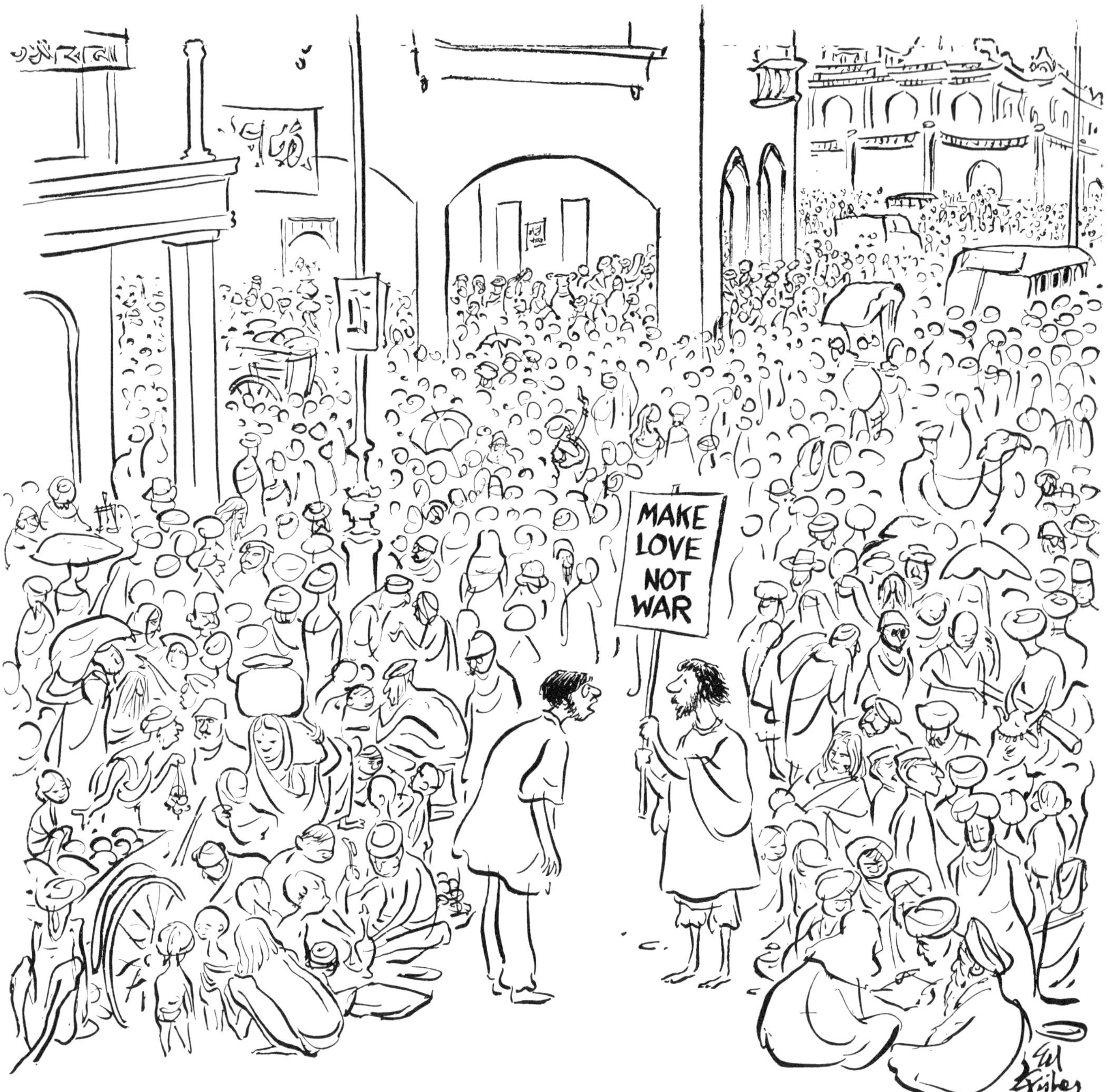
MAKE
LOVE
NOT
WAR

"Are you kidding?"

"All right, prude—you *name* them!"

THELWELL

Norman Thelwell was born in Birkenhead in 1923. He was educated at Liverpool College of Art, then taught art for seven years. He lives with his wife and two children in Braishfield, Hampshire. His two books of cartoons about ponies and horses have been very successful in the United States. There is also a *Penguin Thelwell.*

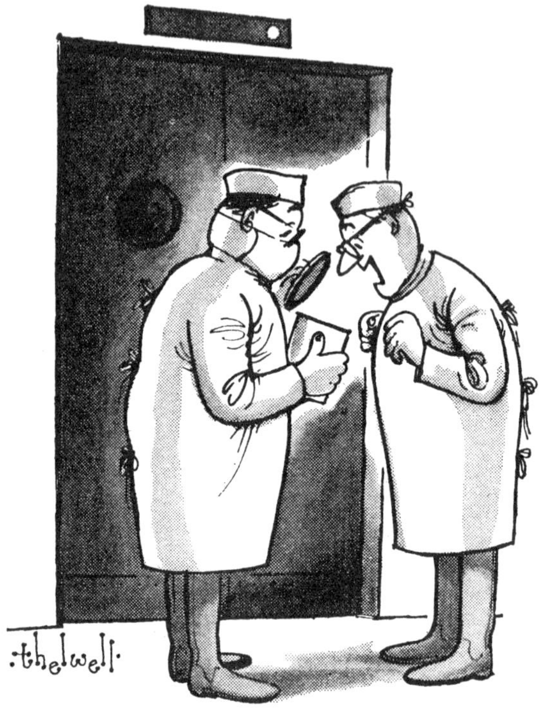
thelwell

"I'll swop you two kidneys for it."

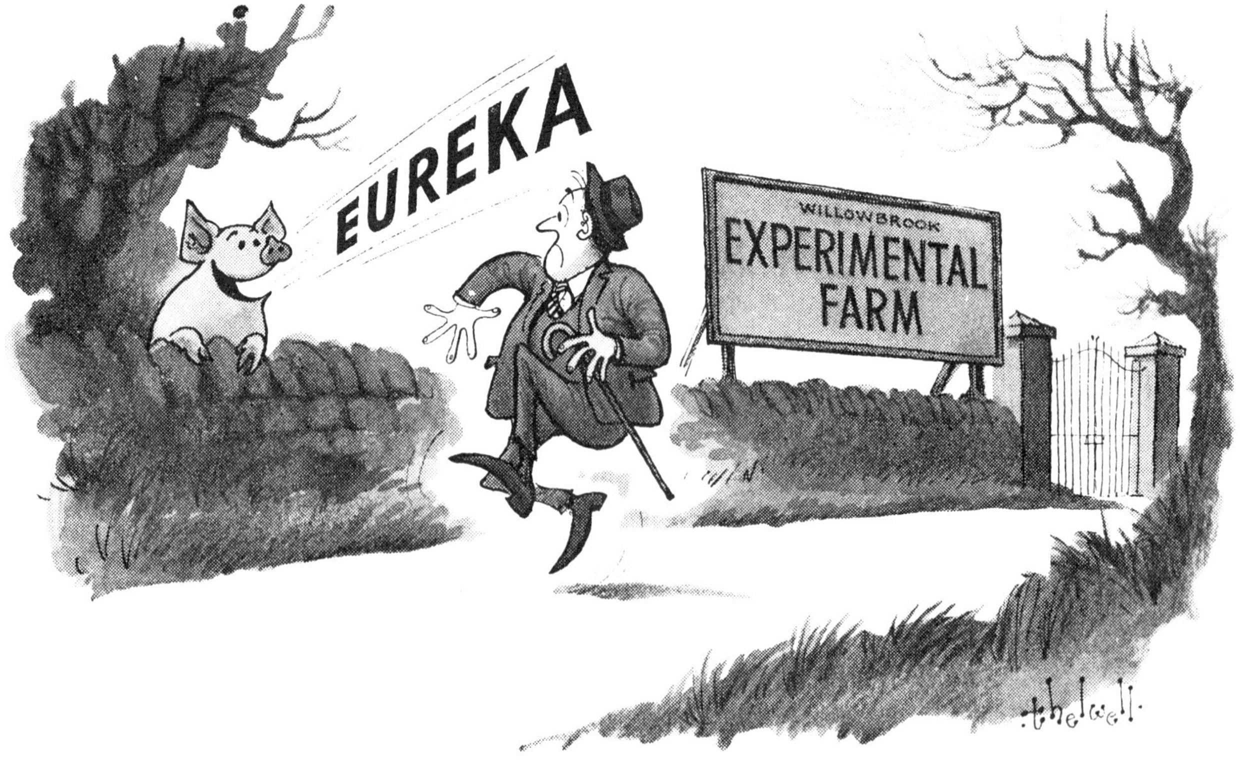
EUREKA
WILLOWBROOK
EXPERIMENTAL FARM
thelwell

"The lock's rusted up."

Weekend Cottage

"You brought them. You take them back."

"I think we've been accepted by the locals."

Drinks by the Pool

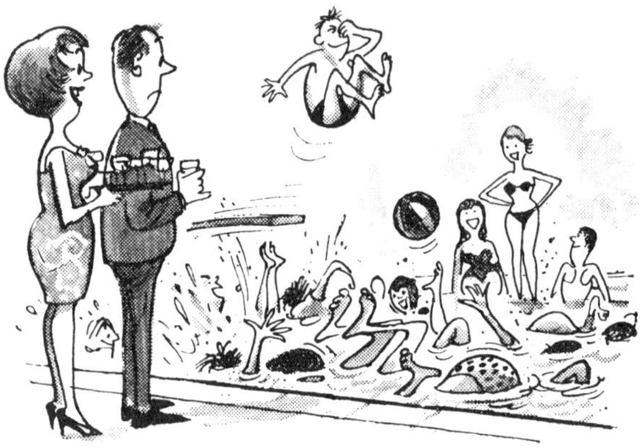

"Is there anyone you don't know?"

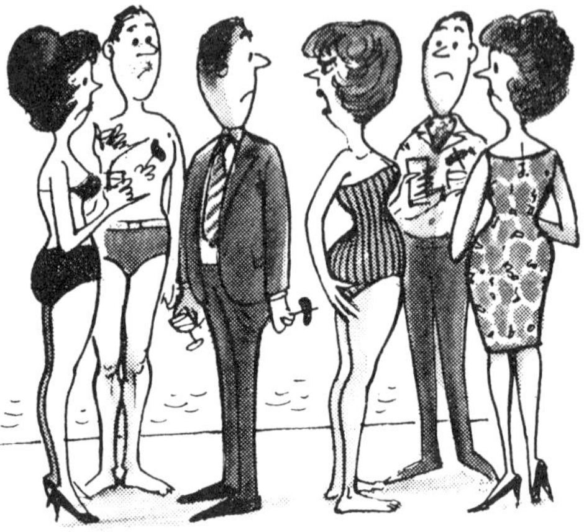

"Careful! Those little sticks are sharp."

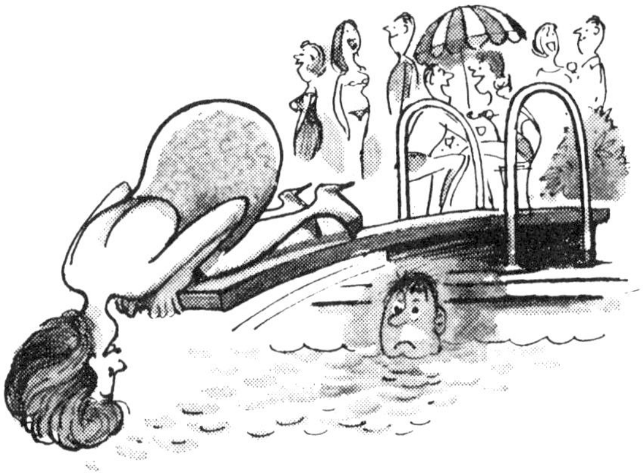

"You're not circulating, Mr. Wilkins."

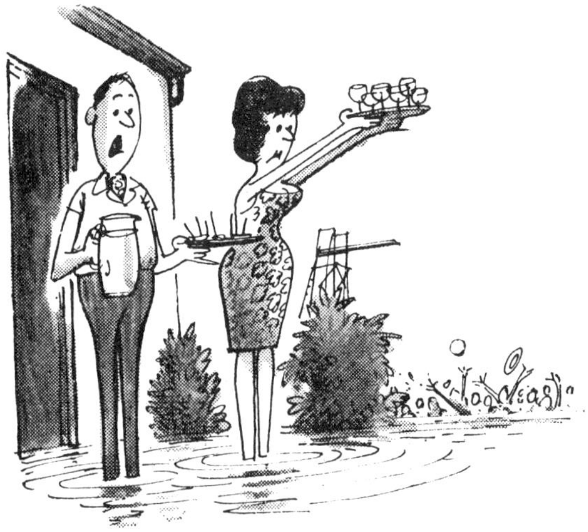

"I didn't think they'd all want to go in."

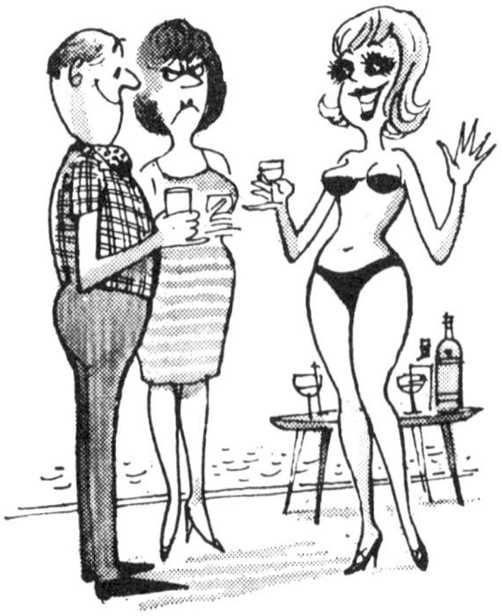

"What! This old thing?"

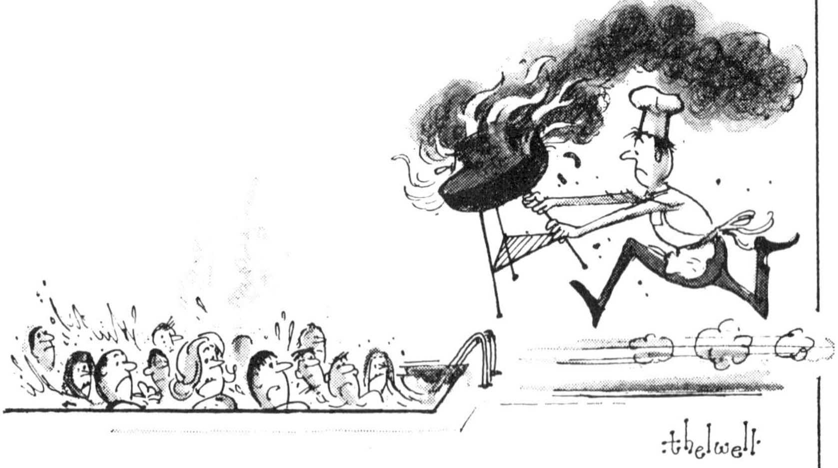
thelwell

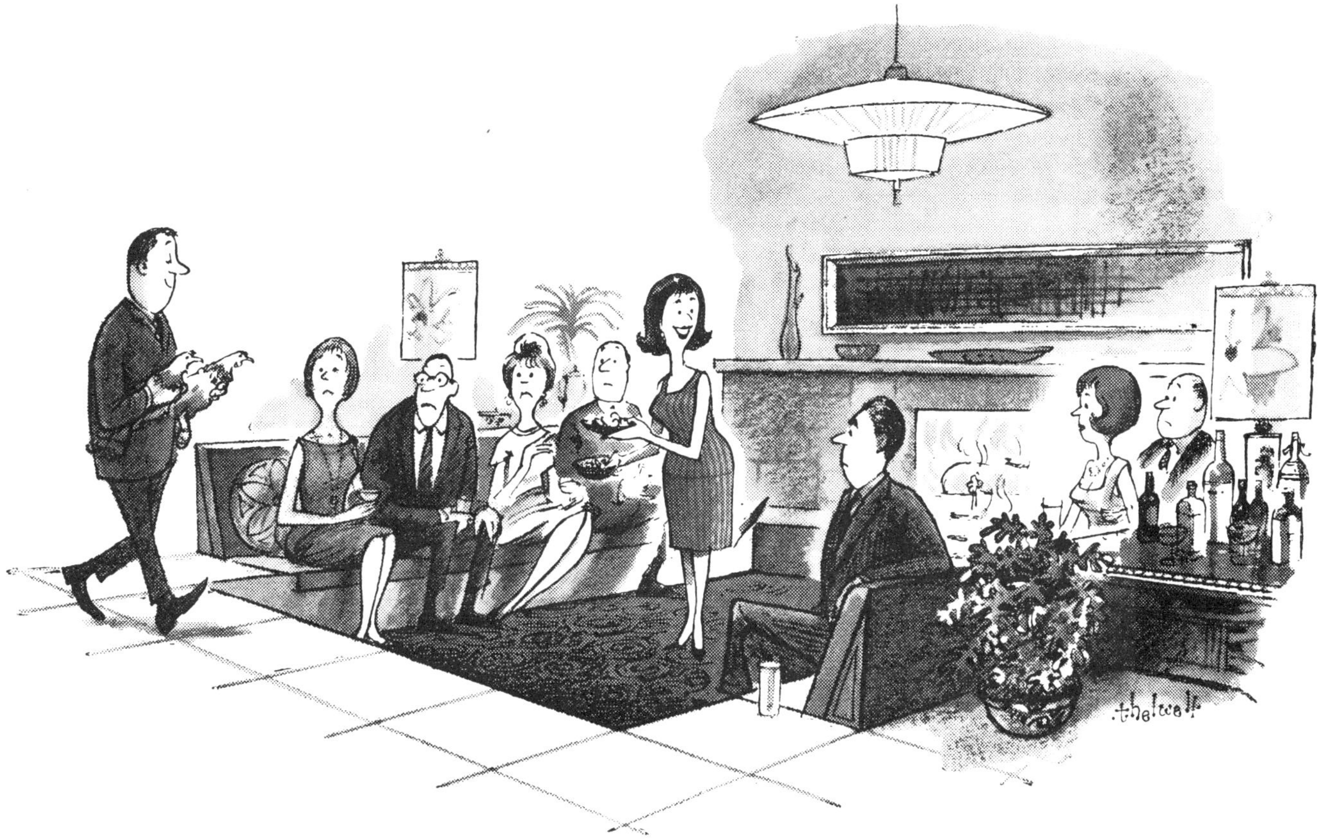
thelwell

"George has planned a little surprise for you."

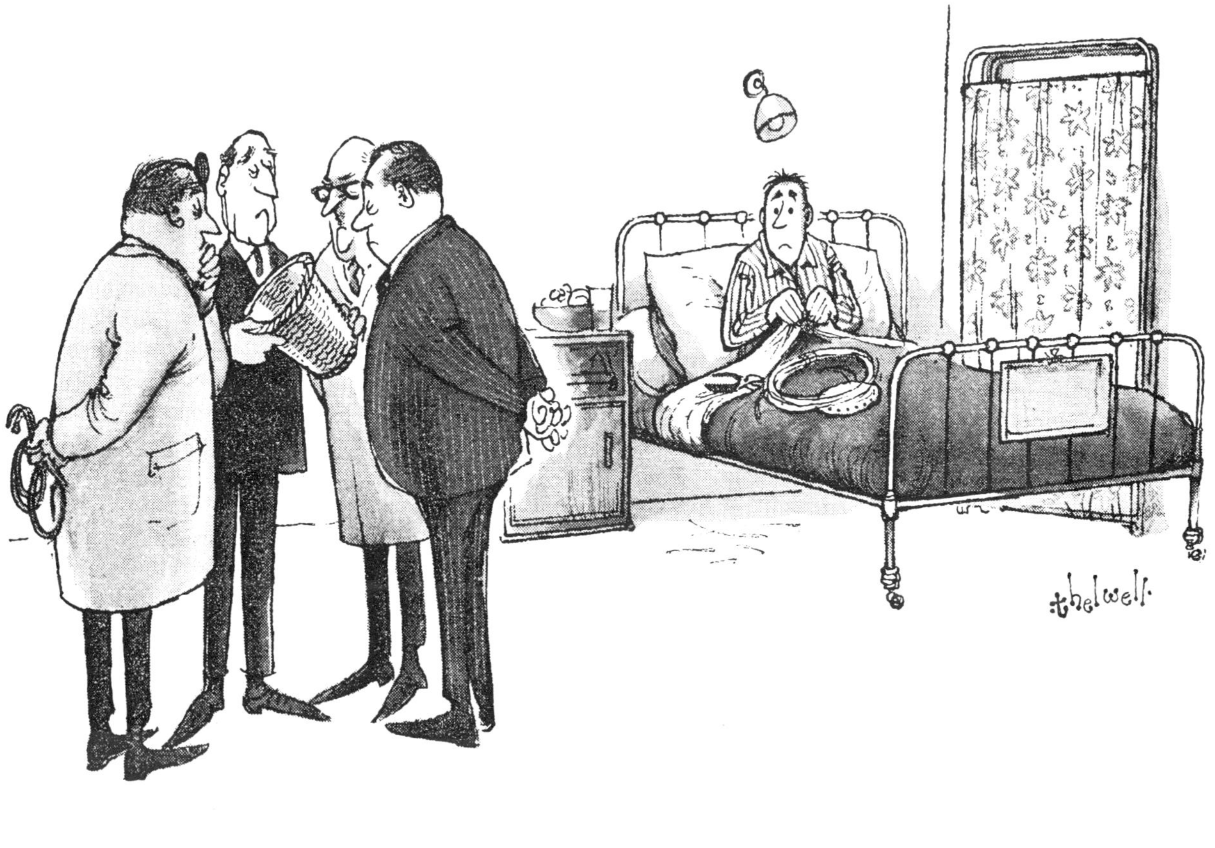
thelwell

LUXURY FLATS
UNITEX
BUILDINGS
LTD
thelwell

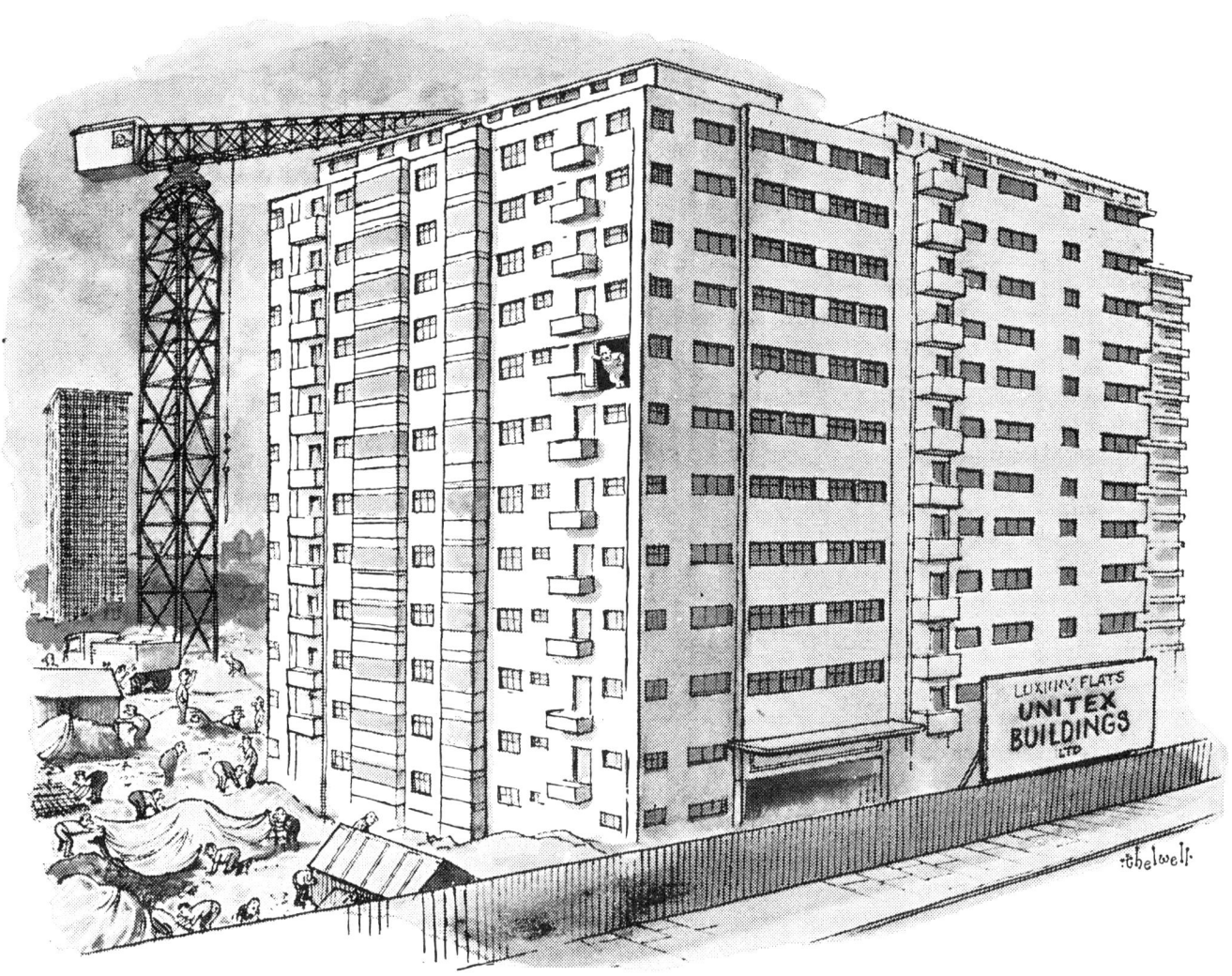

"It's an oblong piece, with a window and a bit of balcony."

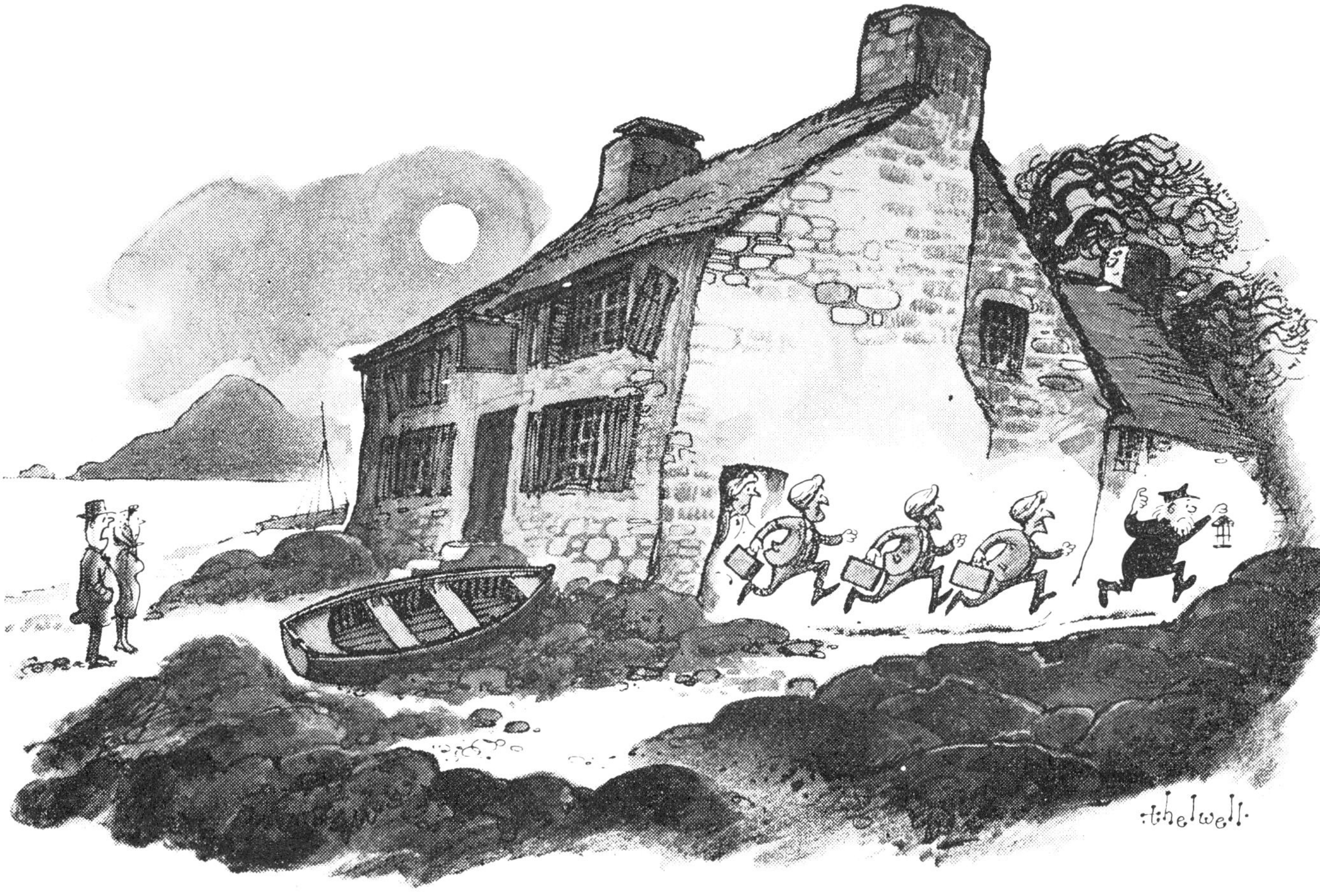
thelwell

"The story goes that the place was once used by smuggl . . ."

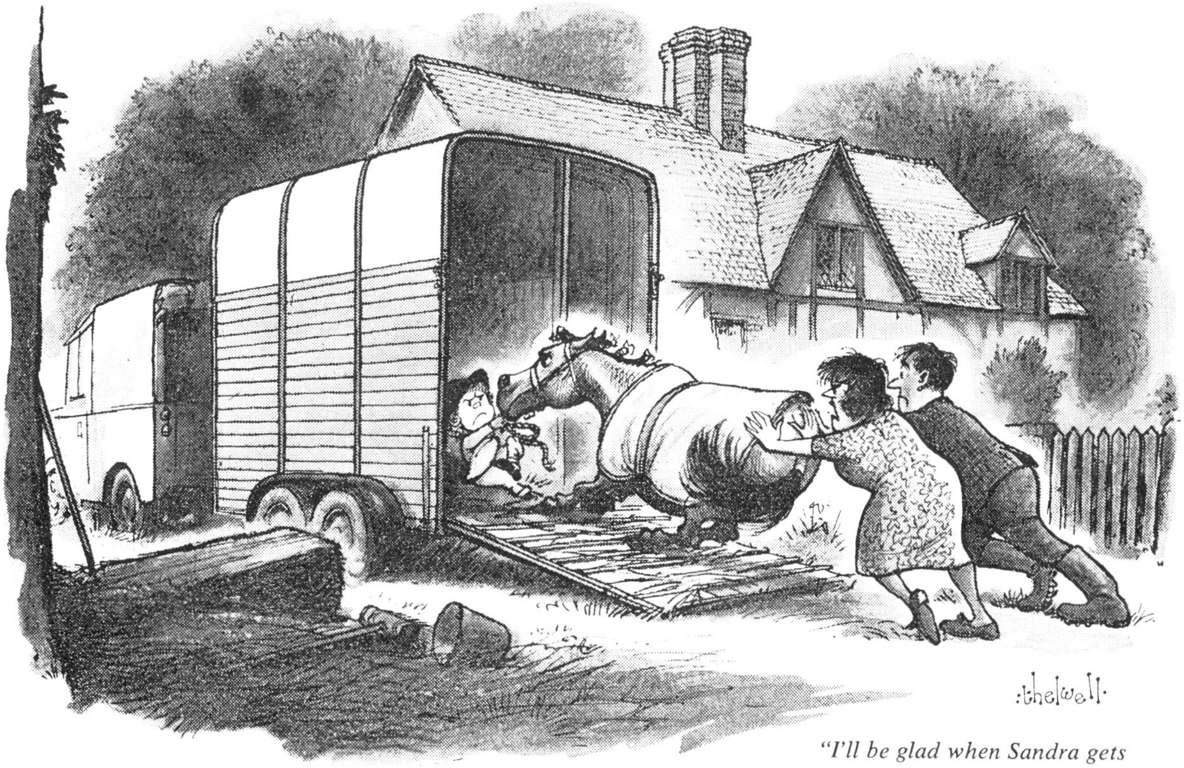
thelwell

"I'll be glad when Sandra gets interested in boys."

DON ROBERTS

Punch can supply no information about Don Roberts. However, if we average out the other contributors, he was born in Maidenhead in 1932, attended the Putney Academy of Art, has worked in advertising, and has one-and-one-half children. He lives in Wormwood Scrubs.

"*He's far too self-critical.*"

"*Seduce me with another helping of veal fricassée.*"

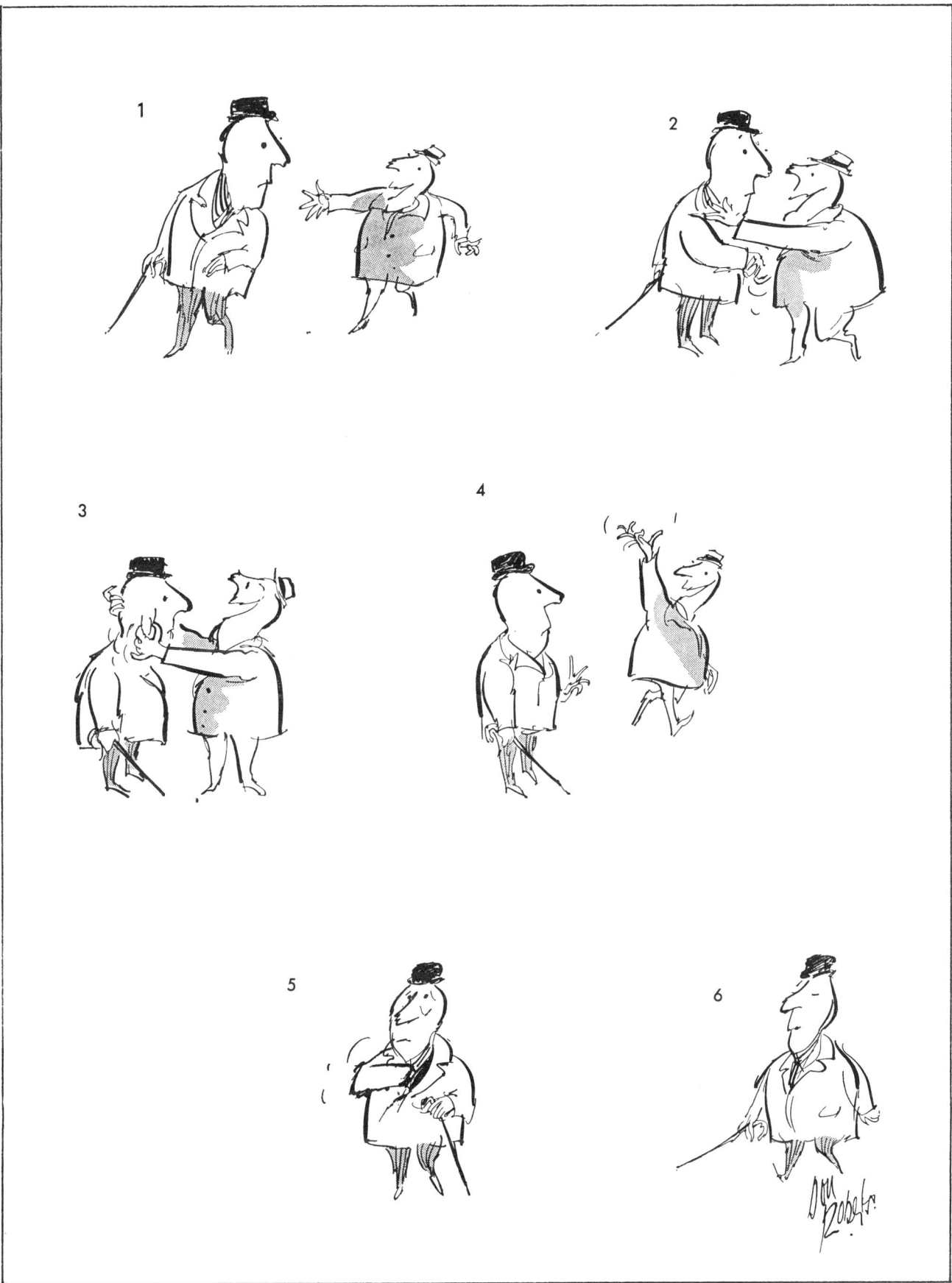

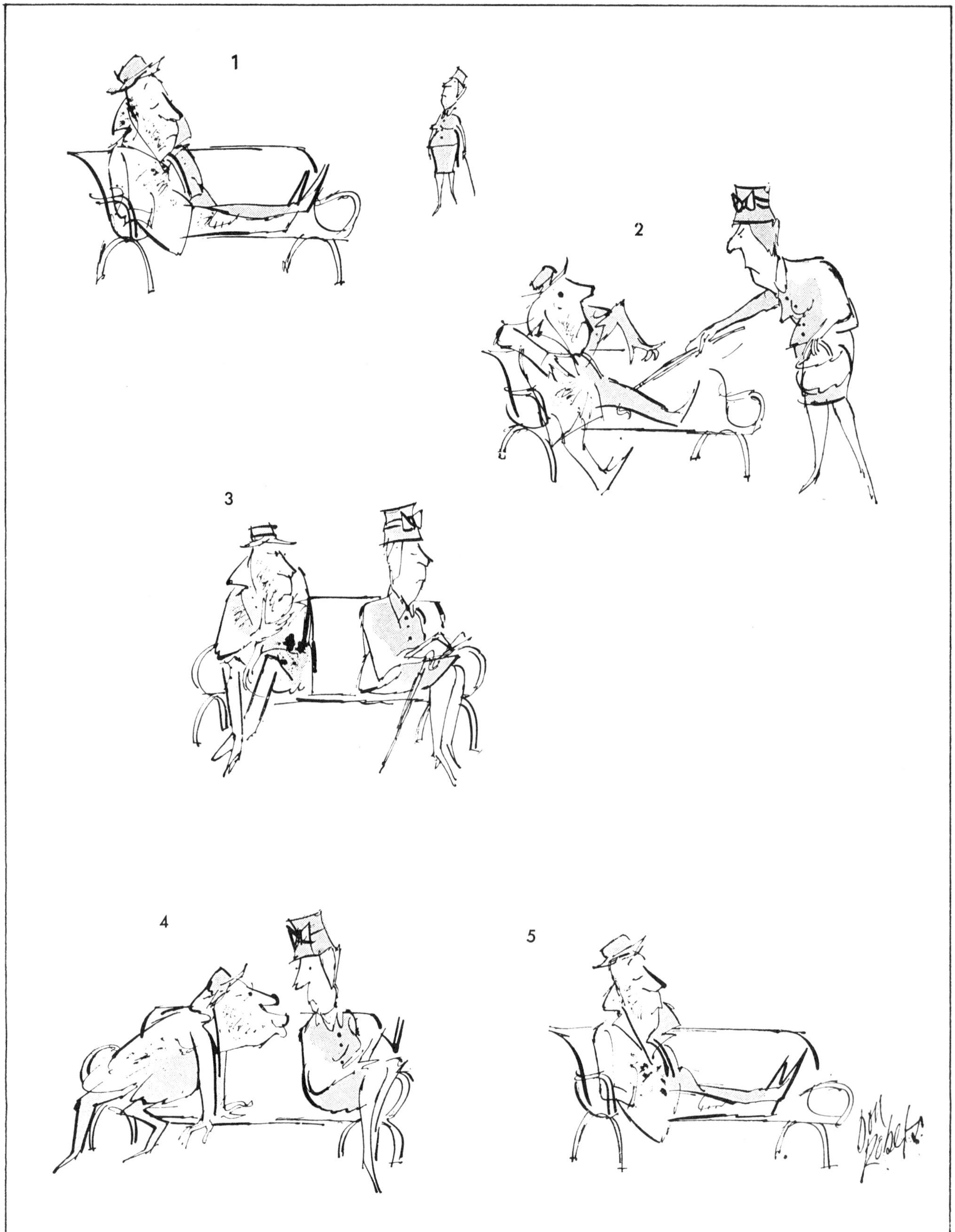
1
2
3
4
5
Don Roberts

ffolkes

Michael ffolkes is the pen name of Brian Davis, who was born in 1925 and attended St. Martin's School of Art. For years he has done *Punch*'s cinema caricatures. He has exhibited his water colors and has published several cartoon collections in England.

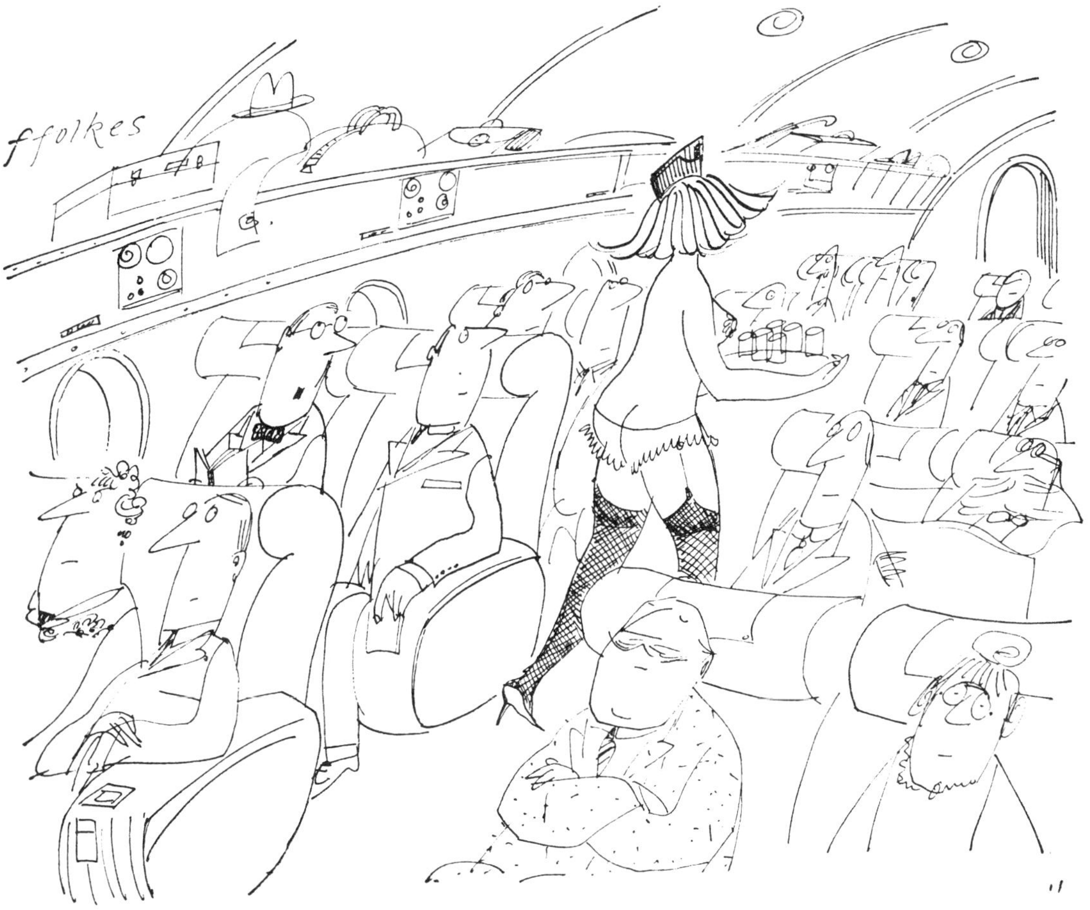
ffolkes

"I had no idea the airlines had become so competitive."

Poetic Licence

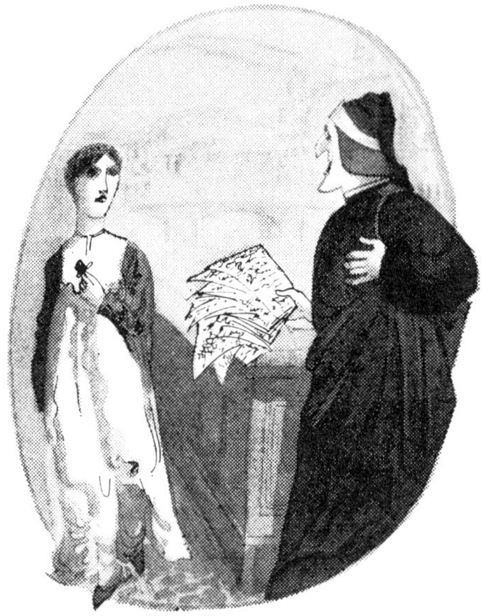

"Please read it. Just for the hell of it."

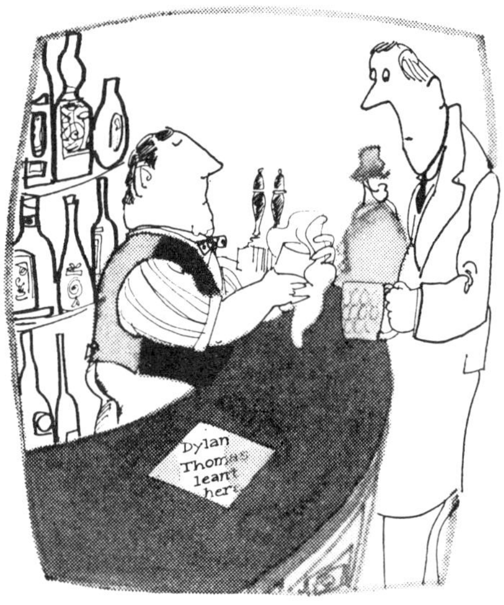
Dylan
Thomas
leant

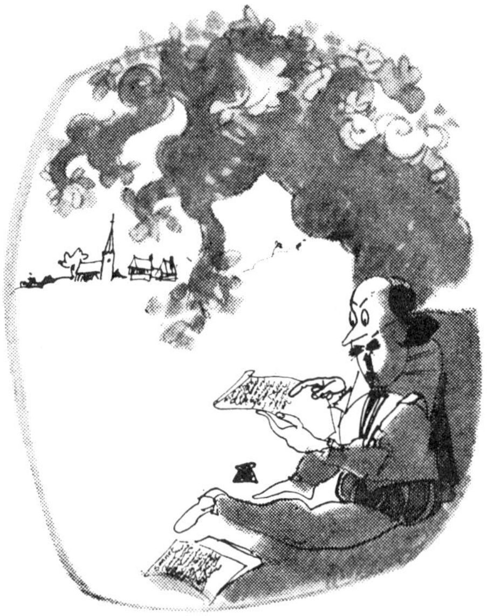

"13 . . . 14 . . . 15 . . . curse it!"

"By the way, what's your name? I can't keep calling you Thou."

"All right, Maud, just come into the garden. I promise there won't be any funny business in the greenhouse."

"I say, Blake, could I speak to you alone?"

Not in the Book
Some undiscovered incidents from between the lines.

"I like you too, Quasimodo, but marriage is a big step."

"Christian, my dear fellow! What are you doing in this God-forsaken slough?"

"Now take the Wife of Bath. I bet she could tell a few stories."

"If that's what we're evolving into, I give up."

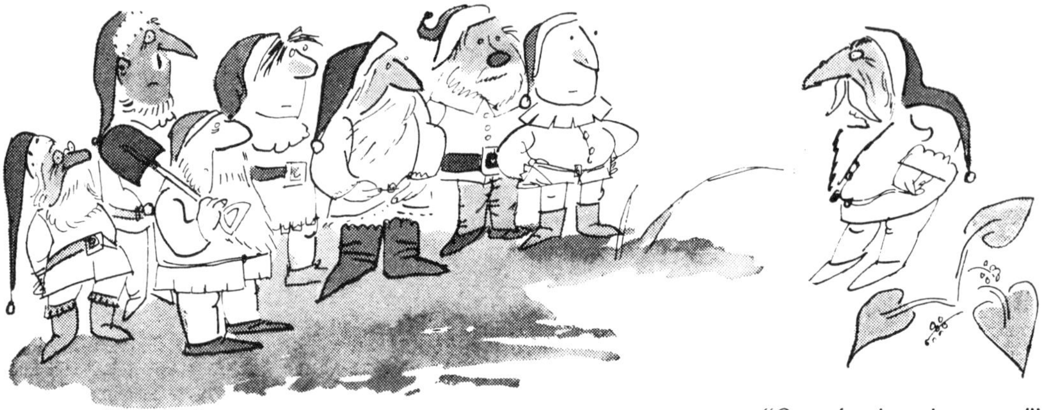

"One of us is an impostor!"

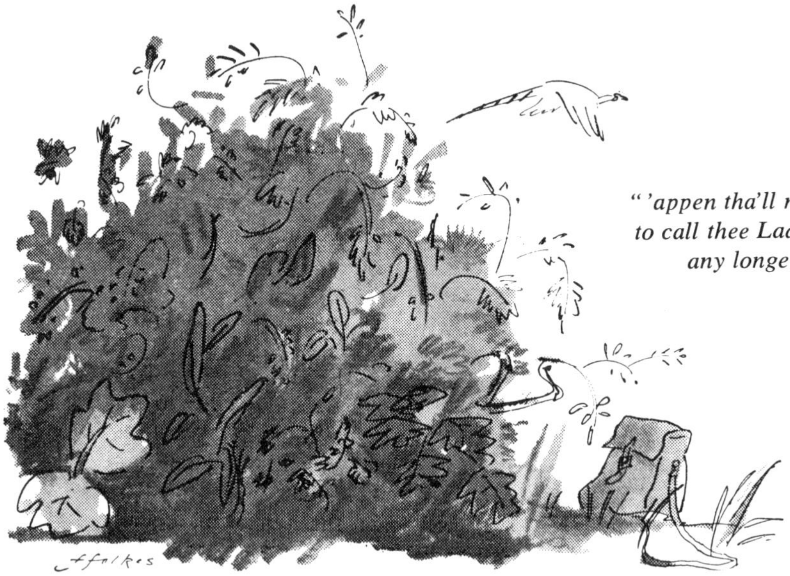
ffolkes

"'appen tha'll not expect me to call thee Lady Chatterley any longer then?"

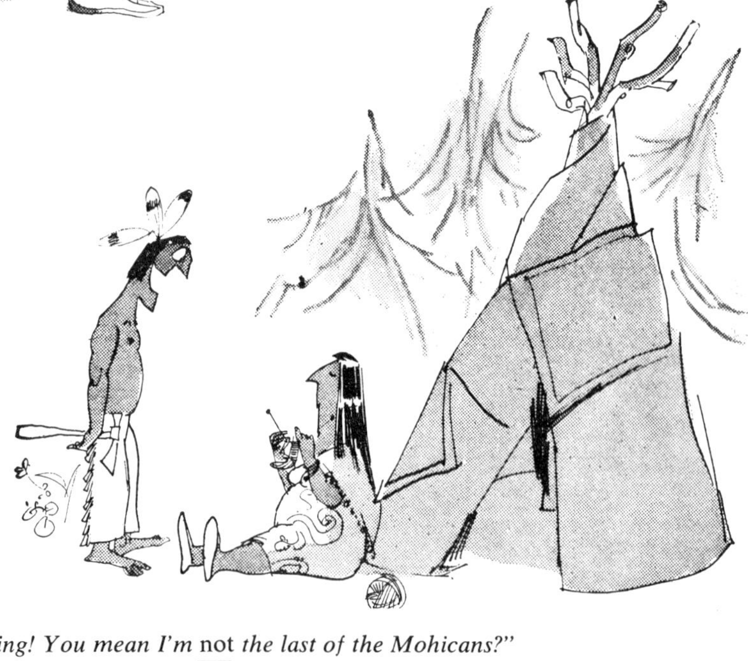

"Darling! You mean I'm not *the last of the Mohicans?"*

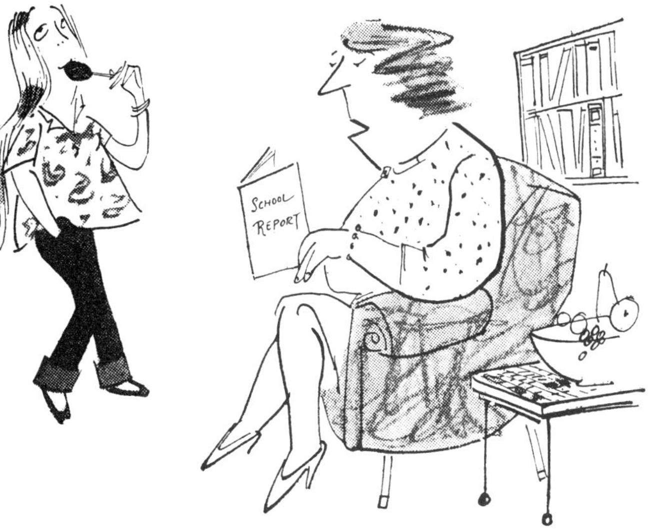
SCHOOL
REPORT

"Lolita, what do they mean in your report by 'precocious'?"

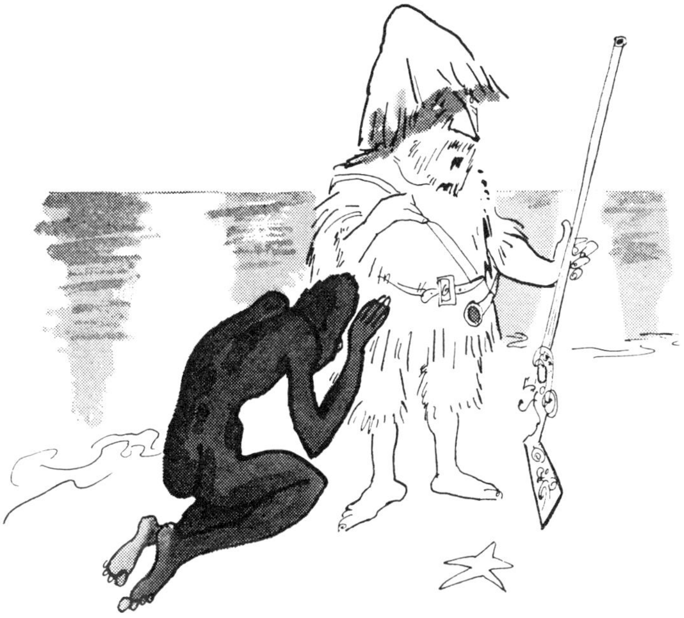

"Segregation, anti-segregation, race riots . . ."

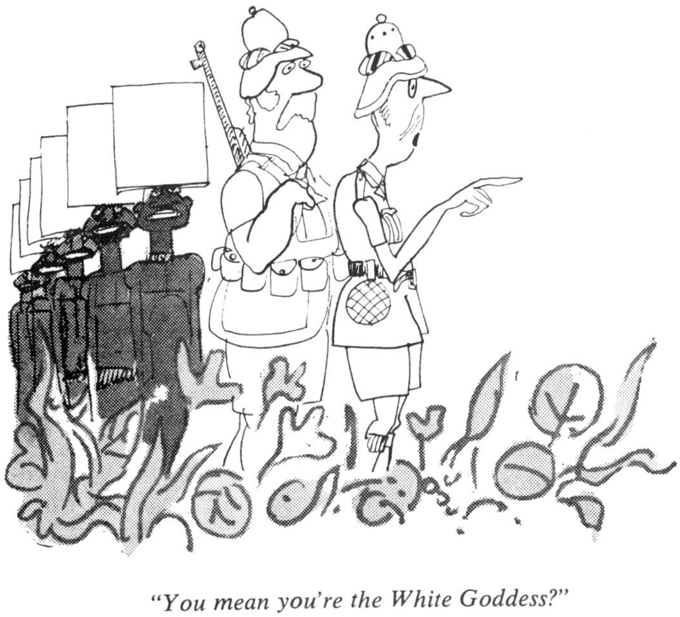

"You mean you're the White Goddess?"

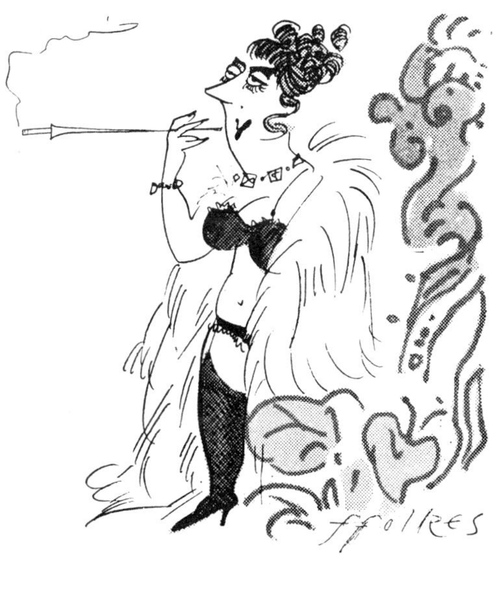
ffolkes

Moments Musicaux

"No, Liszt . . . L as in Leitmotif, I as in Impromptu, S as in Sforzando, Z as in . . ."

"Mr. Britten says you're singing half a tone flat."

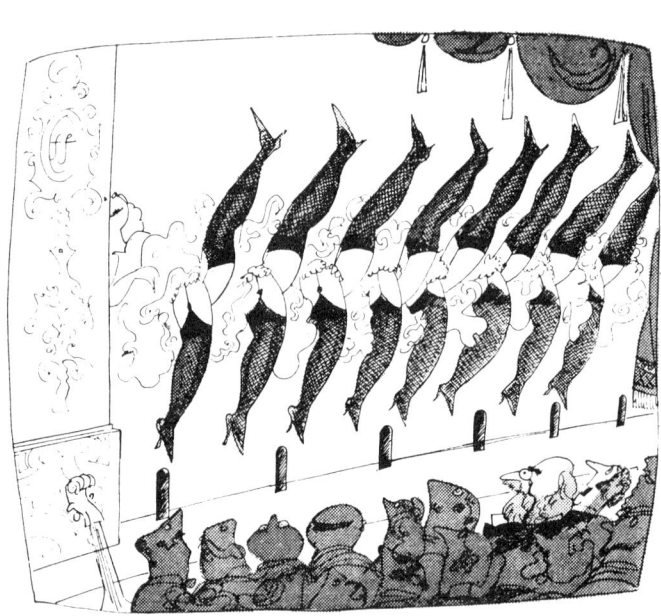

"That's funny, Offenbach. I didn't think I was going to like opera . . ."

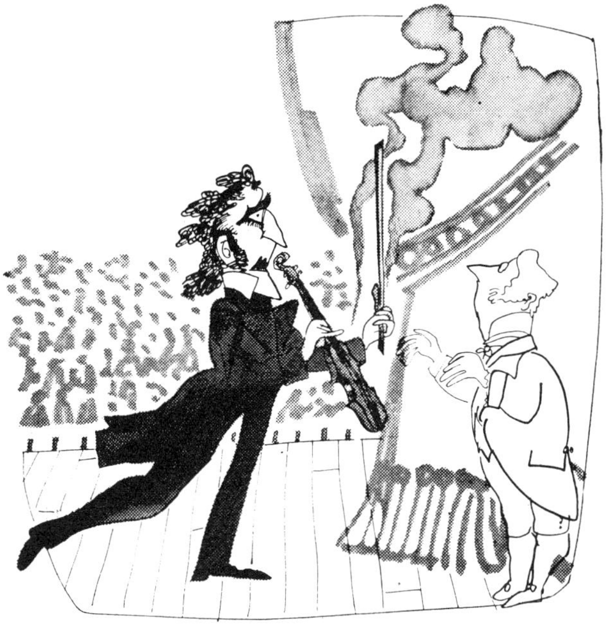

"Be careful of the bow. It's still hot."

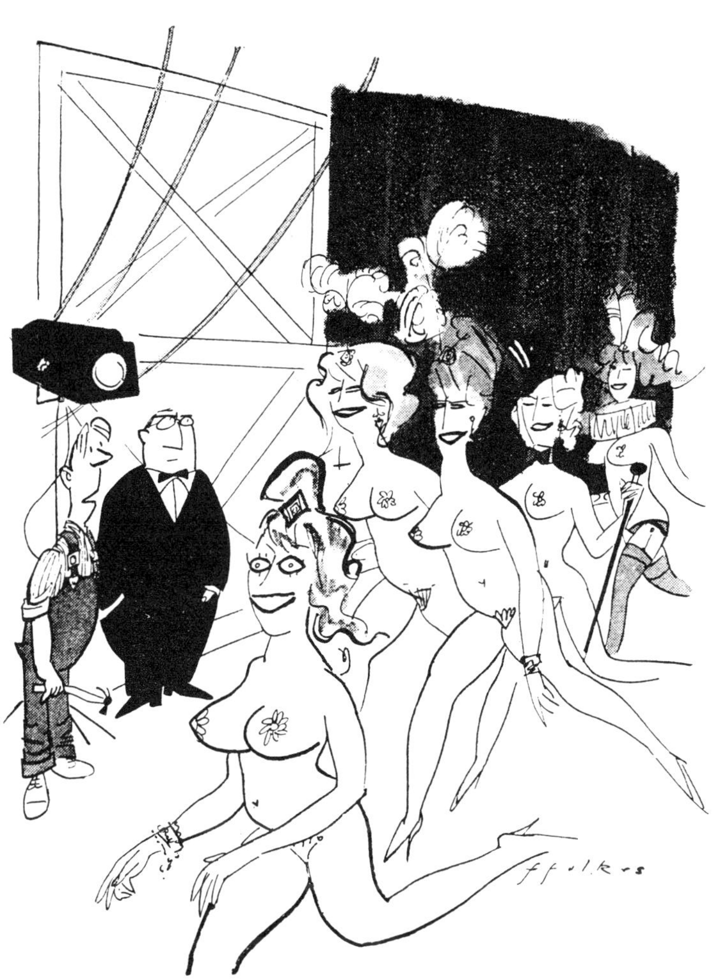

"I'm afraid of the day when it will seem like just another job."

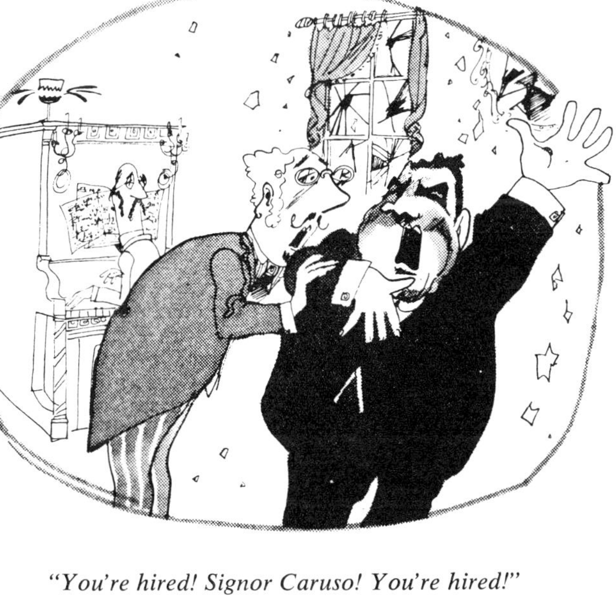

"You're hired! Signor Caruso! You're hired!"

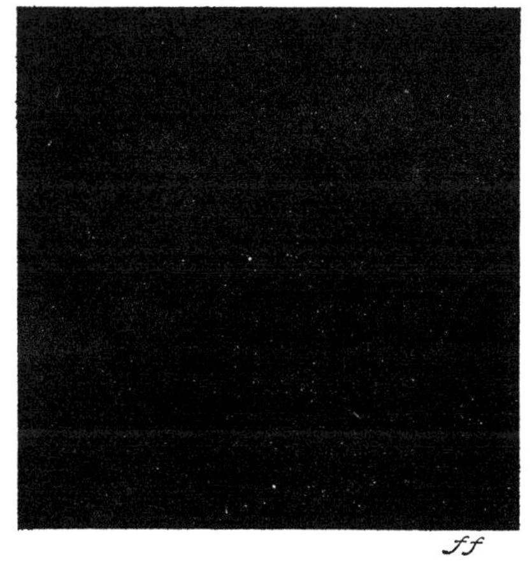

"Cut it out! We're supposed to be hibernating!"

ATCHISON

Michael Atchison was born in Melbourne, Australia, in 1933. He was educated at Kings College, Adelaide, and at the Adelaide School of Arts. Since his arrival in England in 1960, he has been a free-lance artist. He is married.

Five Finger Exercise

"... *and your cerise wallpaper, Cyril* ..."

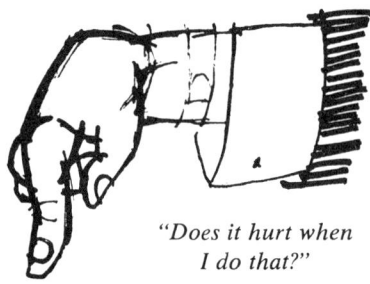

"*Does it hurt when I do that?*"

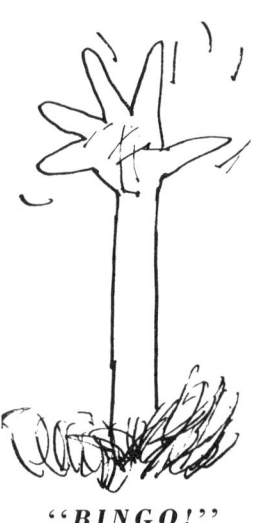

"*BINGO!*"

"*Heil who?*"

"*I want a volunteer.*"

"Another double, George."

"Perhaps if you look again . . . You may have missed an empty table?"

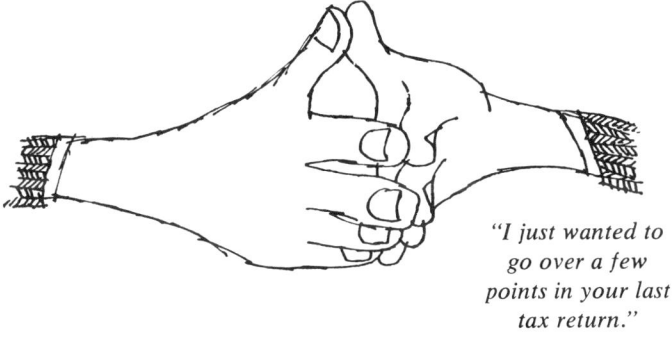

"I just wanted to go over a few points in your last tax return."

"Come and sit next to me, dearie! I won't eat you."

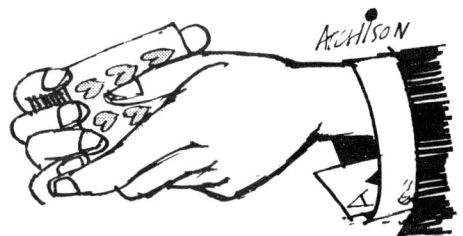

"Shall I shuffle them for you again?"

Seating Capacity

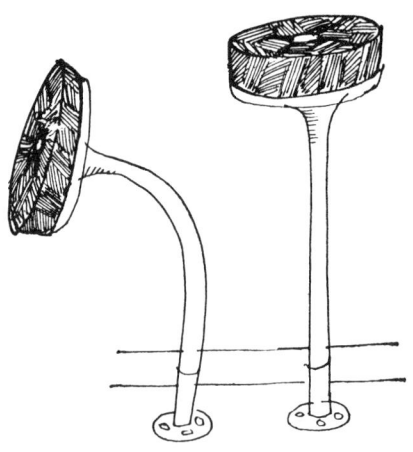

"I only drink to be sociable."

"My feet are killing me."

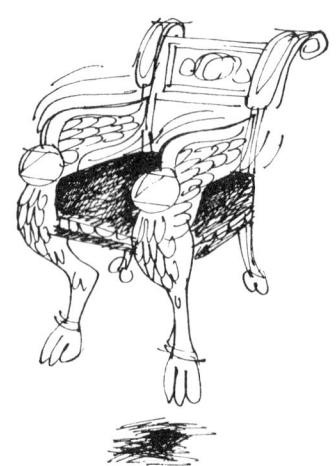

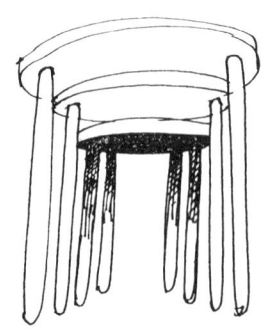

"My analyst says I have an inferiority complex."

"I feel sick."

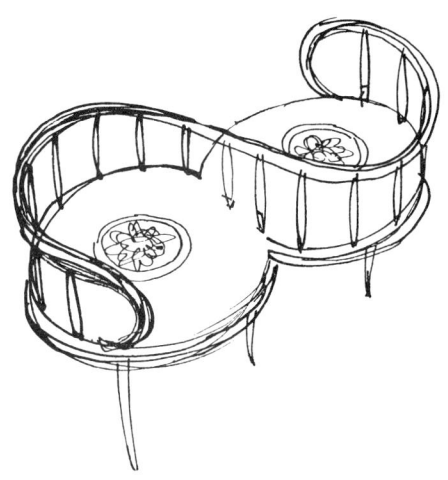
"I just don't know whether I'm coming or going."

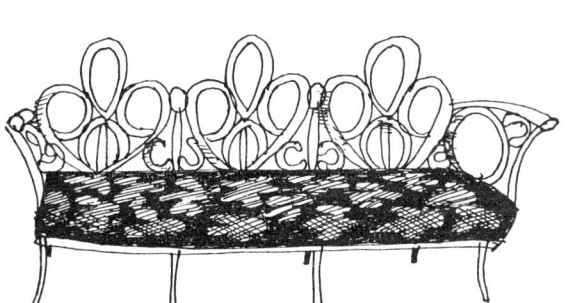
"Two's company . . ."

"Wheeee!"

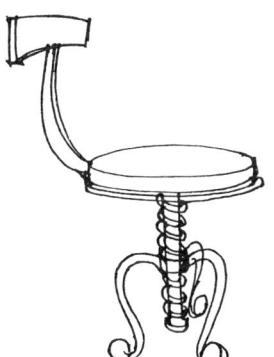
"I've been going around in circles all day."

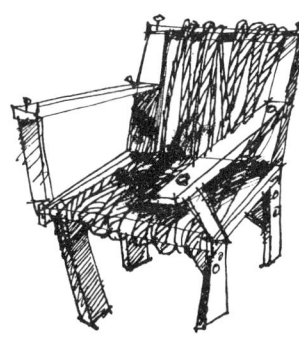
"One electric power drill kit and he thinks he's Charles Eames."

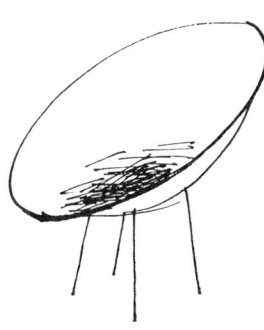
"I think I've contacted Mars."

LARRY

Larry is Terence Parks, born in Birmingham in 1927. He studied at Birmingham Art School and subsequently taught art for four years. He lives with his wife and two children in Solihull, Warwickshire. His books of domestic comedy—*Man in Apron, Man in Garden* and others—have been successful in England and the United States.

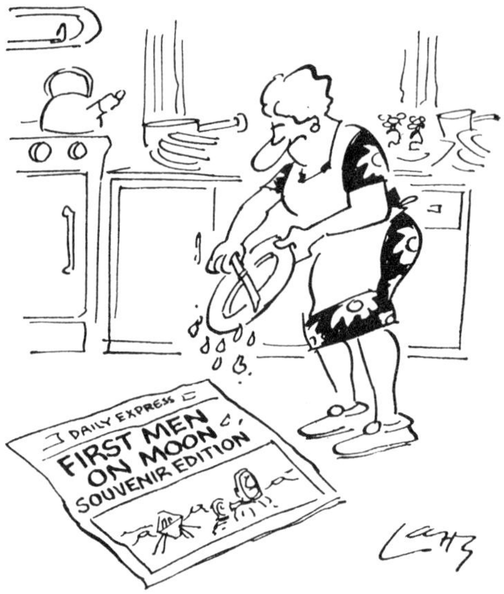
DAILY EXPRESS
FIRST MEN ON MOON
SOUVENIR EDITION
Larry

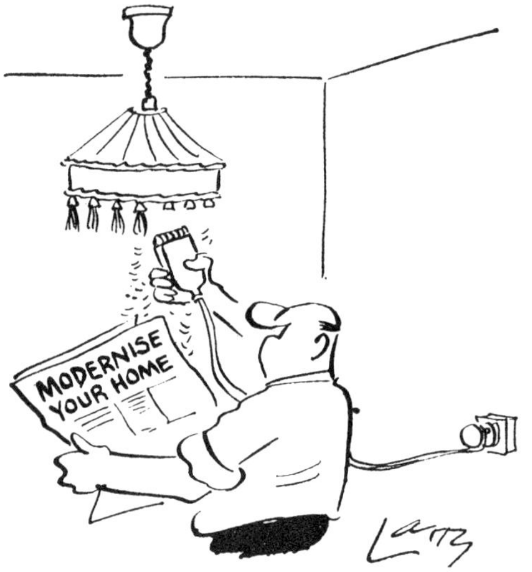
MODERNISE YOUR HOME
Larry

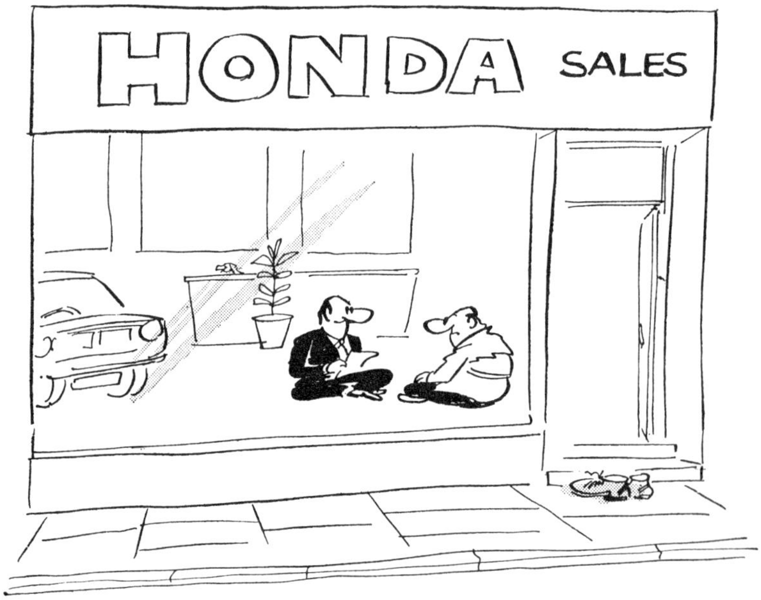
HONDA SALES

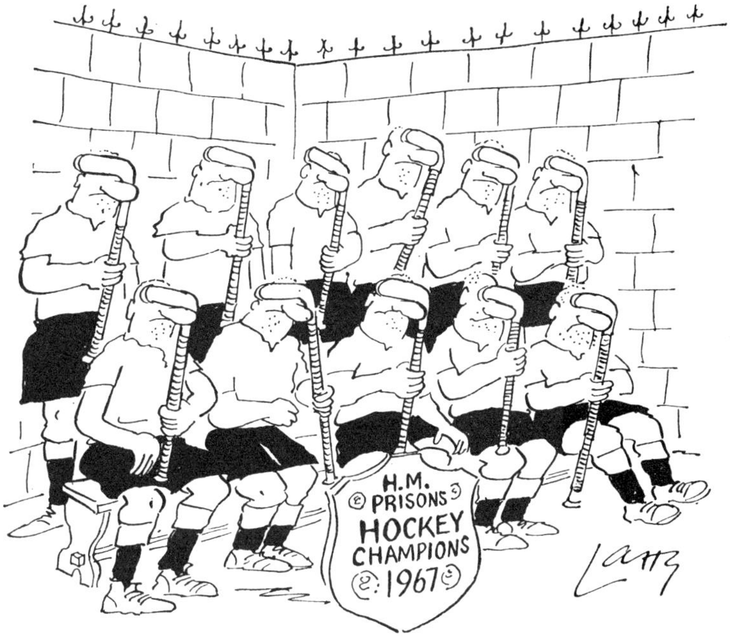
H.M.
PRISONS
HOCKEY
CHAMPIONS
1967
Larry

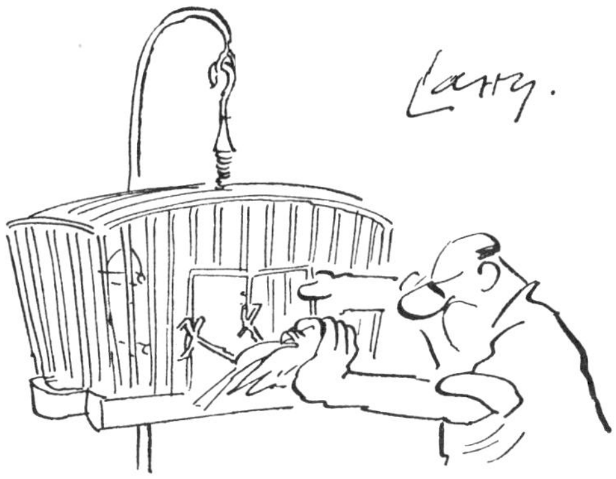
Larry.

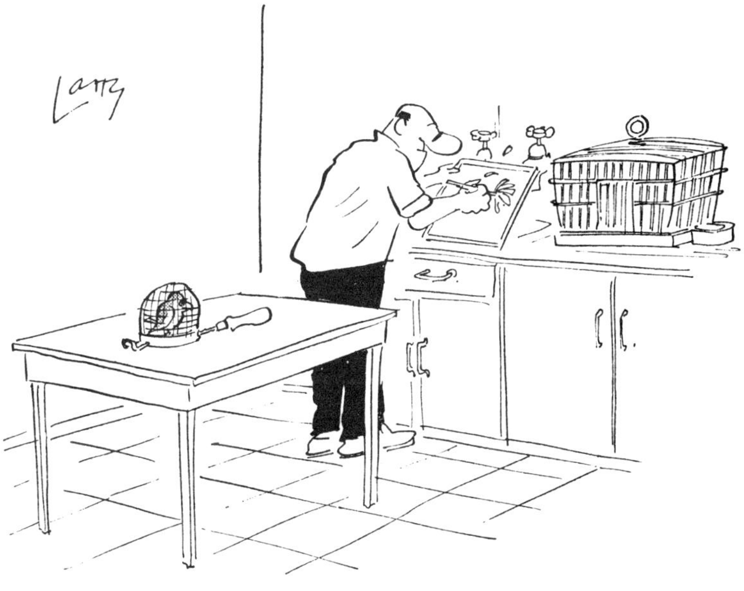
Larry

Man in Garden

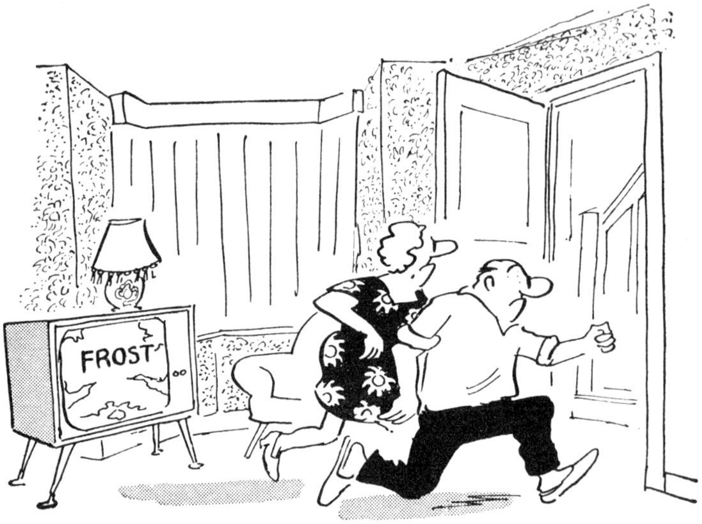
FROST

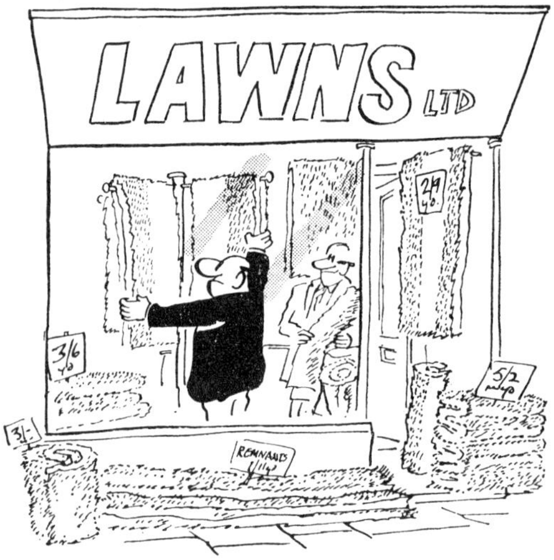
LAWNS LTD

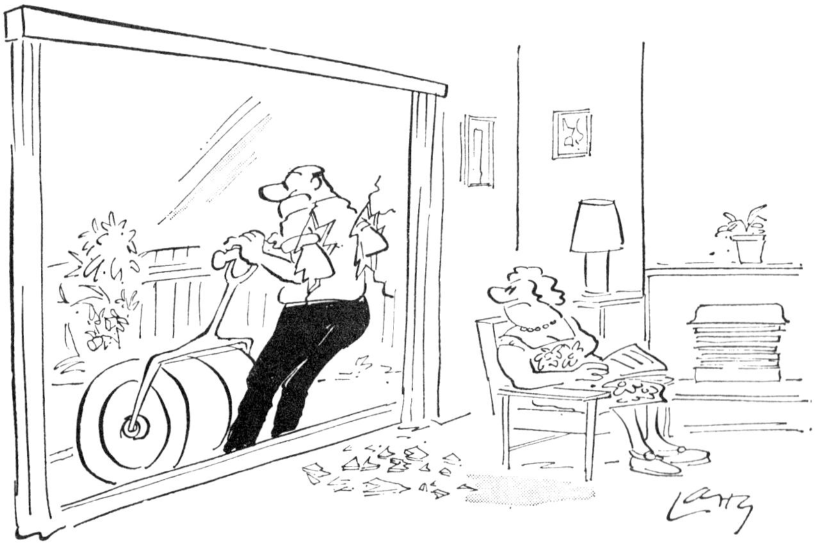

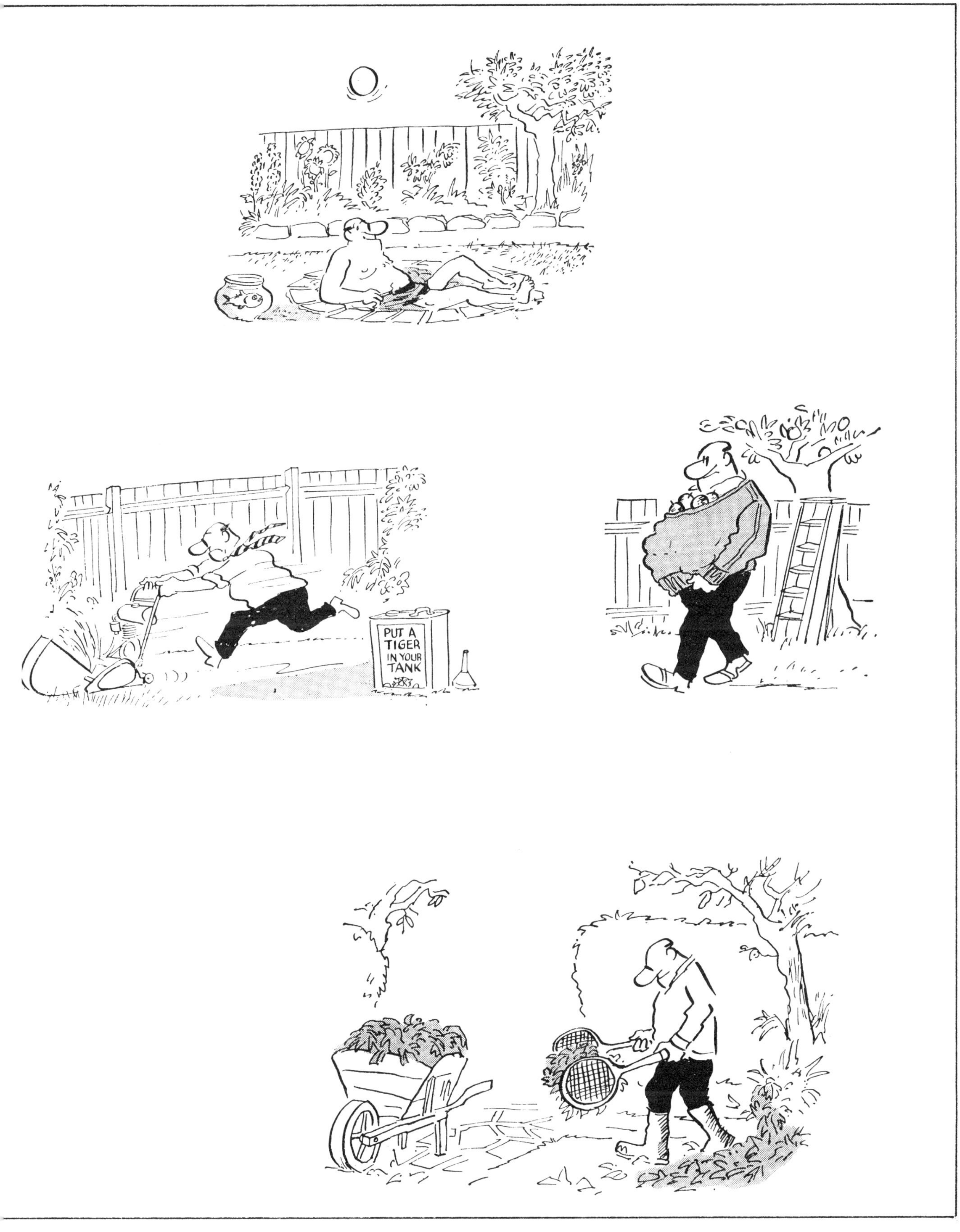
PUT A TIGER IN YOUR TANK

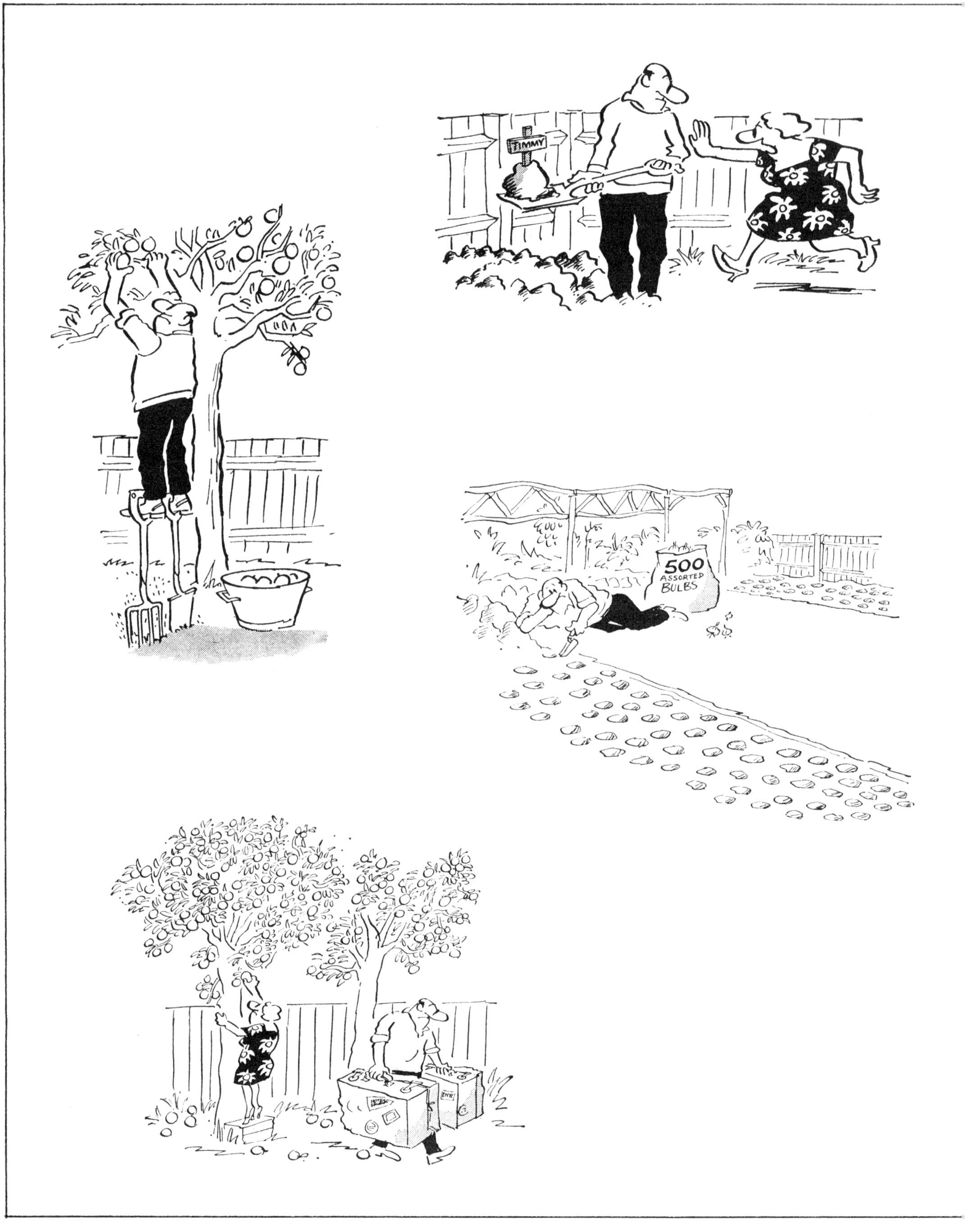
TIMMY
500
ASSORTED
BULBS

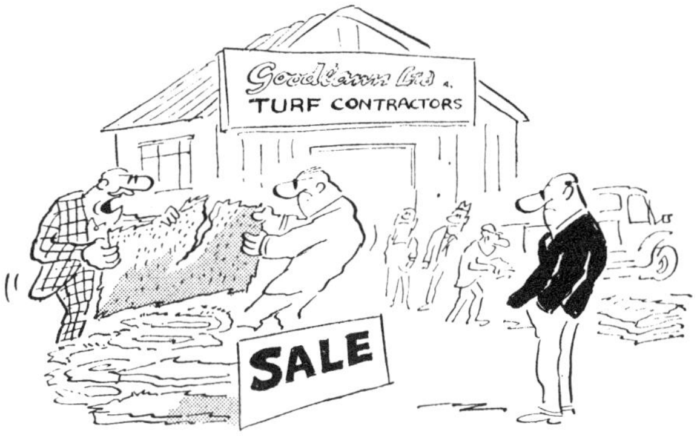
TURF CONTRACTORS
SALE

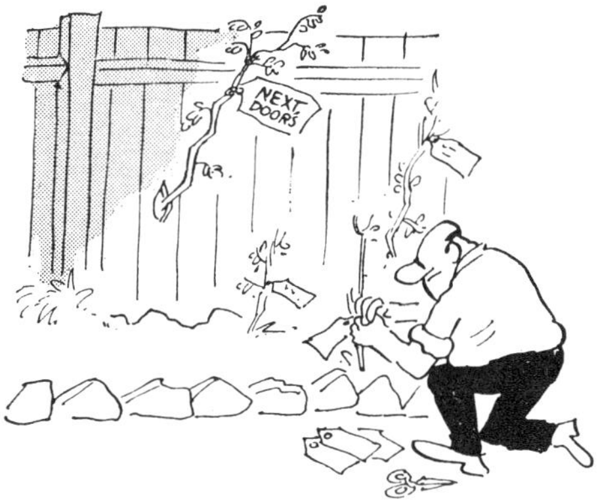
NEXT DOORS

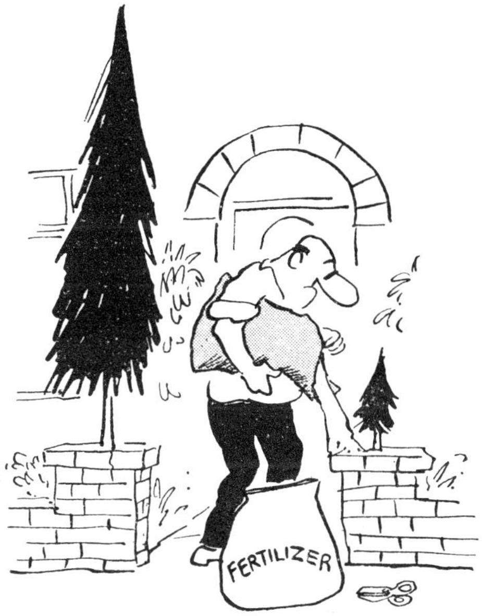
FERTILIZER

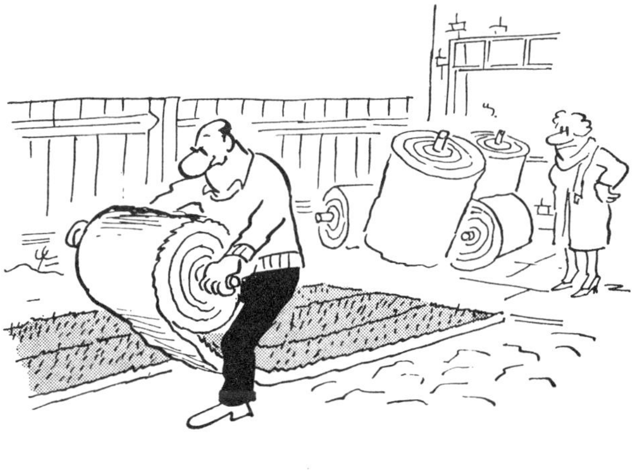

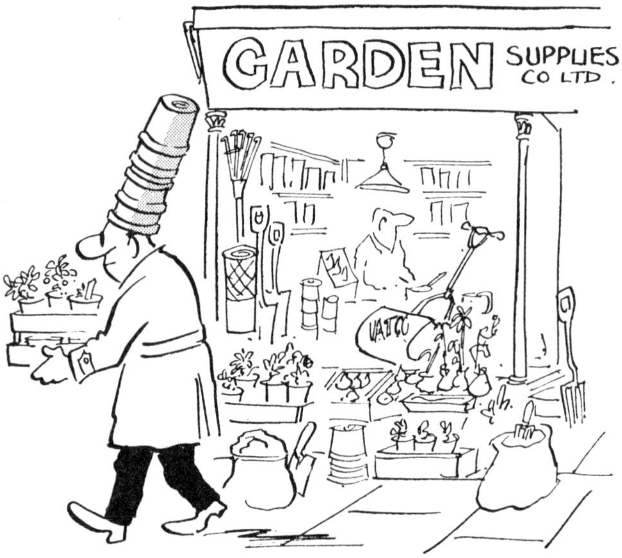
GARDEN SUPPLIES
CO LTD.

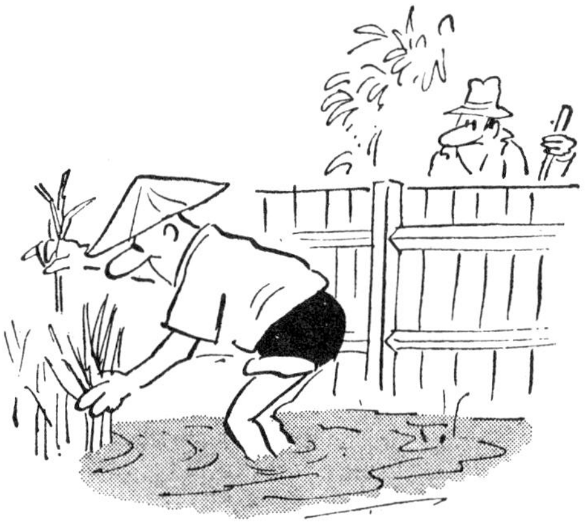

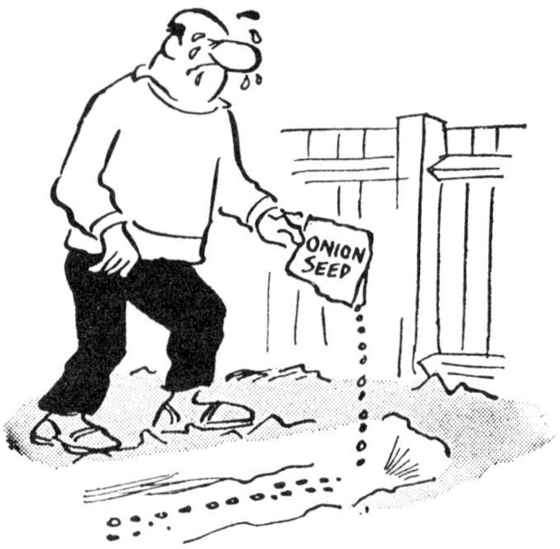
ONION
SEED

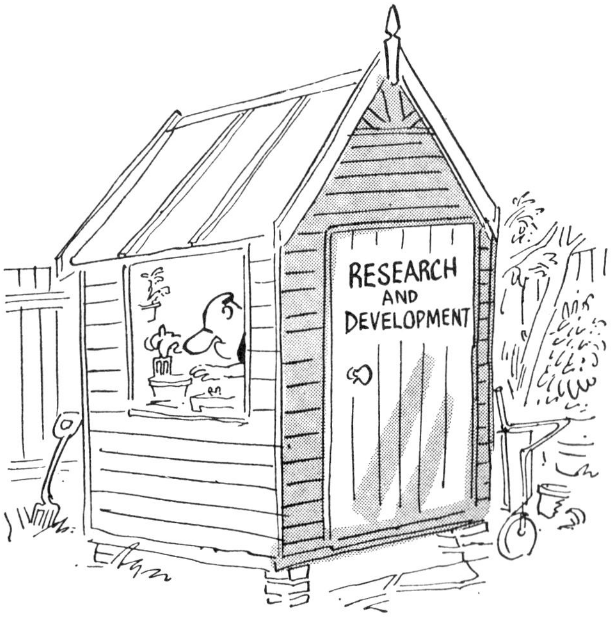
RESEARCH
AND
DEVELOPMENT

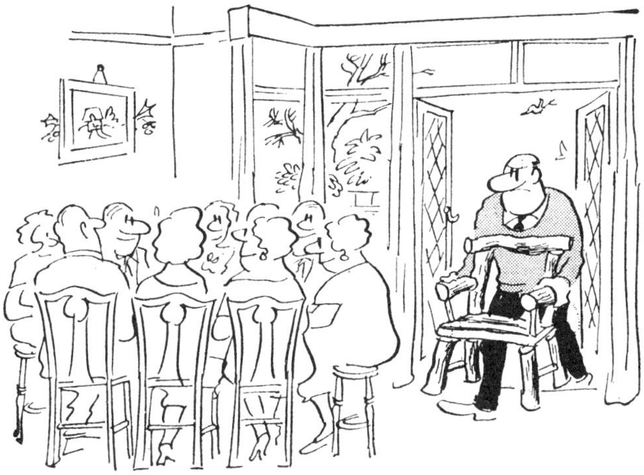

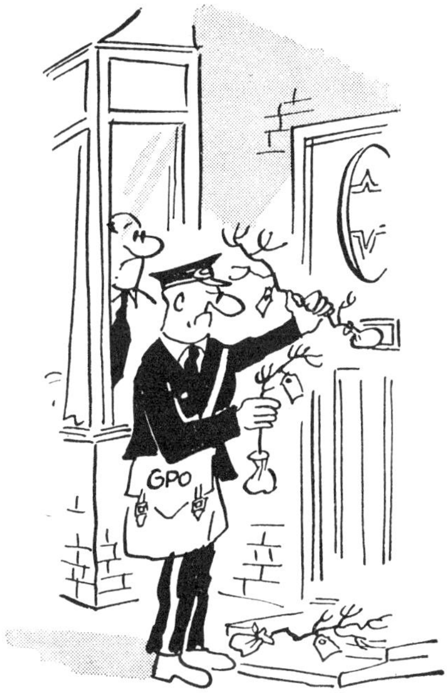
GPO

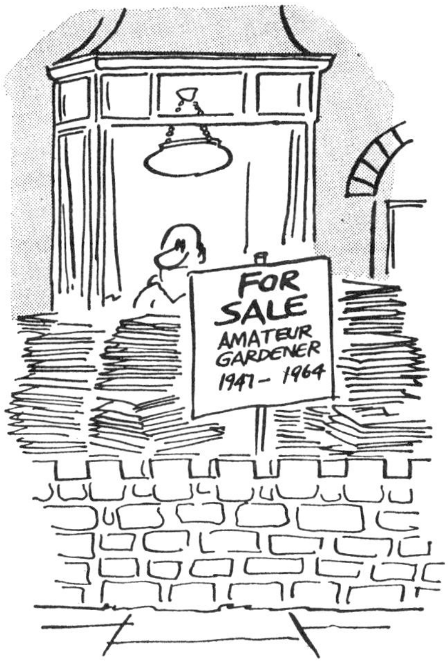
FOR SALE
AMATEUR GARDENER
1947 - 1964

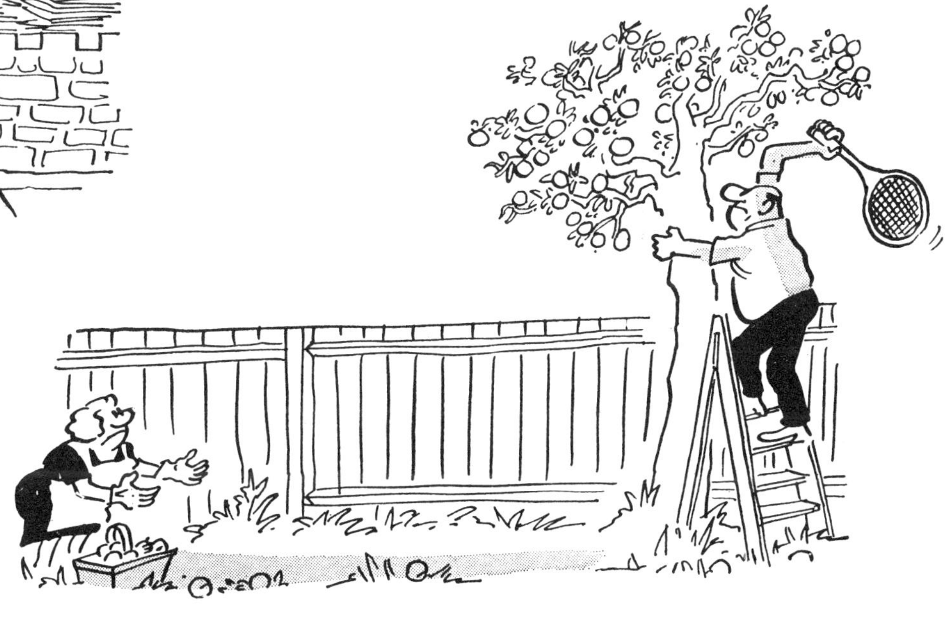

Man in Hospital

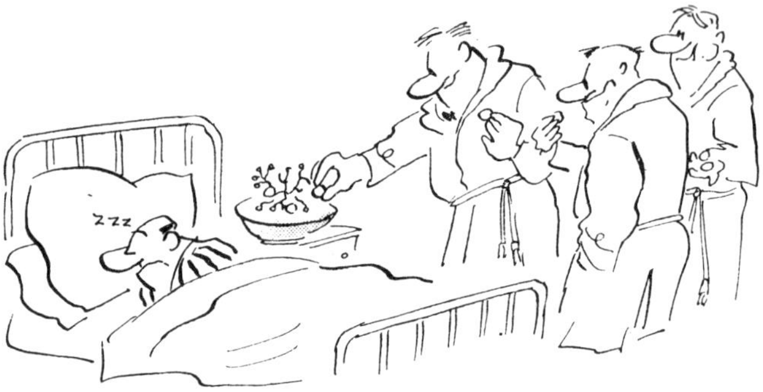
zzz

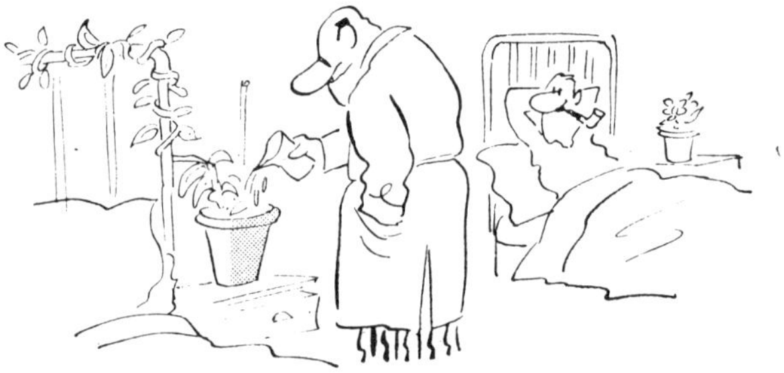

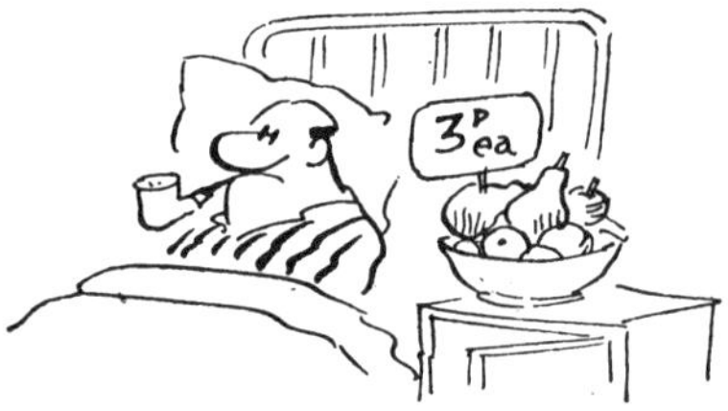
3D ea

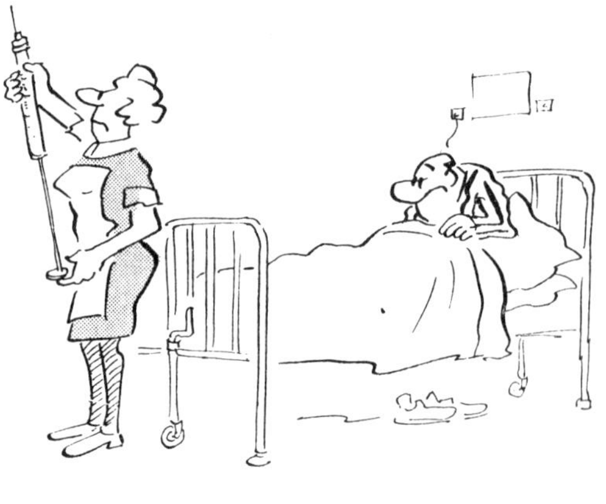

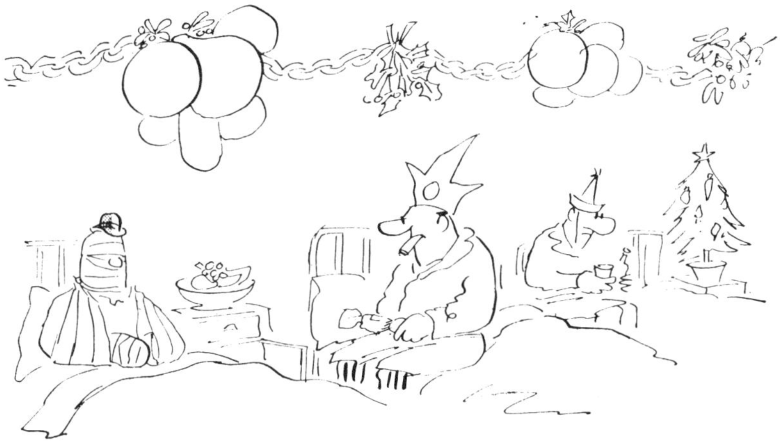

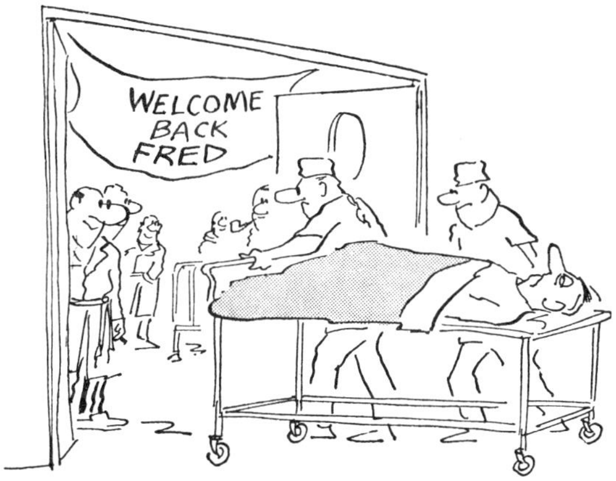
WELCOME
BACK
FRED

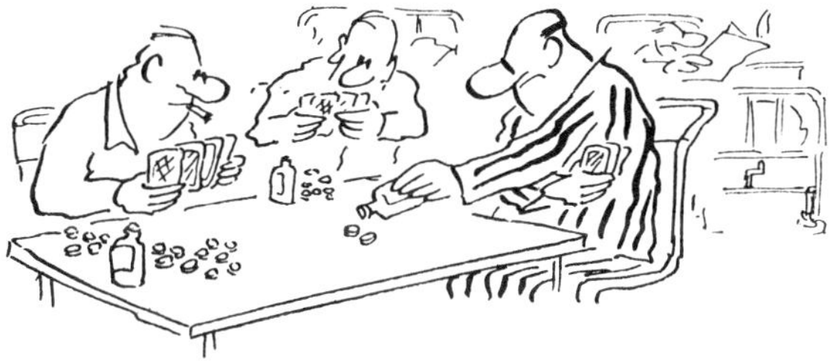

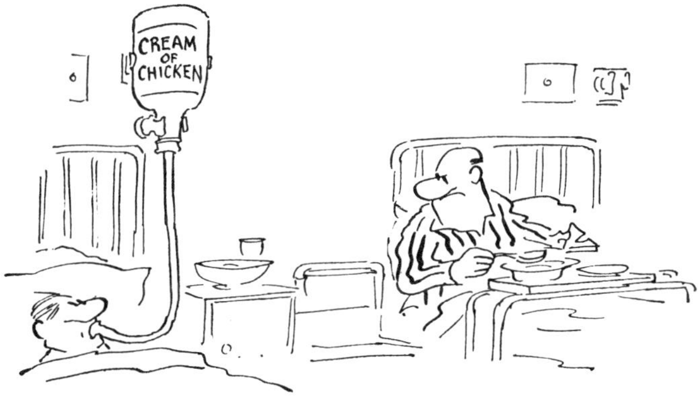
CREAM
OF
CHICKEN

WARD
COMEDIAN

OVERCROWDED
WARDS DISGRACE
IN CITY HOSPITAL

NURSE
NURSE
NURSE

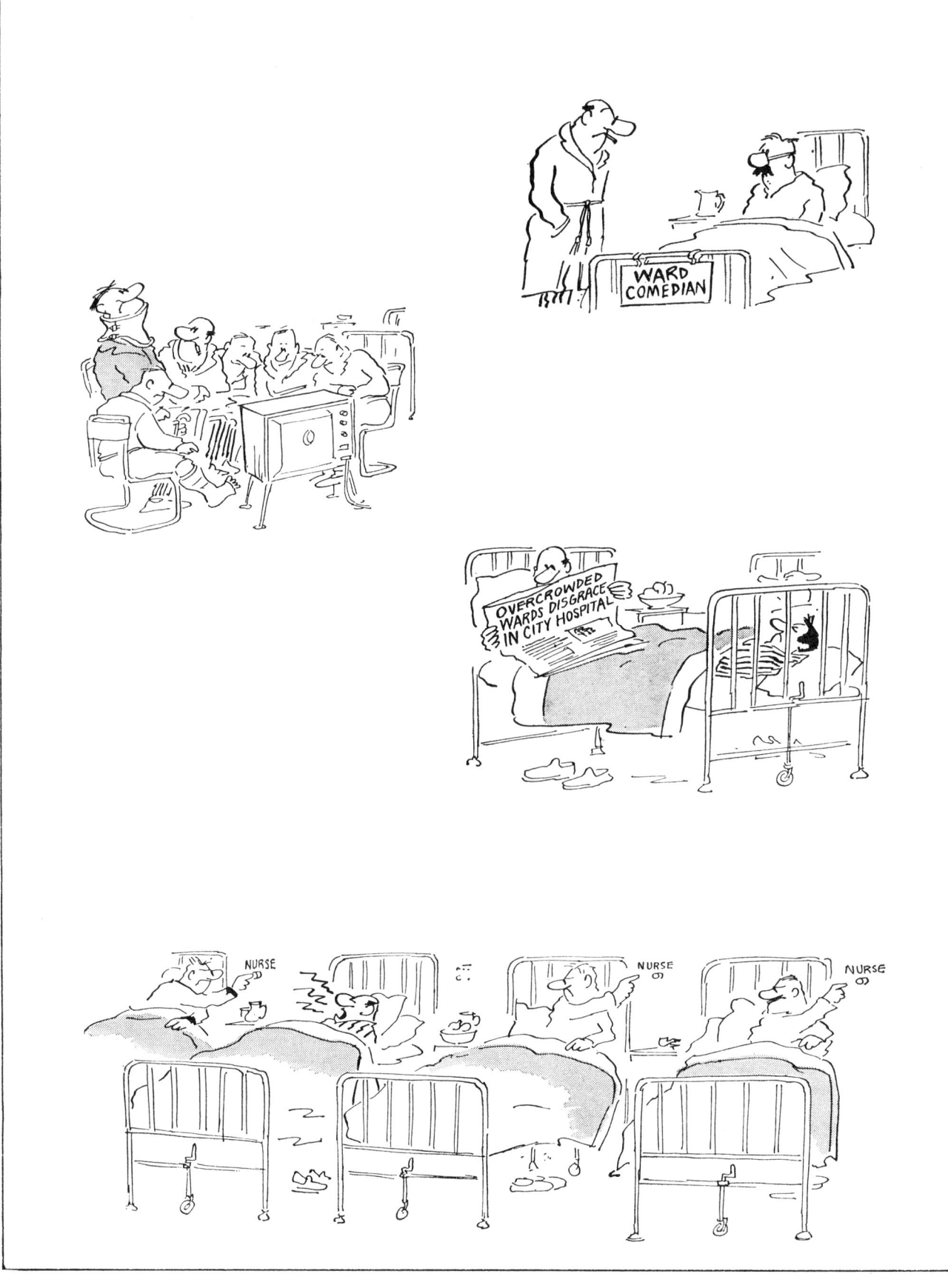

J. W. TAYLOR

J. W. Taylor is a long-time *Punch* contributor. He was born in 1908 and had a career as a teacher and headmaster at various schools. He retired in 1968 and is now a full time free-lance cartoonist. He is married, with two children, and lives in Stoke-on-Trent.

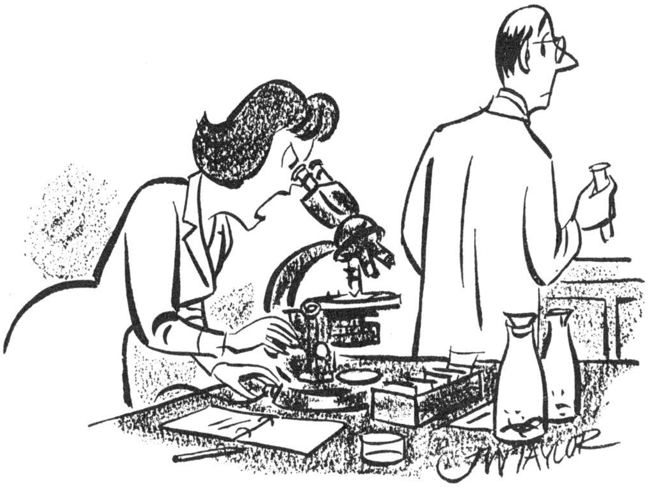
JWTAYLOR

"You males are all alike!"

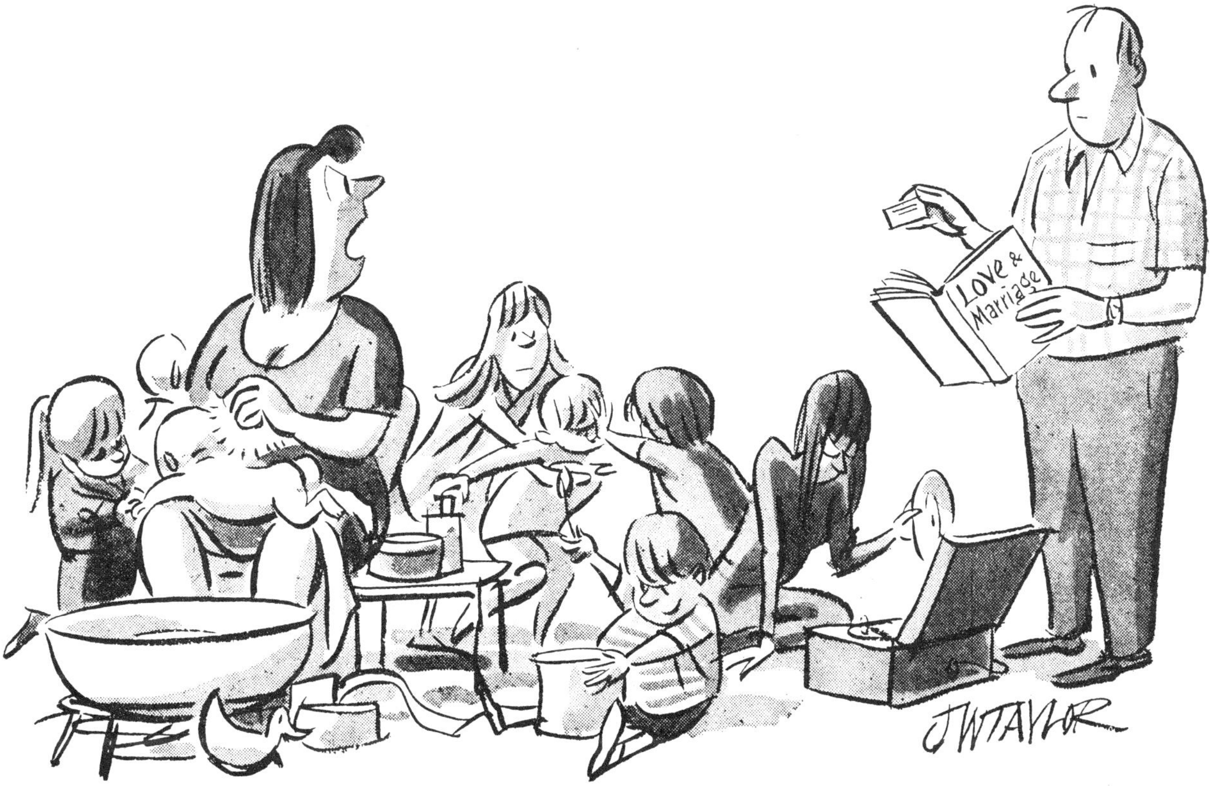
Love & Marriage
JWTAYLOR

"Now *you find the erratum slip!"*

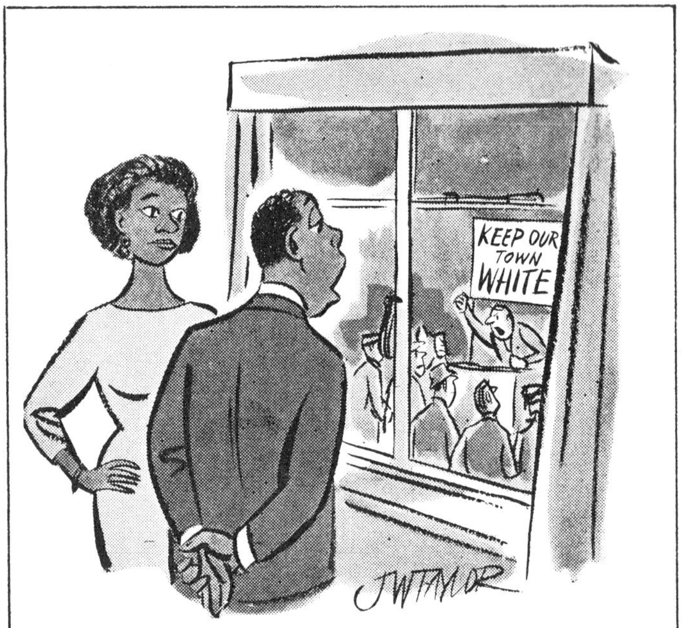
KEEP OUR
TOWN
WHITE
JWTAYLOR

"The natives are restless tonight."

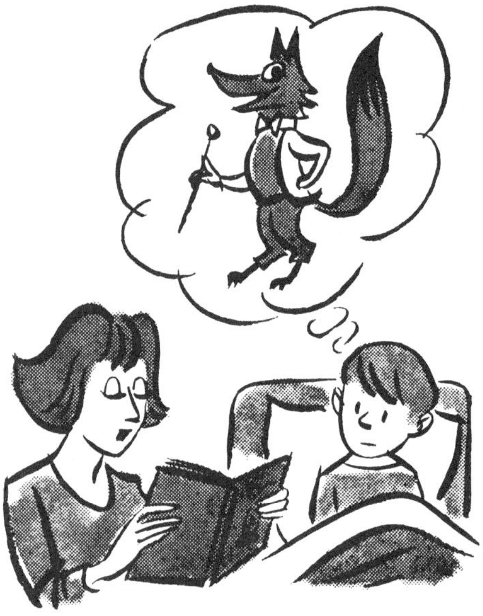

"This is the story of Freddie Fox . . .

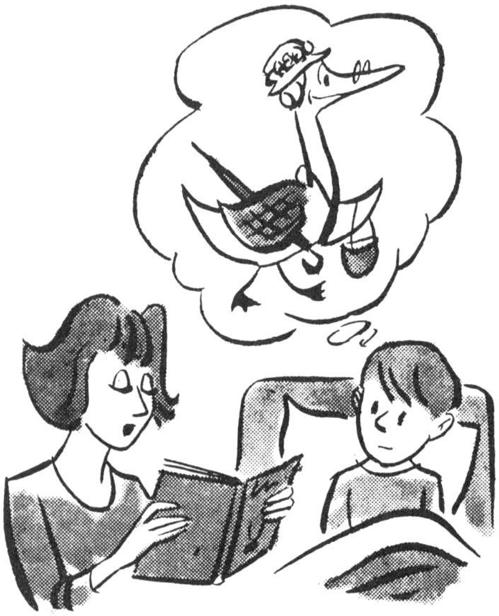

. . . Grandma Goose . . .

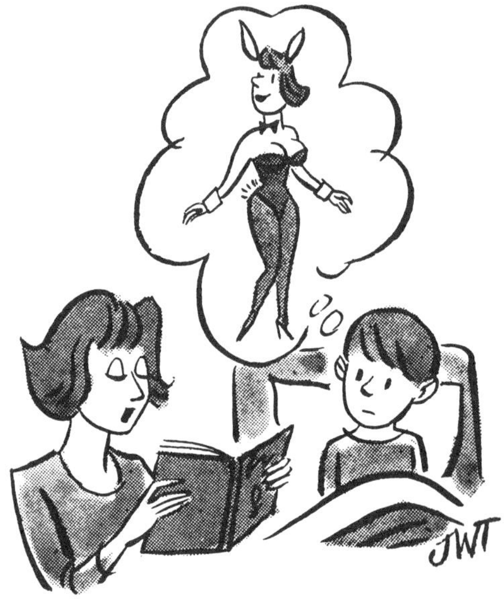
JWT

. . . and Barbara Bunny."

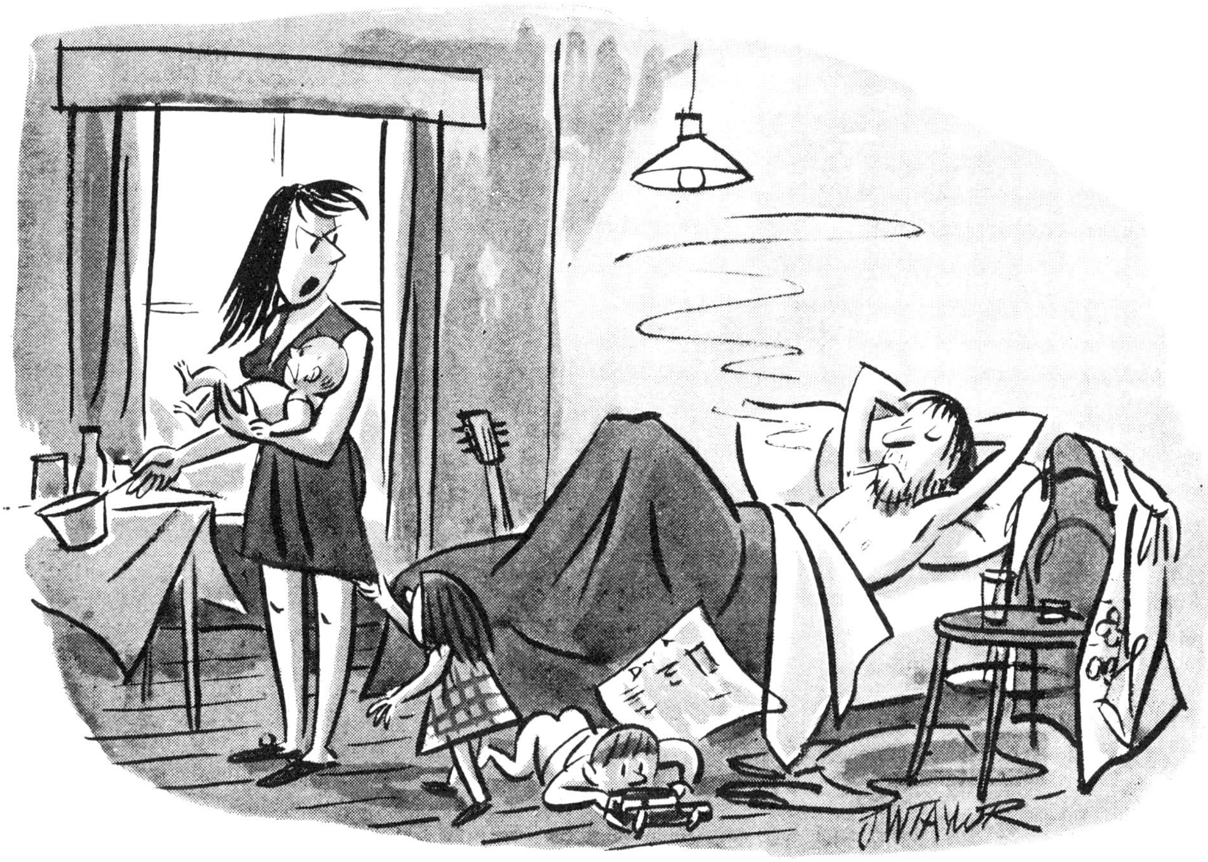
J W TAYLOR

"I pity the girl that marries you."

HARGREAVES

Harry Hargreaves was born in Manchester in 1922 and he worked as a film-cartoon animator and free-lance artist from 1946 to 1950. He has published three books about his famous birds. He lives with his wife and two daughters in Penselwood, Surrey.

"I like to make a weekly call on . . .

. . . an unfortunate who lives on a pinch of food a day . . .

. . . who never leaves his tiny abode . . .

. . . and seldom sees a cheerful face . . .

. . . so I give him a weekly smile . . .

. . . and somehow it makes me feel better."

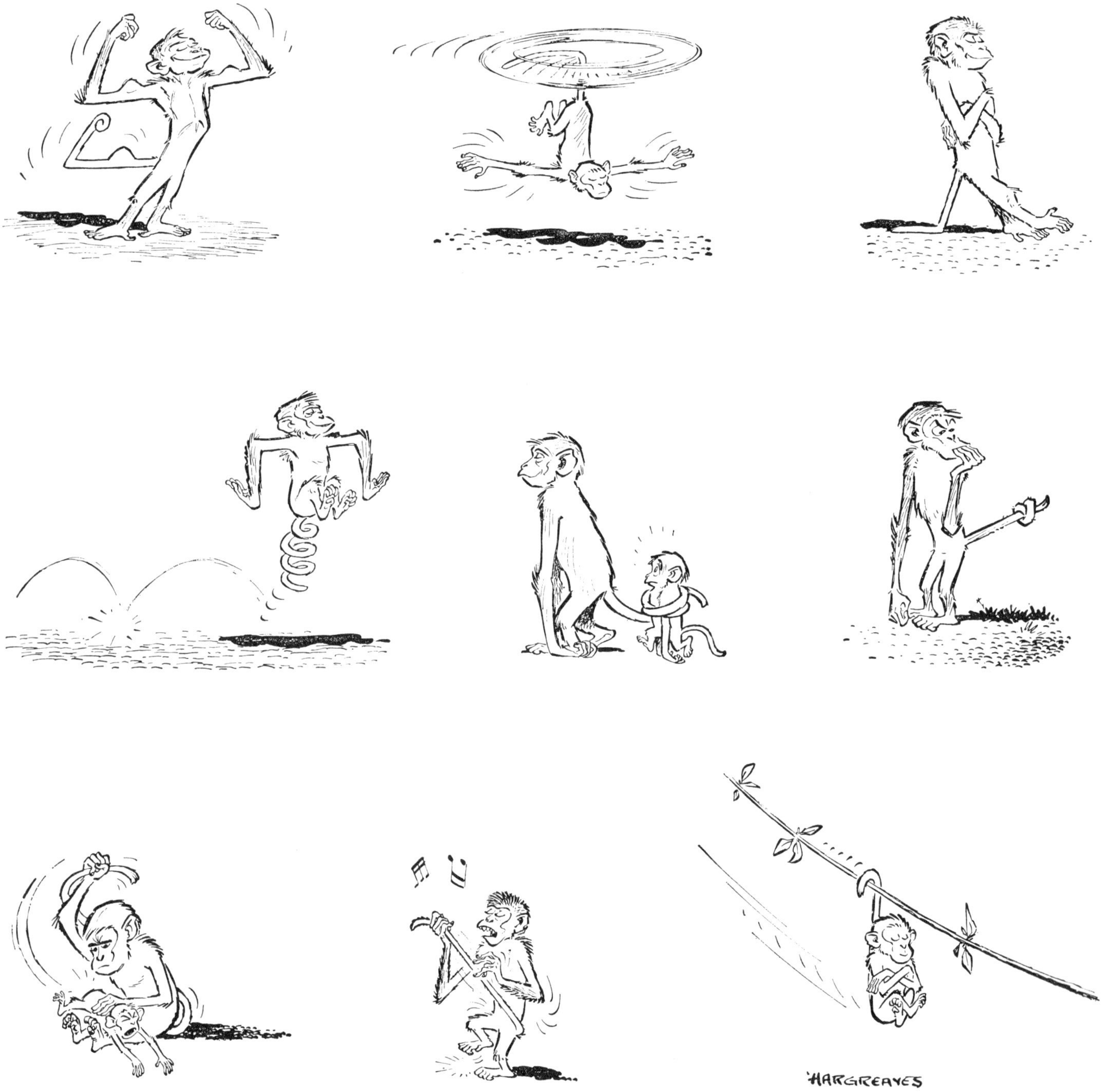
HARGREAVES

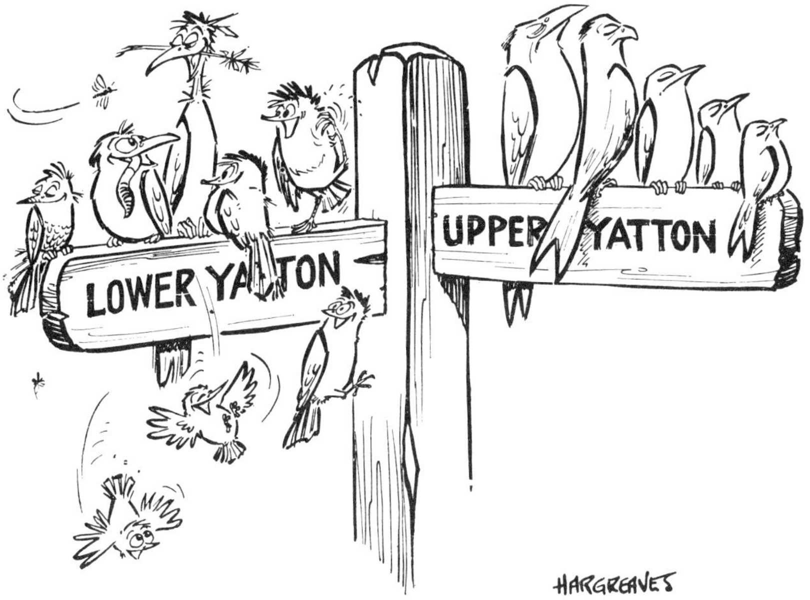
LOWER YA TON
UPPER YATTON
HARGREAVES

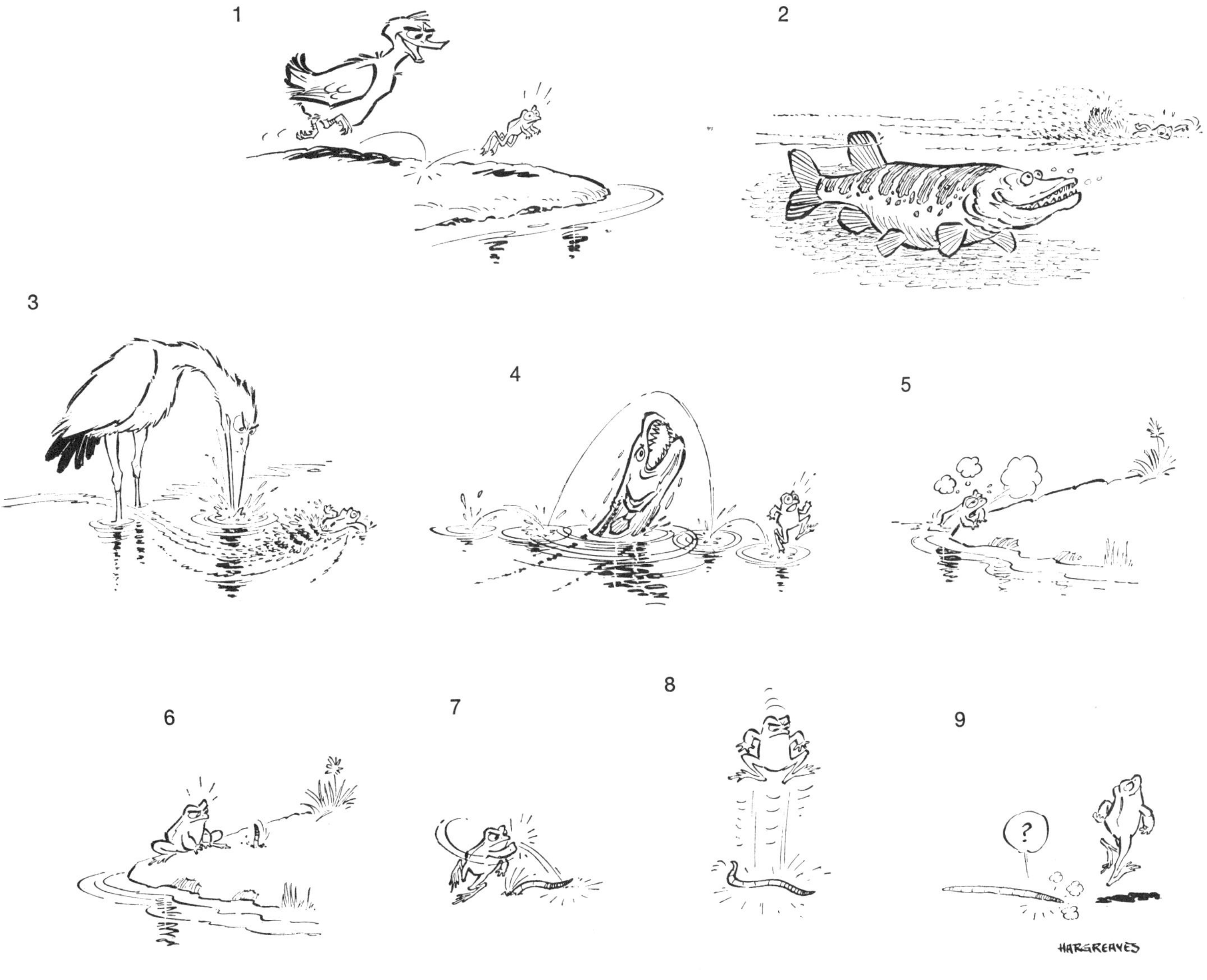
1
2
3
4
5
6
7
8
9
?
HARGREAVES

ERIC BURGIN

Eric Burgin was born in Maidenhead in 1926 and spent some time as an engineering apprentice. He has been a full-time cartoonist since 1954. He lives in Maidenhead with his wife and two children.

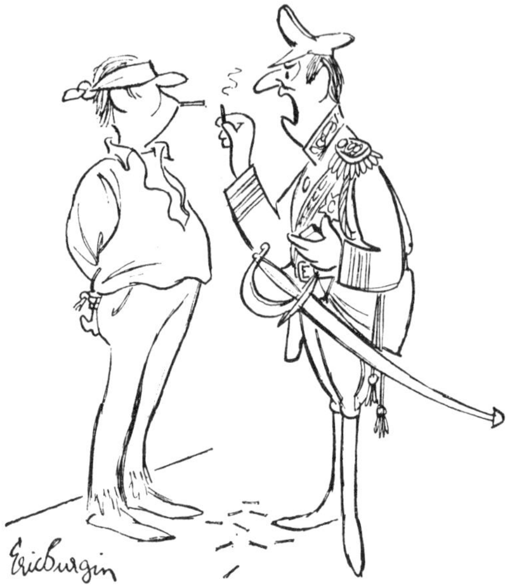

"Stop blowing the match out."

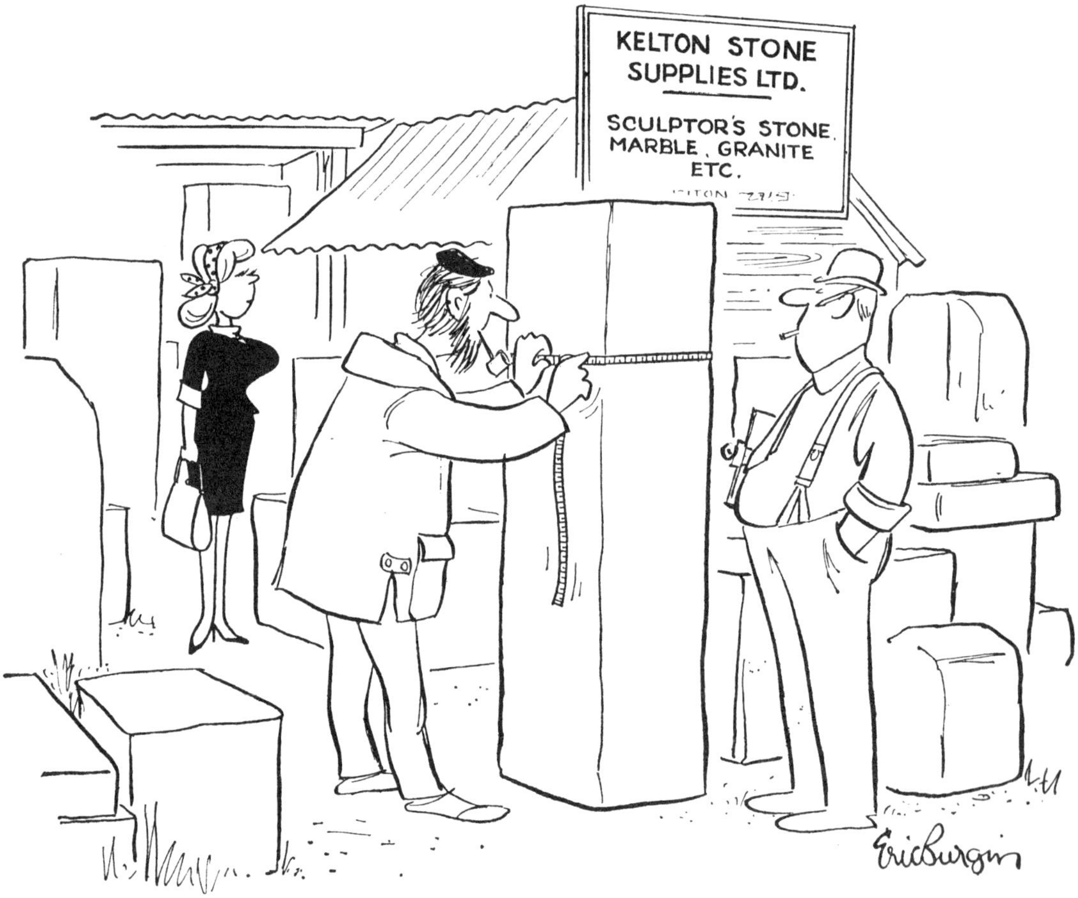
KELTON STONE
SUPPLIES LTD.
SCULPTOR'S STONE,
MARBLE, GRANITE
ETC.

THE FUN SHOP
OP
CLOSED
PRACTICAL JOKES FOR ALL OCCASIONS
Eric Burgin

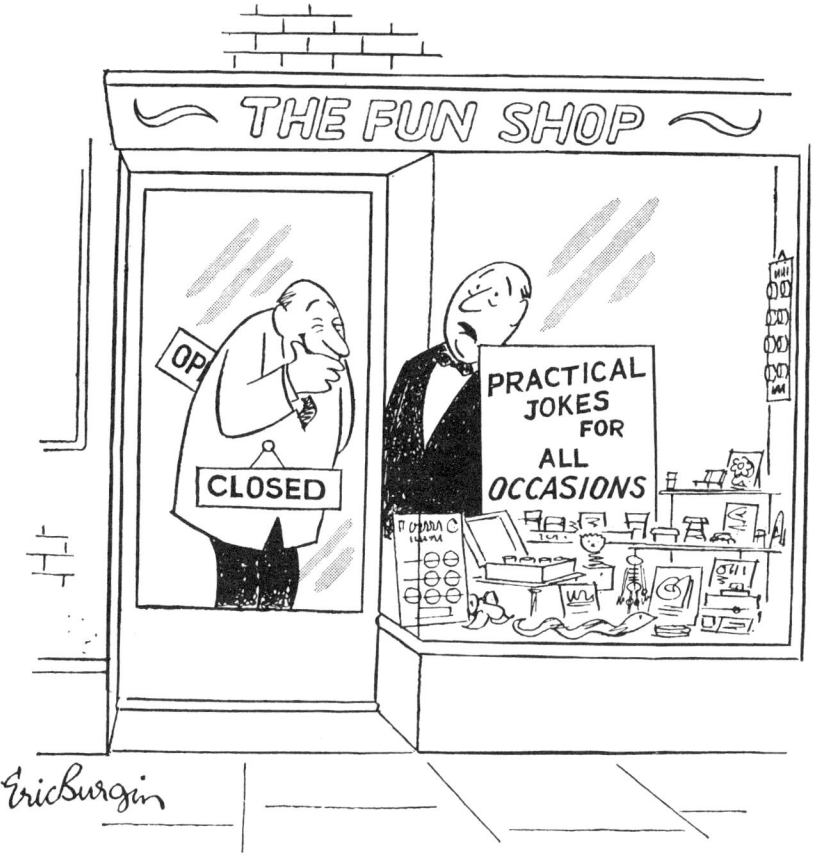

"I can't understand it—we've never been this slack."

Eric Burgin

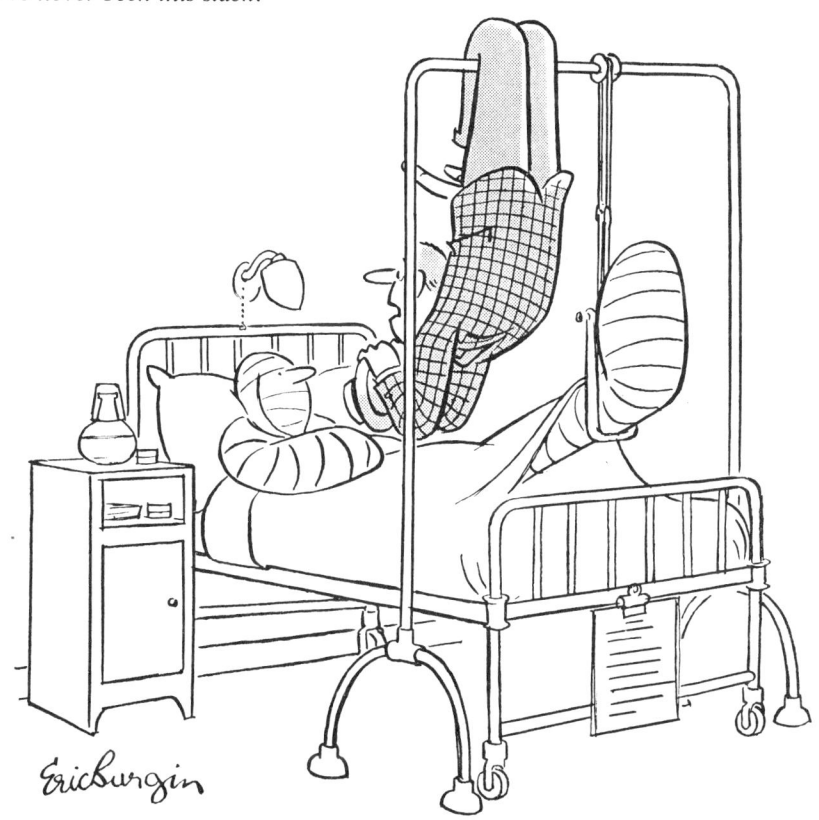

"Gosh, Bertel, the Flying Farinis just don't seem the same without you."

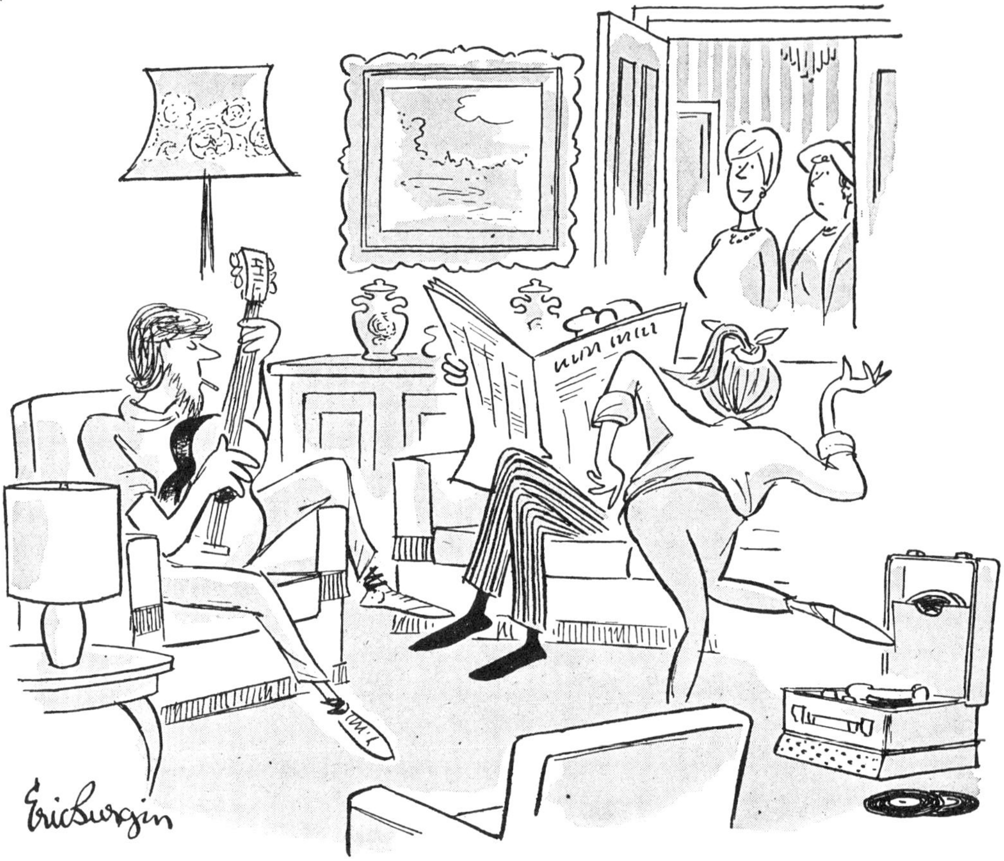
Eric Burgin

"Maurice has a wonderful understanding with the children—they don't try to understand him and he doesn't try to understand them."

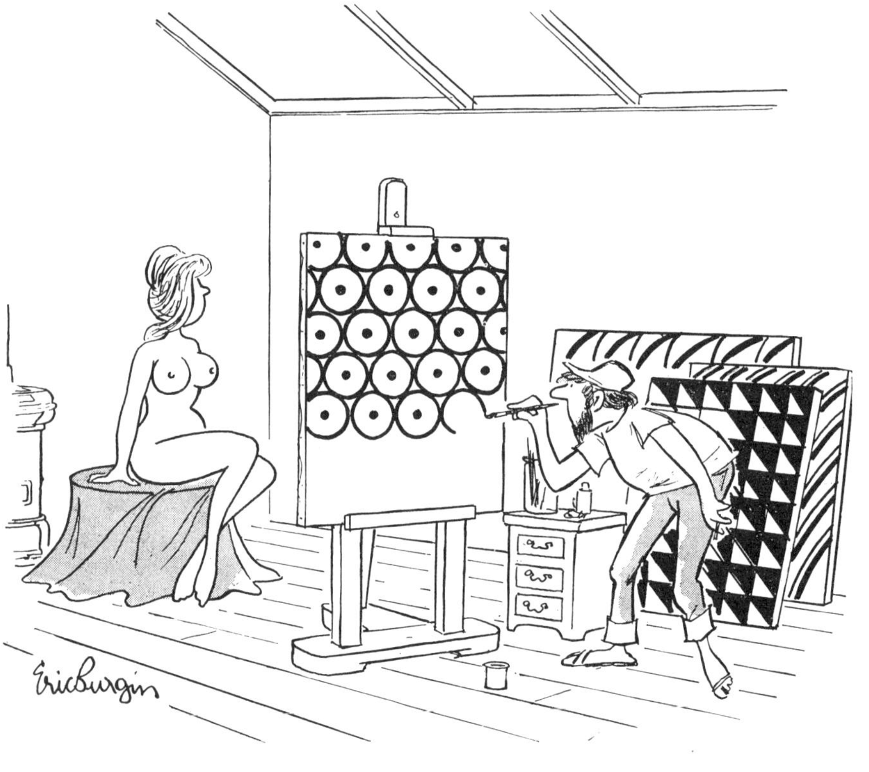
Eric Burgin

GRAHAM

Alex Graham was born in Glasgow in 1918 and attended the Glasgow School of Art. He has had a number of successful newspaper strips in various papers. He lives with his wife and two sons in East Sussex.

"I've been worried sick . . ."

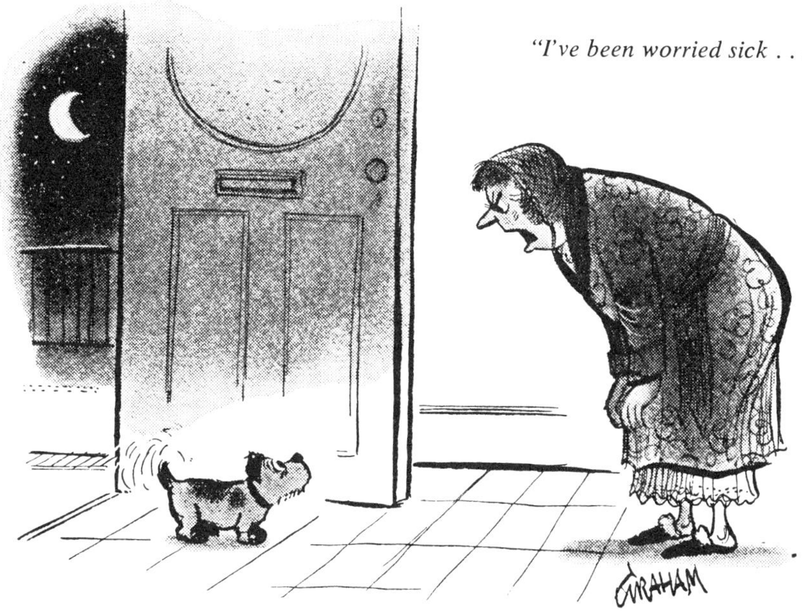
GRAHAM

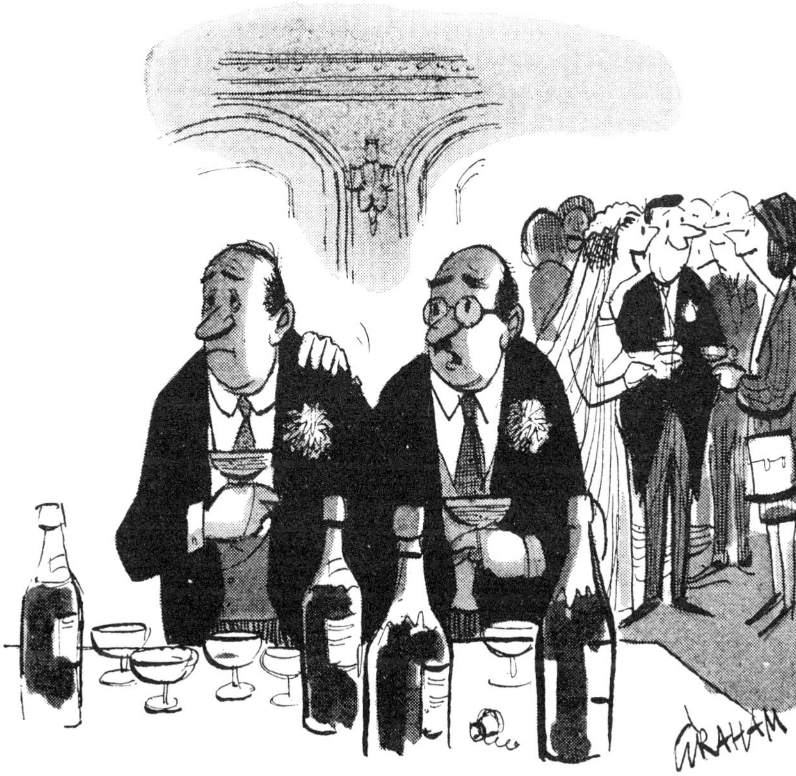
GRAHAM

"As I see it, Sid, you've lost a daughter and gained a nit."

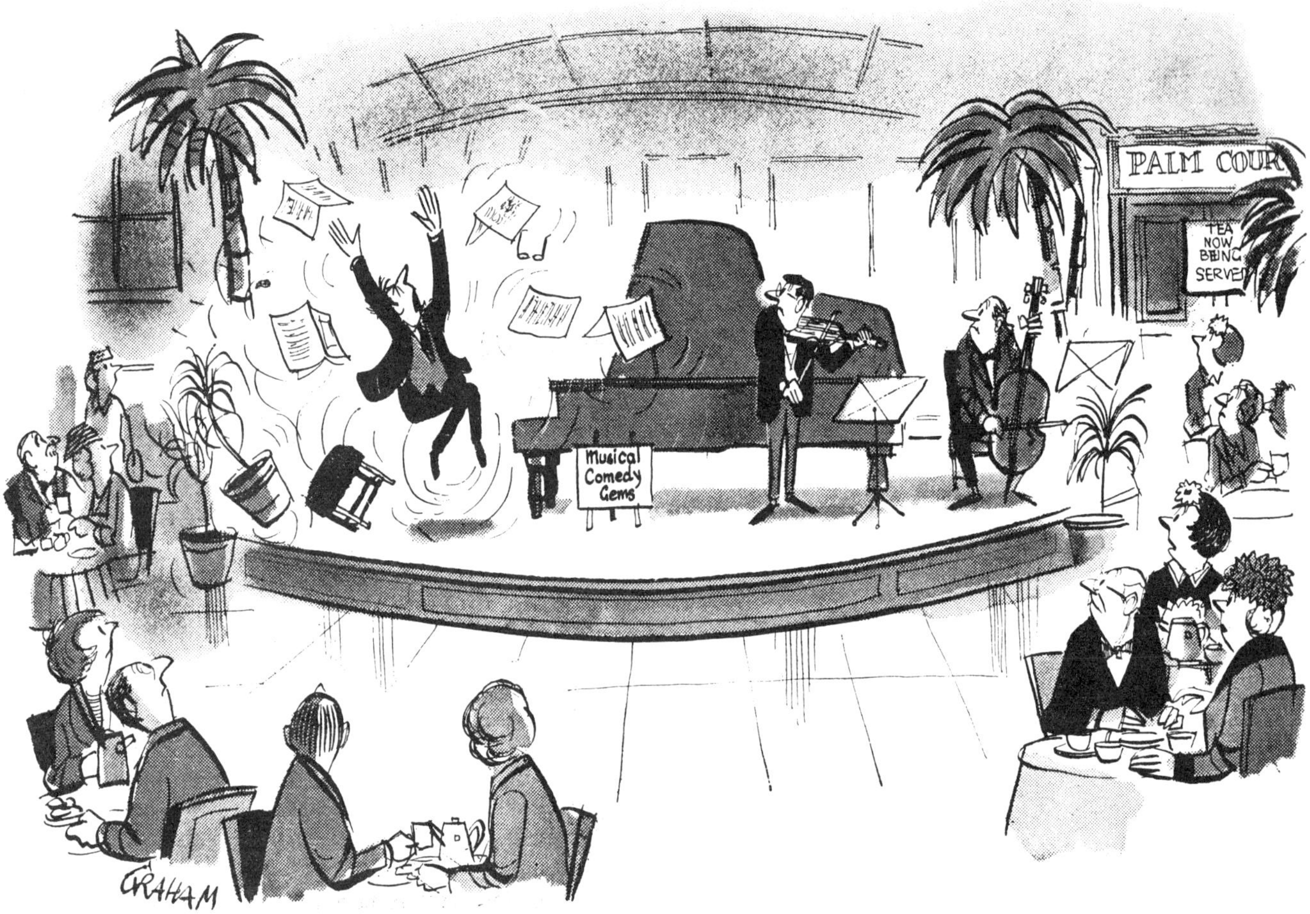
PALM COUR
TEA NOW BEING SERVED
Musical Comedy Gems
GRAHAM

"They often crack towards the end of the season."

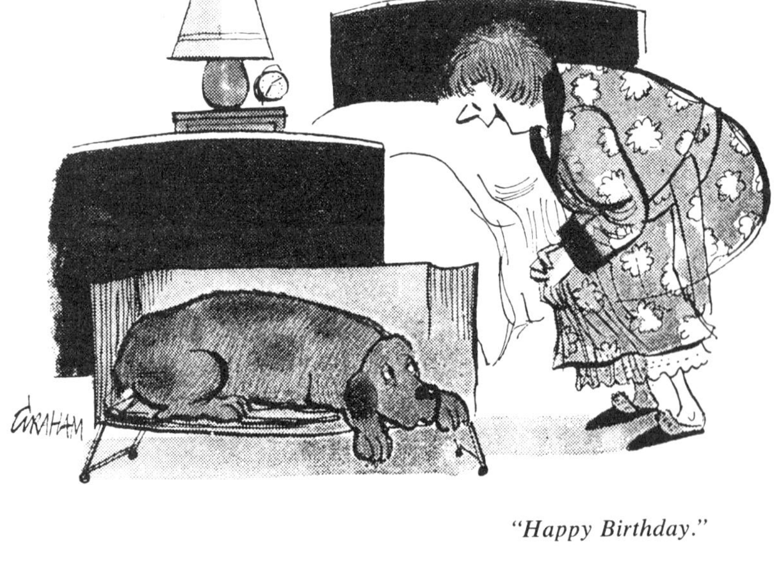
GRAHAM

"Happy Birthday."

Party Spirit

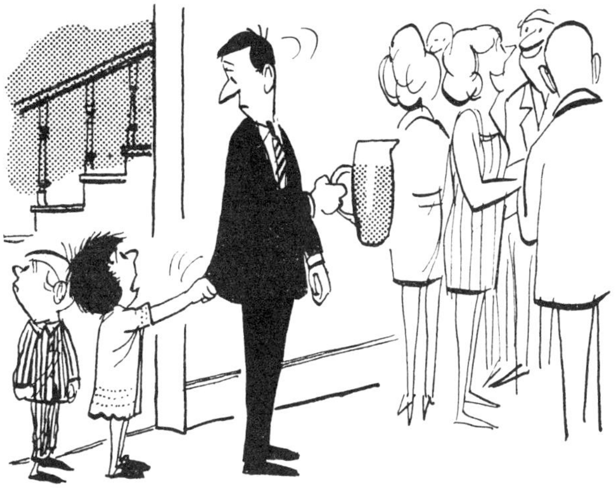

"There's something very peculiar going on in the spare bedroom!"

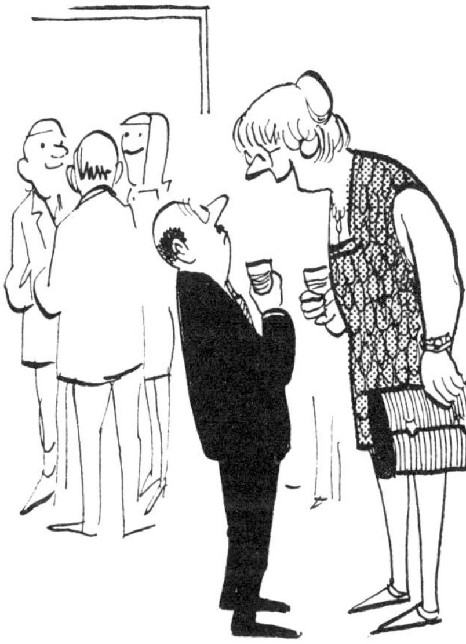

"My friends all call me Liz."

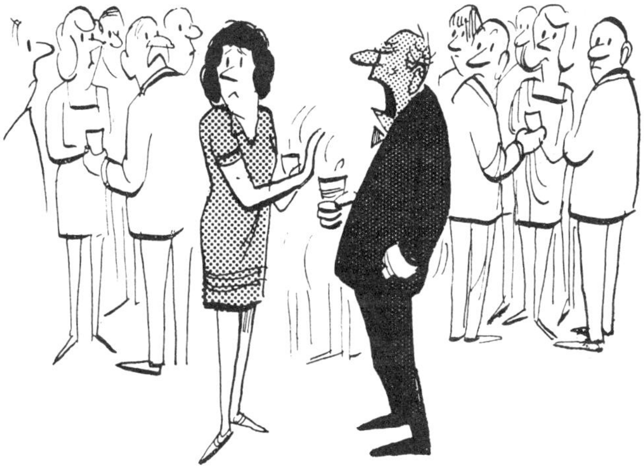

"I . . . am . . . not . . . sloshed!"

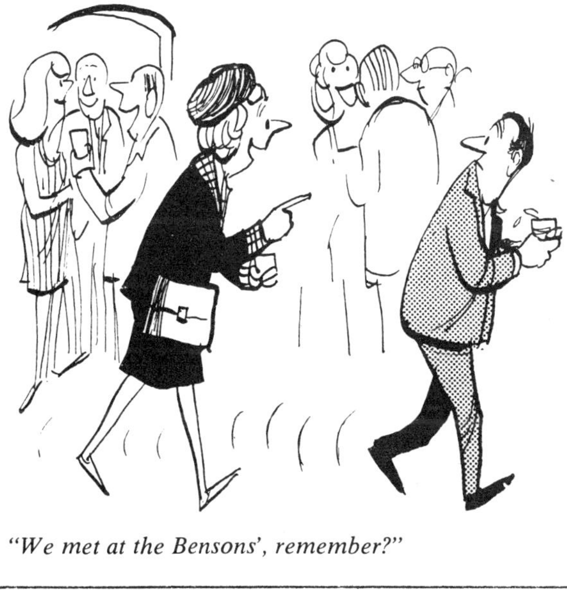

"We met at the Bensons', remember?"

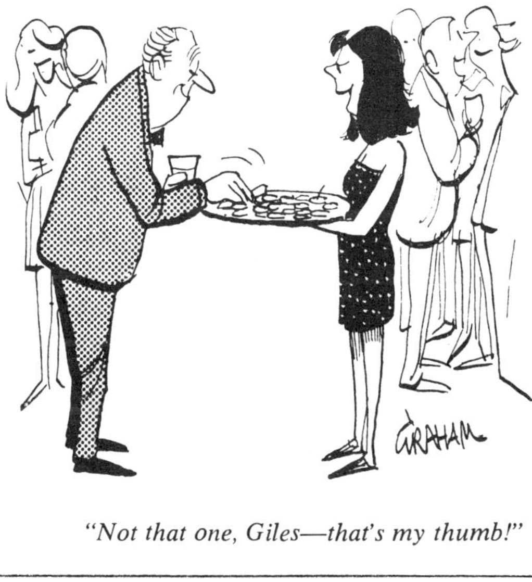
GRAHAM

"Not that one, Giles—that's my thumb!"

Daughter in the House

"Dad been looking after you all right?"

"... and you plug in over here, Bill."

"It's for you."

"It's the one with glasses."

"Somehow Daddy and I had imagined Dirk as being a little—you know—younger."

EDWARD McLACHLAN

Edward McLachlan was born in Leicester in 1940. He attended Leicester College of Art, then worked in design and advertising. He teaches art part time, and is political cartoonist for the *Sunday Mirror*. He is married, has one child, and lives in Leicestershire.

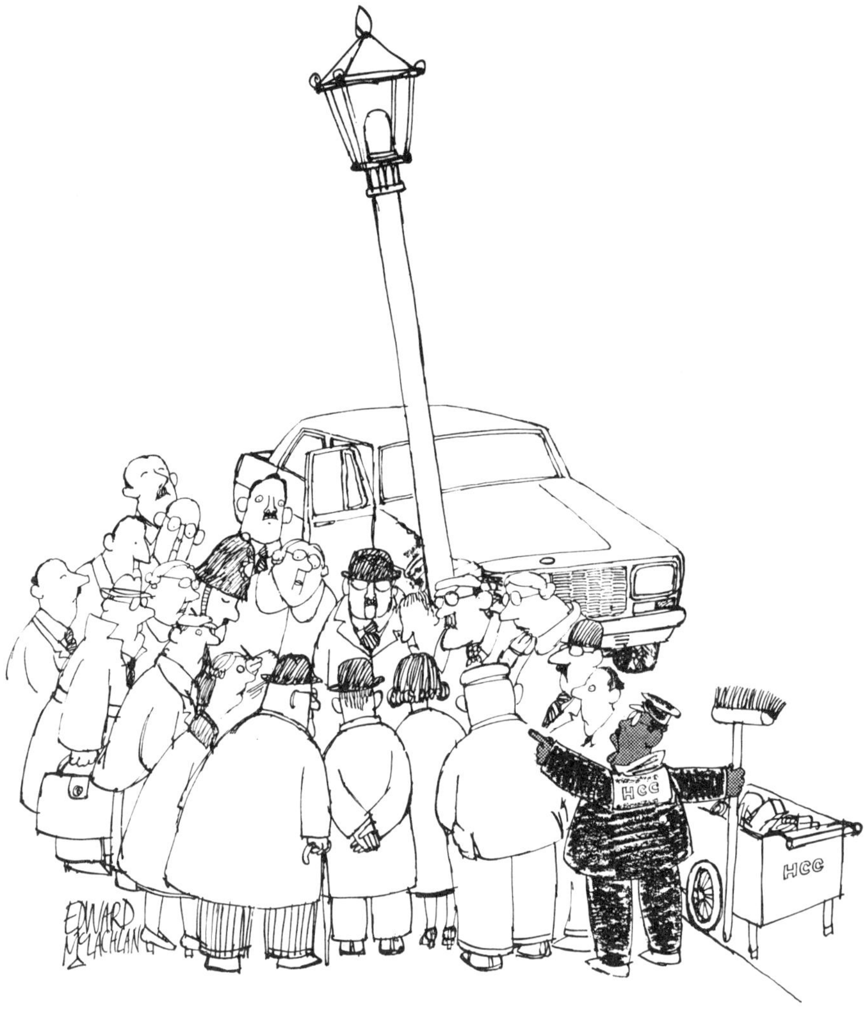
HCC
HCC
EDWARD McLACHLAN

"Let me through, please! I'm a doctor!"

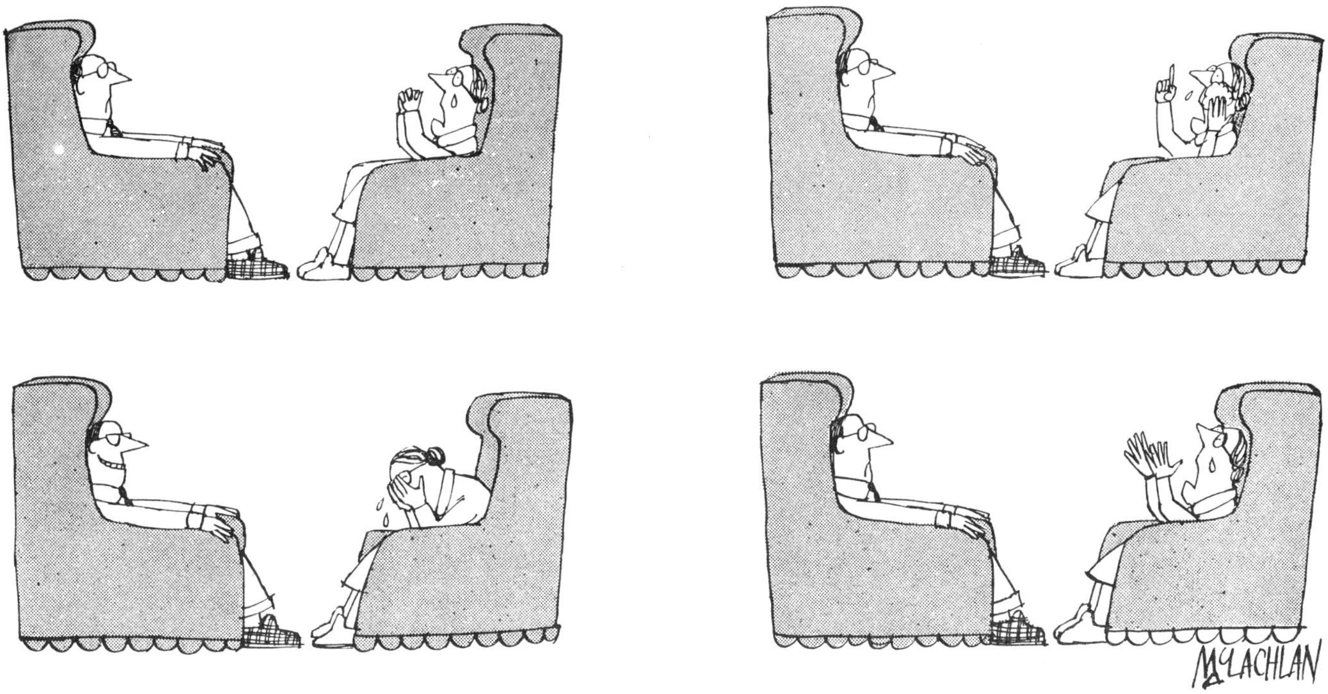
McLACHLAN

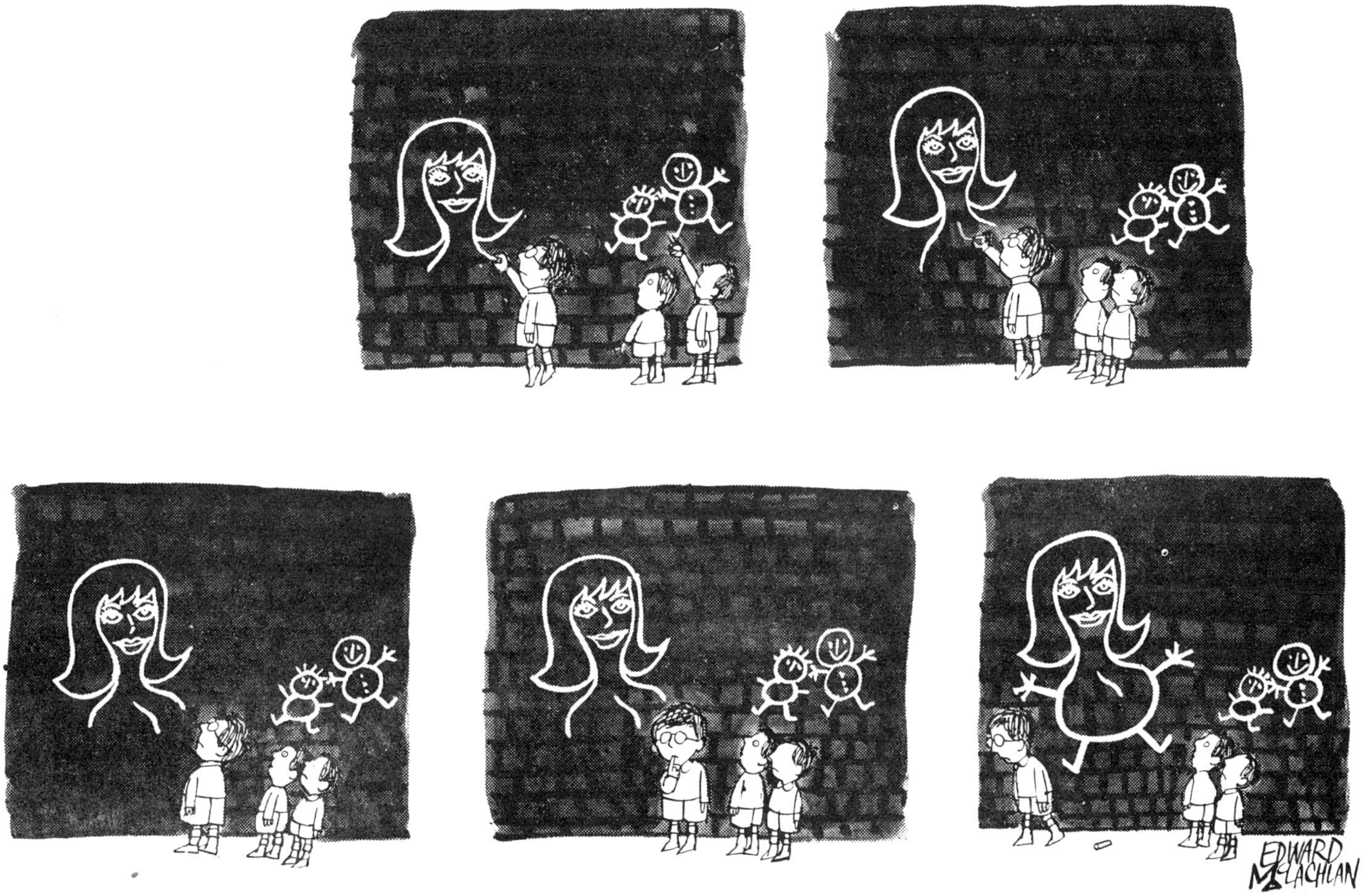
EDWARD McLACHLAN

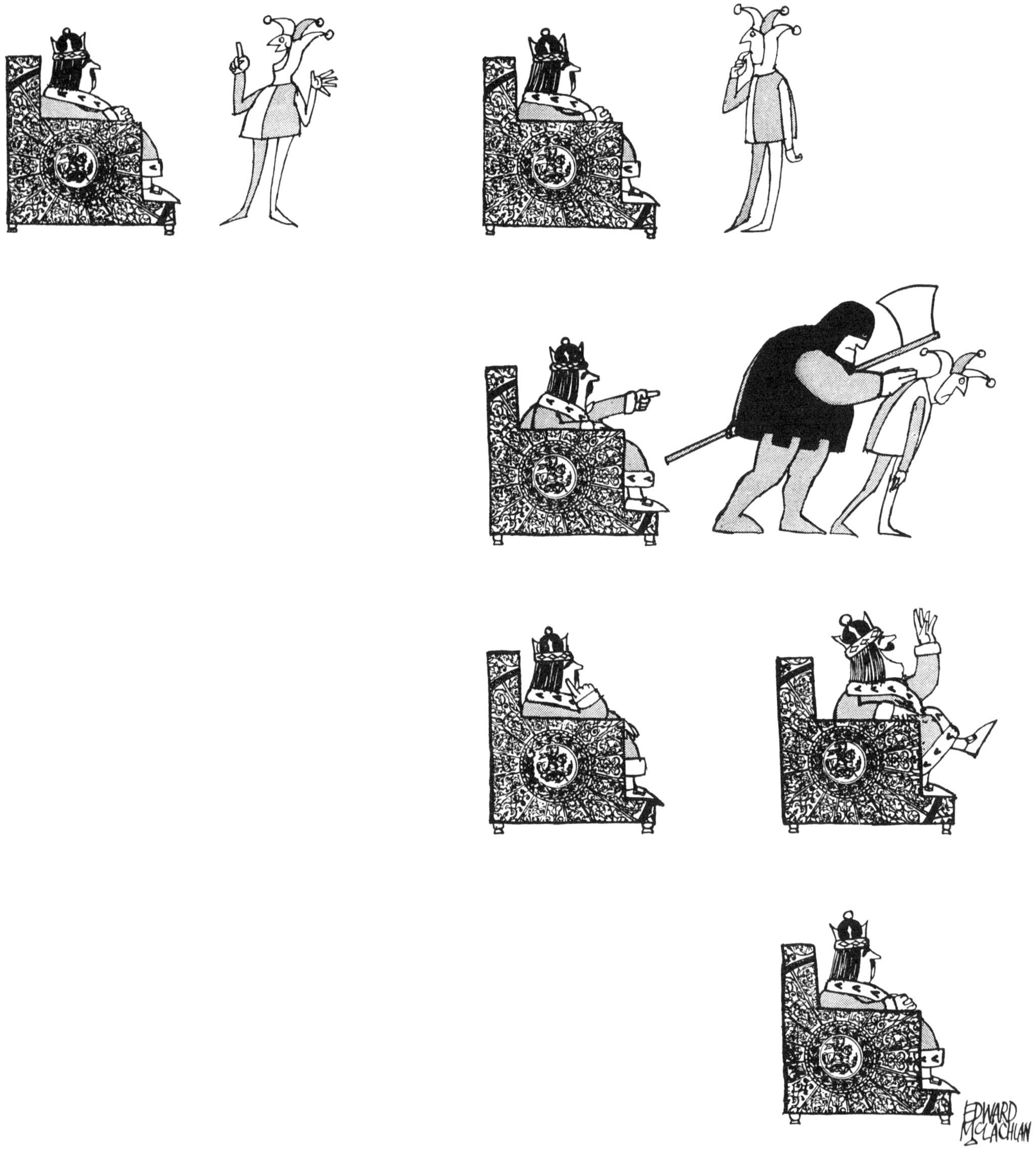
EDWARD McLACHLAN

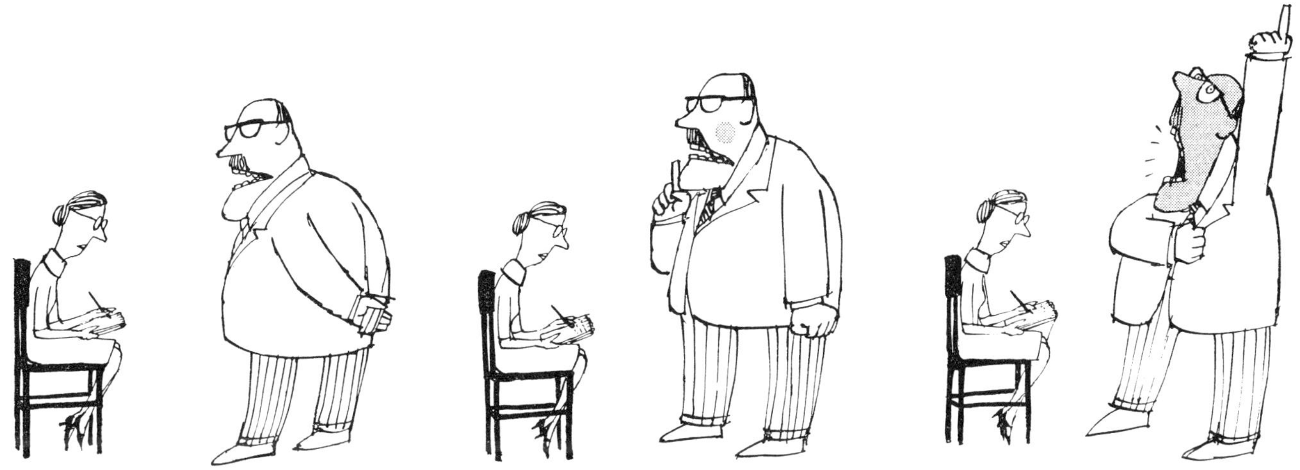

"Take a letter, Miss Roper.

'Dear Sir . . .'

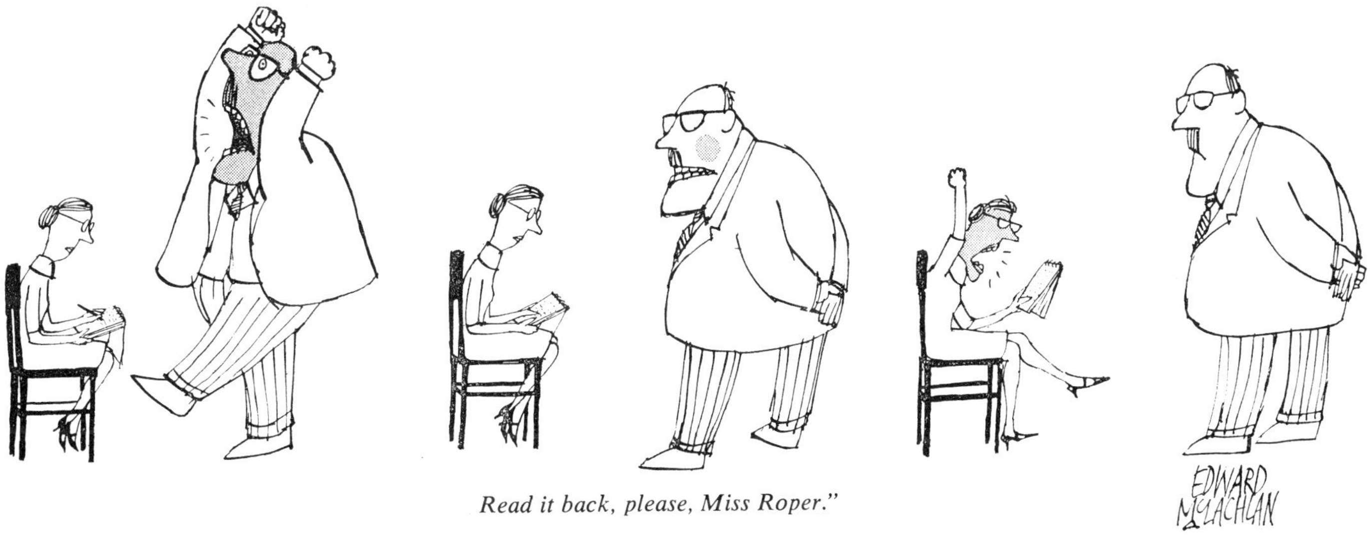
EDWARD
McLACHLAN

Read it back, please, Miss Roper."

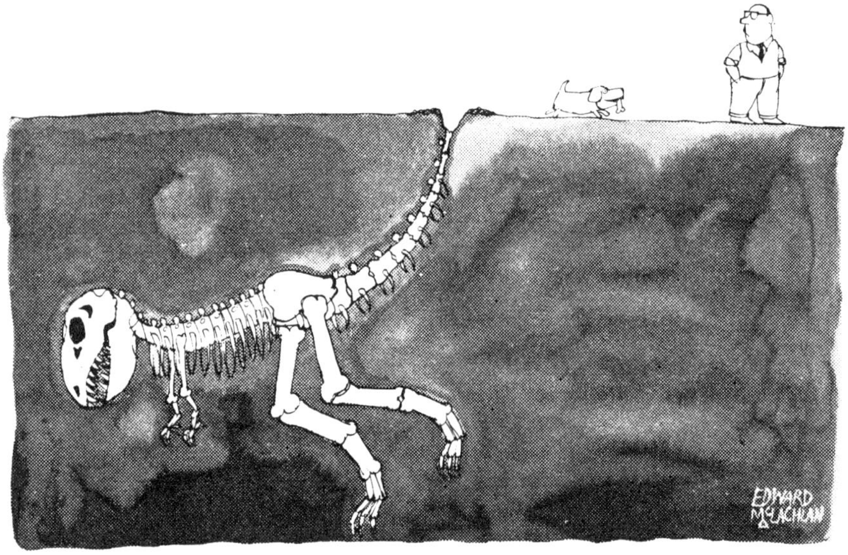
EDWARD
McLACHLAN

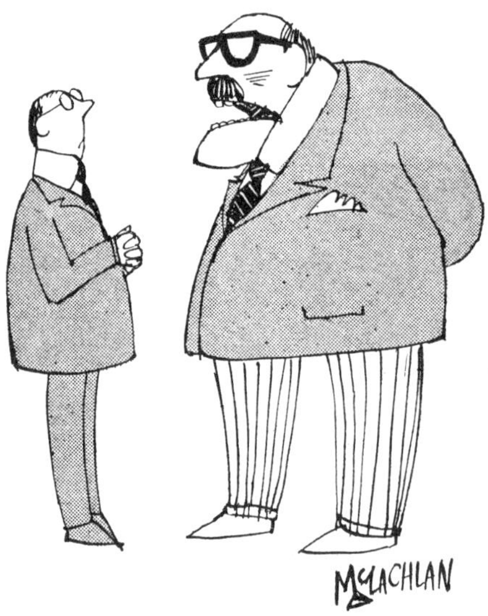
McLACHLAN

"Yes sir, yes sir, yes sir. That's all I hear from you. You're a director now, Festerton, so you can drop the 'sir'!"

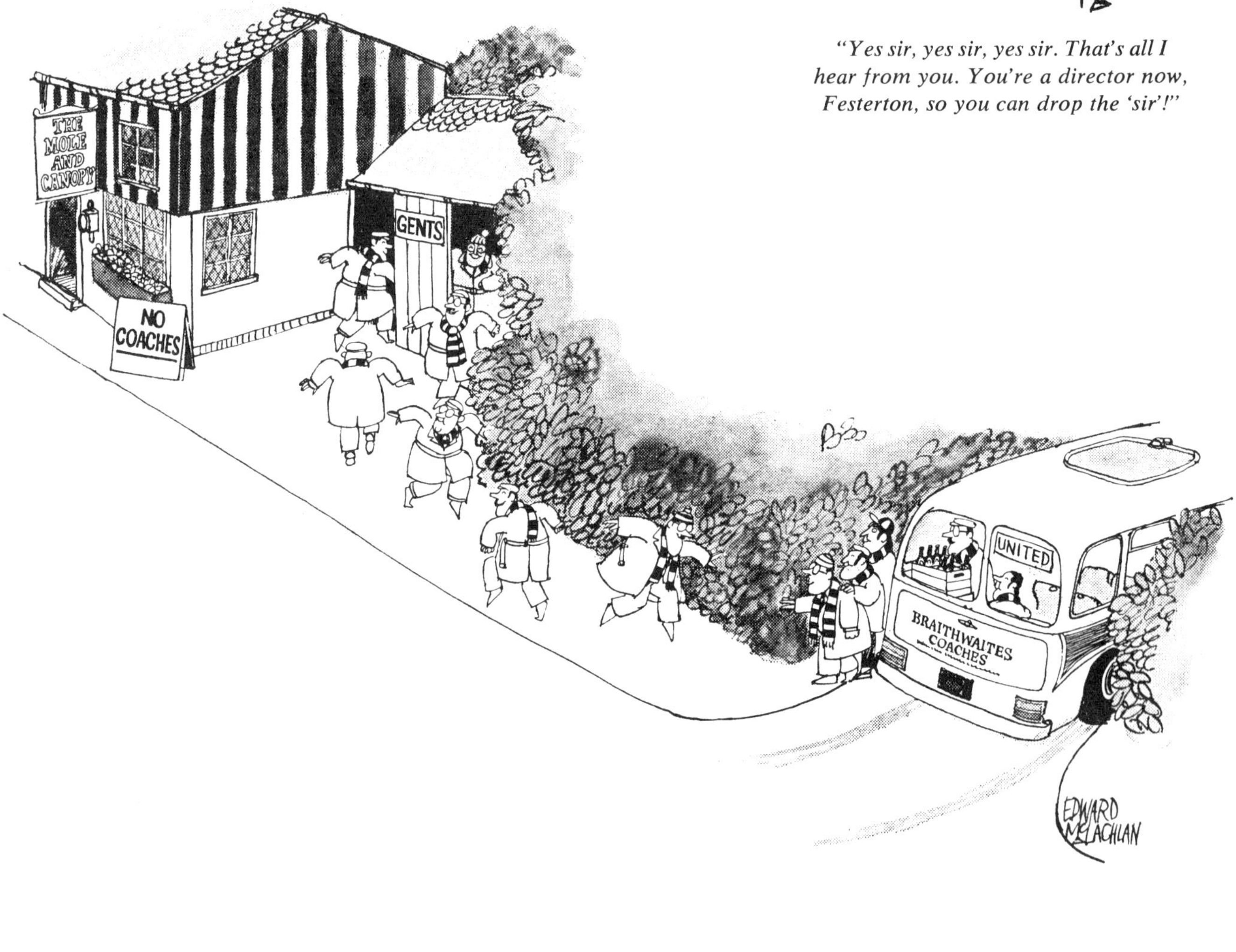
THE
MOLE
AND
CANOPY
GENTS
NO
COACHES
UNITED
BRAITHWAITES
COACHES
EDWARD
McLACHLAN

EDWARD MCLACHLAN 85

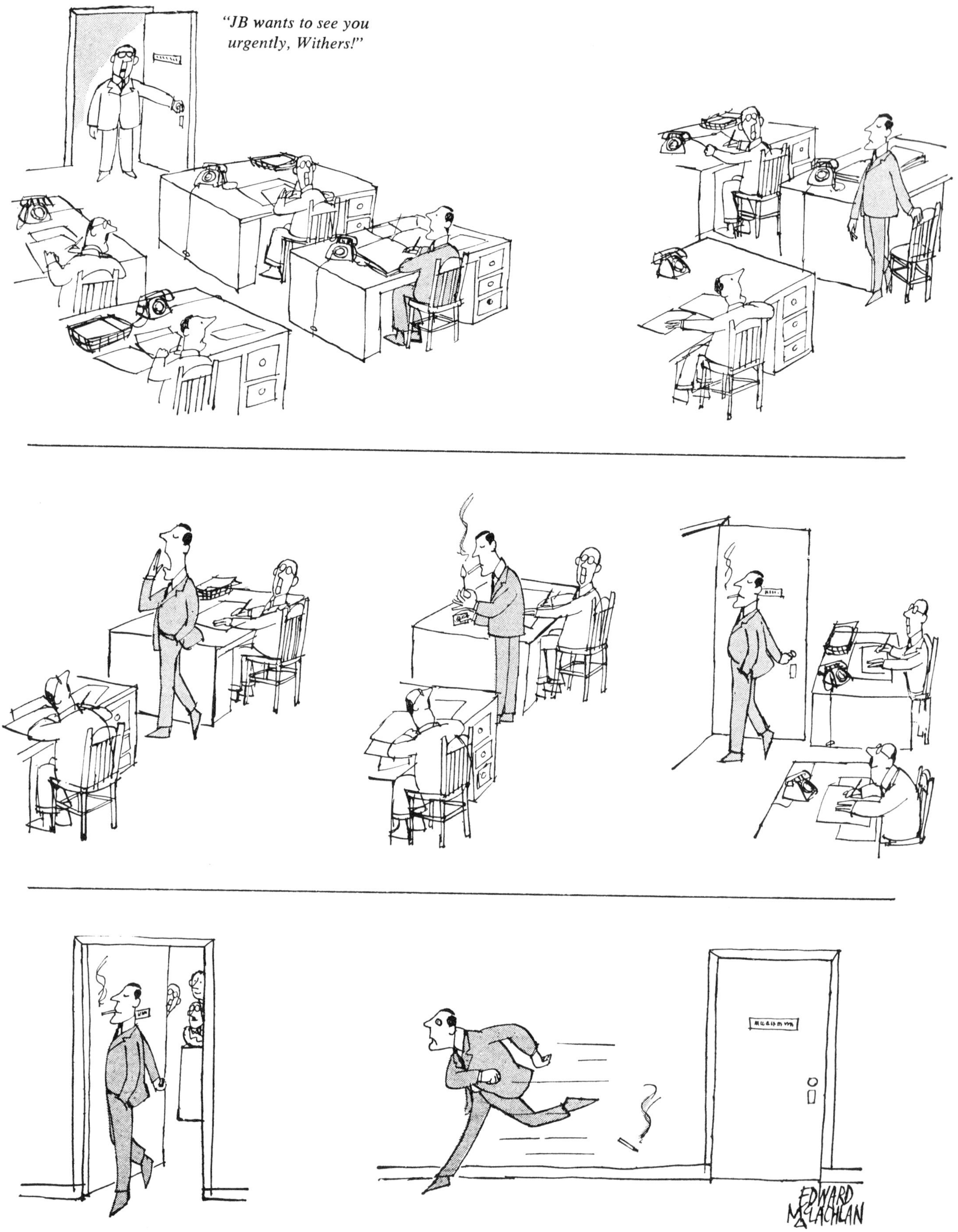
"JB wants to see you urgently, Withers!"
EDWARD McLACHLAN

STARKE

Leslie Starke was born in Scotland in 1905. He had no formal art training, yet has illustrated several books as well as having three collections of his own cartoons published. He is married and lives in London.

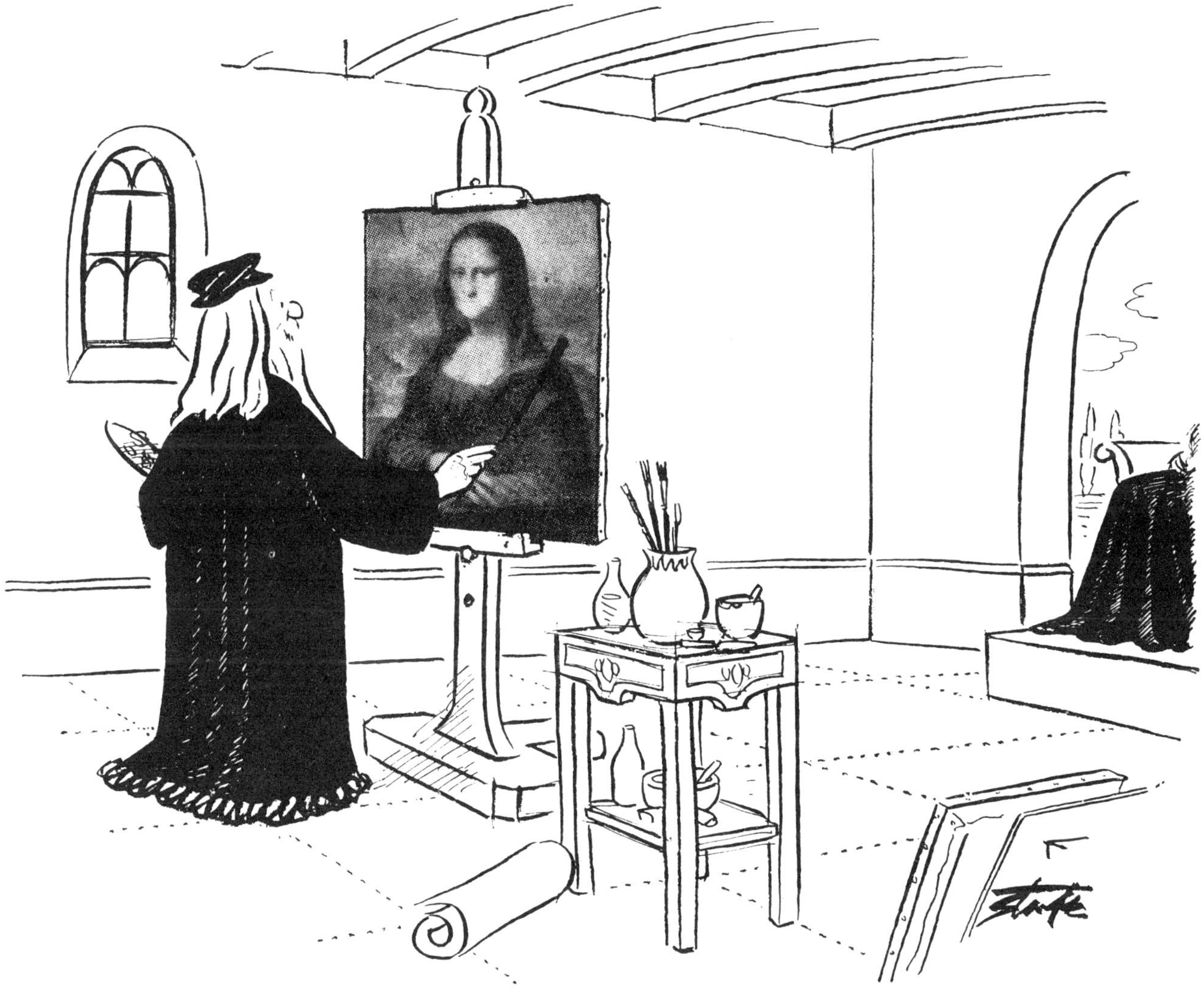
Starke

"Then there's the one about the Armenian, the Hungarian and the Sicilian . . ."

"Come back—I haven't finished with you yet."

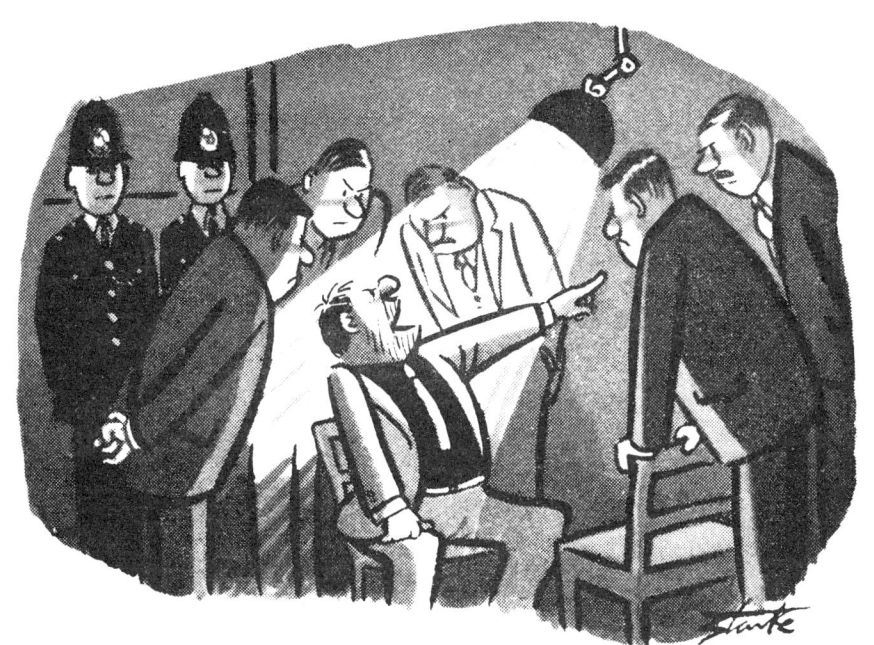

"Now you, sir—<u>you</u> have a question?"

"My forgiveness to the Chef."

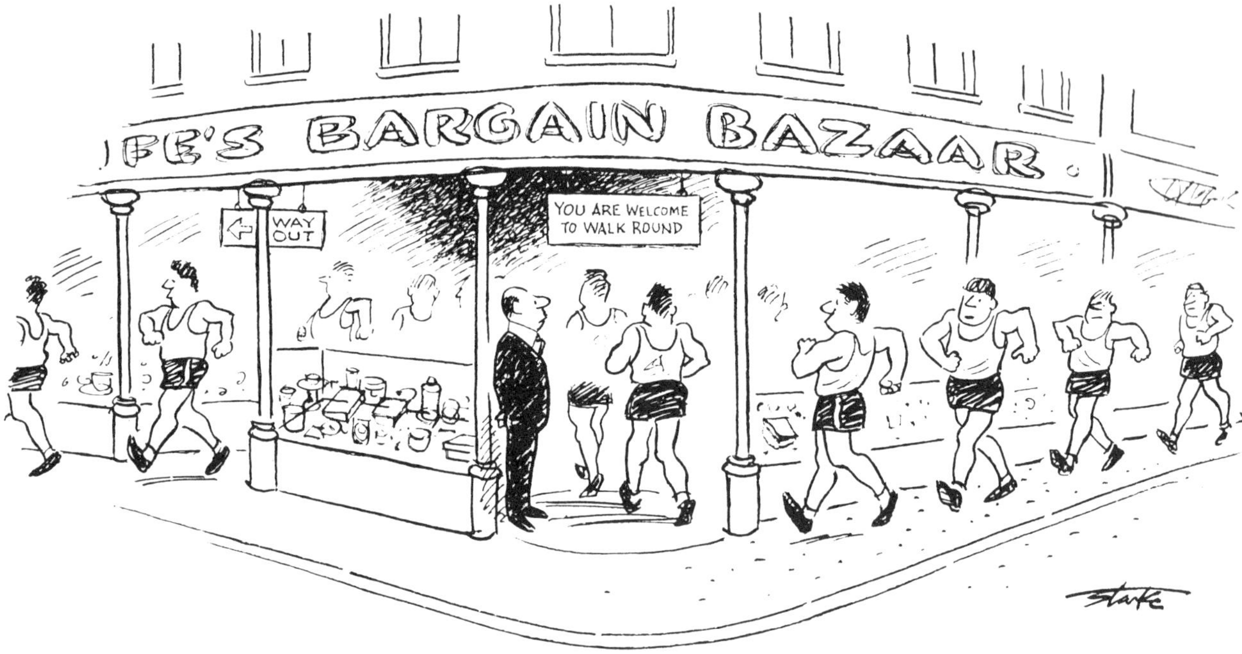
FE'S BARGAIN BAZAAR
WAY OUT
YOU ARE WELCOME TO WALK ROUND
Starke

"Ignore them, Alice."

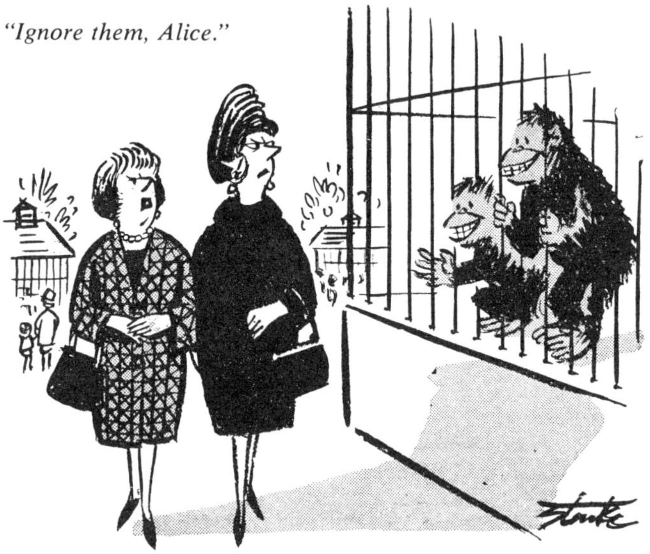
Starke

"Pay attention, Brogan, and answer the questions!"

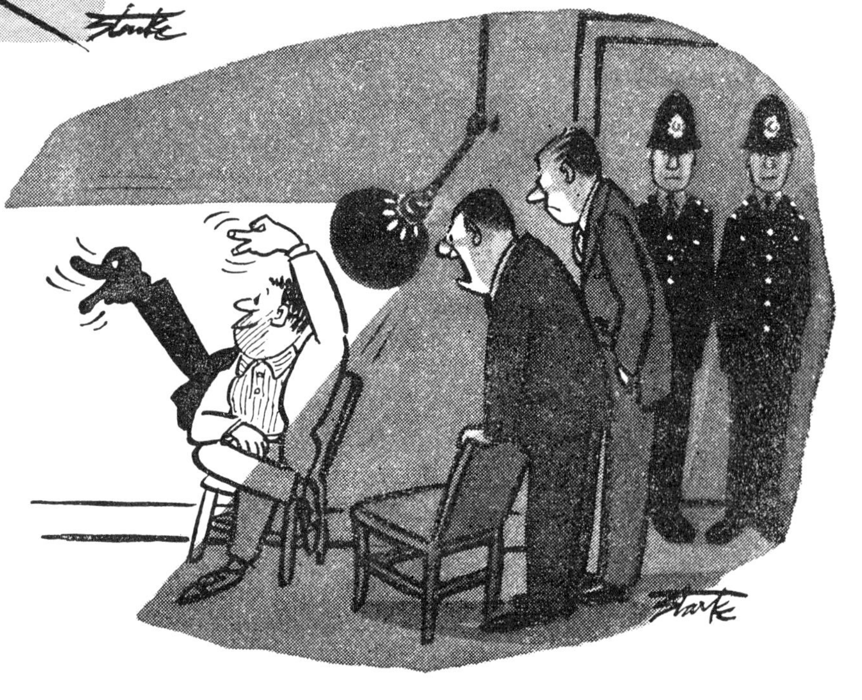
Starke

"Mrs. Angelo! Triplets!"

HITCHINS

M. Hitchins was born in London in 1924. He has worked in film animation with the Rank organization and has also worked in television advertising. He is married and has two children.

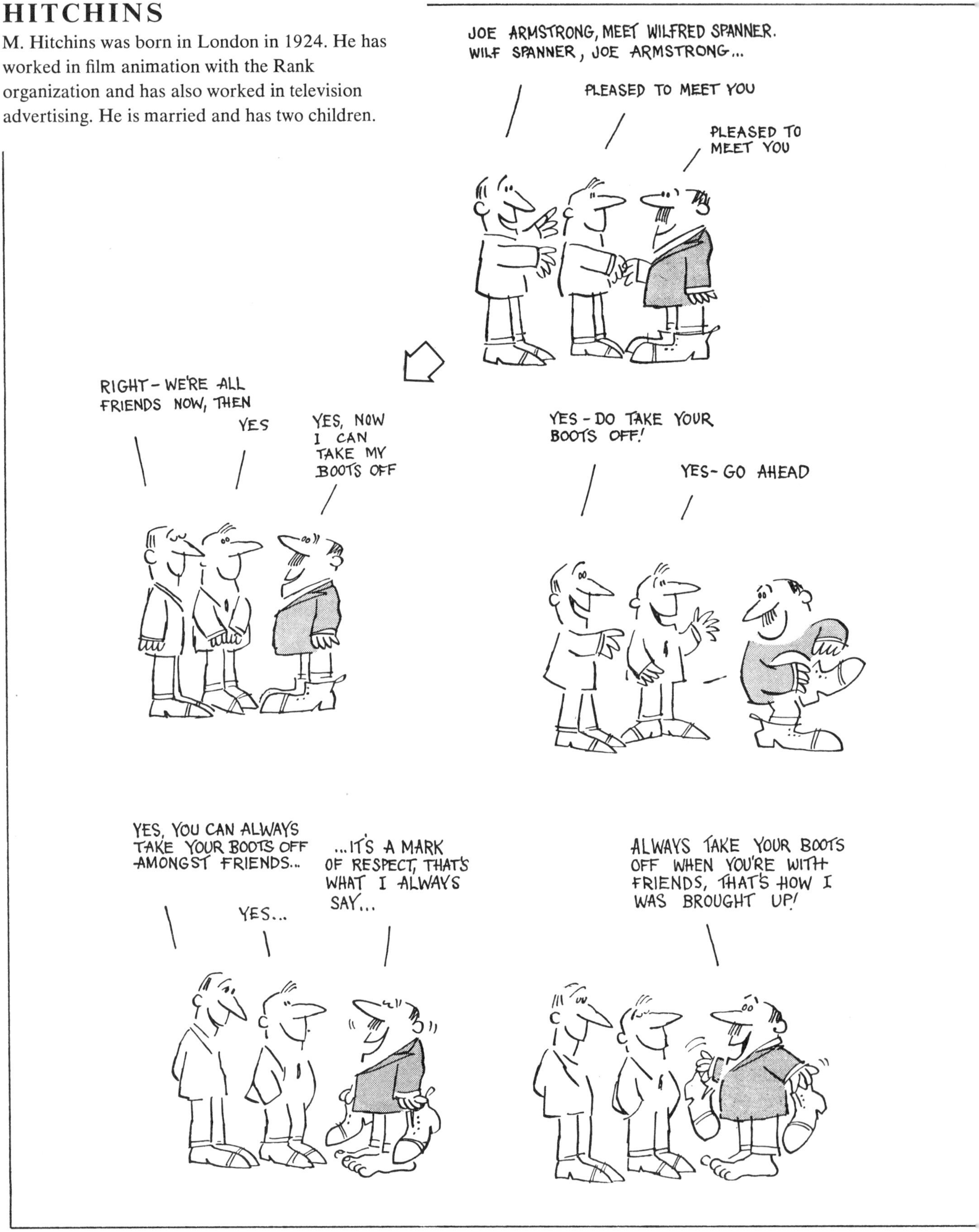
JOE ARMSTRONG, MEET WILFRED SPANNER. WILF SPANNER, JOE ARMSTRONG...
PLEASED TO MEET YOU
PLEASED TO MEET YOU
RIGHT - WE'RE ALL FRIENDS NOW, THEN
YES
YES, NOW I CAN TAKE MY BOOTS OFF
YES - DO TAKE YOUR BOOTS OFF!
YES- GO AHEAD
YES, YOU CAN ALWAYS TAKE YOUR BOOTS OFF AMONGST FRIENDS...
YES...
...IT'S A MARK OF RESPECT, THAT'S WHAT I ALWAYS SAY...
ALWAYS TAKE YOUR BOOTS OFF WHEN YOU'RE WITH FRIENDS, THAT'S HOW I WAS BROUGHT UP!

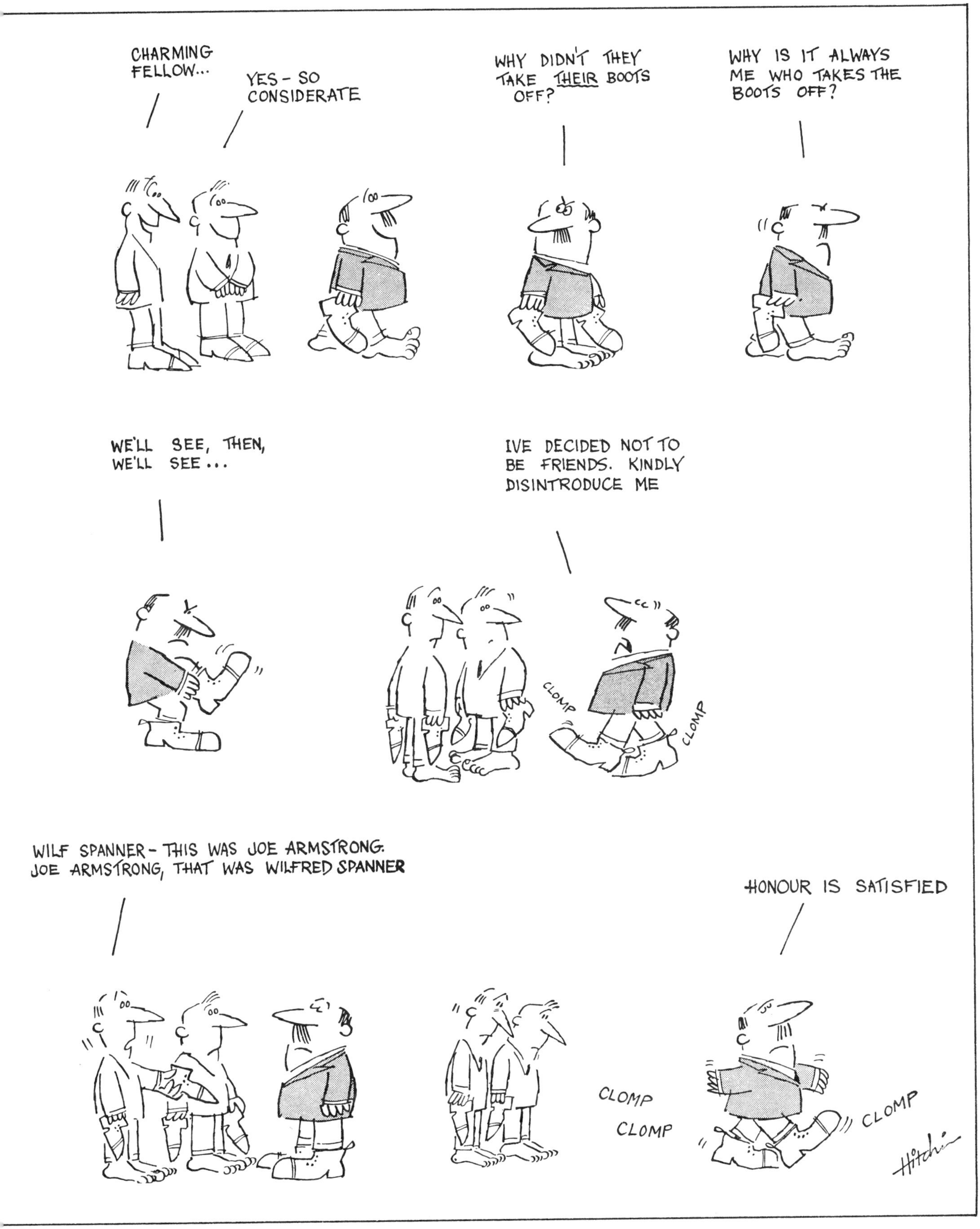
CHARMING FELLOW...
YES - SO CONSIDERATE
WHY DIDN'T THEY TAKE THEIR BOOTS OFF?
WHY IS IT ALWAYS ME WHO TAKES THE BOOTS OFF?
WE'LL SEE, THEN, WE'LL SEE...
IVE DECIDED NOT TO BE FRIENDS. KINDLY DISINTRODUCE ME
CLOMP
CLOMP
WILF SPANNER - THIS WAS JOE ARMSTRONG. JOE ARMSTRONG, THAT WAS WILFRED SPANNER
HONOUR IS SATISFIED
CLOMP
CLOMP
CLOMP
Hitchins

...Yes, that's a good idea, Mr Blethers...
COME, COME, FUDLEIGH—THAT ATTITUDE WILL GET YOU NOWHERE!
NOW, THUMP ME ON THE BACK, BOY—TELL ME IT'S A MARVELLOUS IDEA!
IT'S A GREAT IDEA, MR BLETHERS! BRILLIANT!
Better, better... You may call me Edward
IT'S SENSATIONAL TED! YOU'RE A GENIUS!
SPLENDID! I THINK YOU'VE GOT A FUTURE HERE, LAD...
...YES-YOU'VE A NATURAL TALENT FOR SINCERE FLATTERY- THE ONLY THING YOU HAVE TO LEARN NOW IS...
THAT'S MY BOY! I KNEW YOU HAD IT IN YOU...
Hitchins

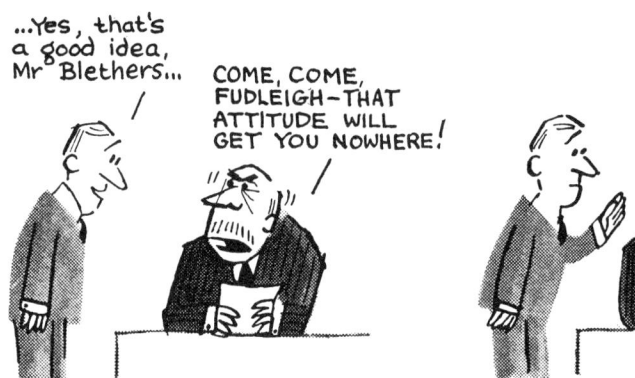

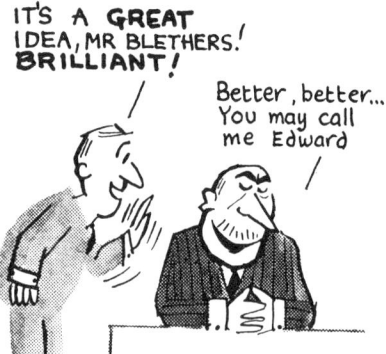

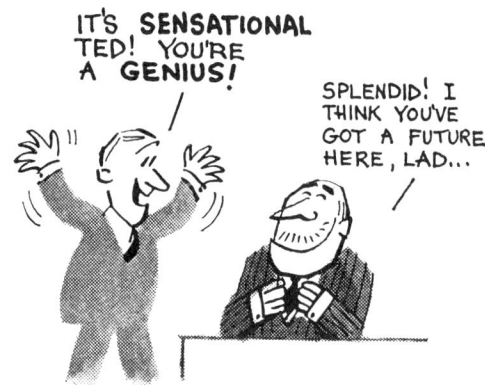

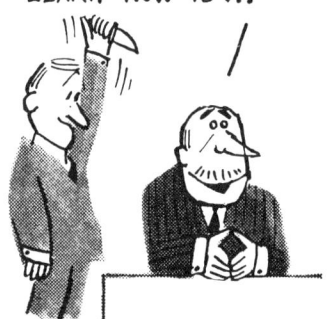

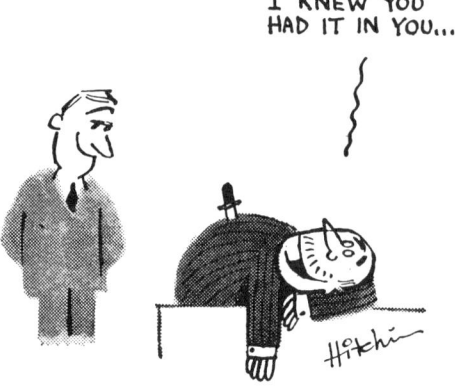

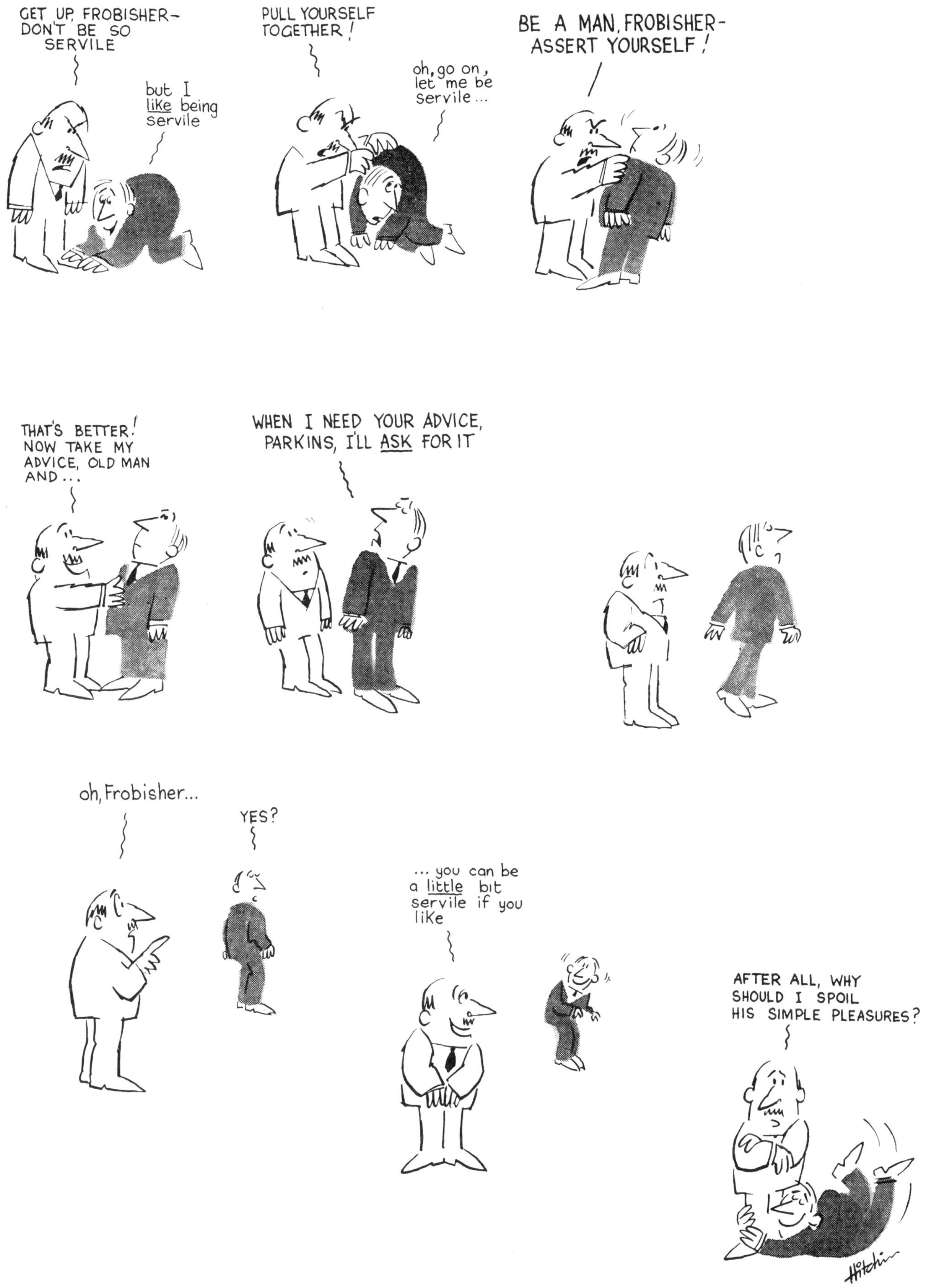
GET UP, FROBISHER-
DON'T BE SO
SERVILE
but I
like being
servile
PULL YOURSELF
TOGETHER!
oh, go on,
let me be
servile...
BE A MAN, FROBISHER-
ASSERT YOURSELF!
THAT'S BETTER!
NOW TAKE MY
ADVICE, OLD MAN
AND...
WHEN I NEED YOUR ADVICE,
PARKINS, I'LL ASK FOR IT
oh, Frobisher...
YES?
... you can be
a little bit
servile if you
like
AFTER ALL, WHY
SHOULD I SPOIL
HIS SIMPLE PLEASURES?
Hitchins

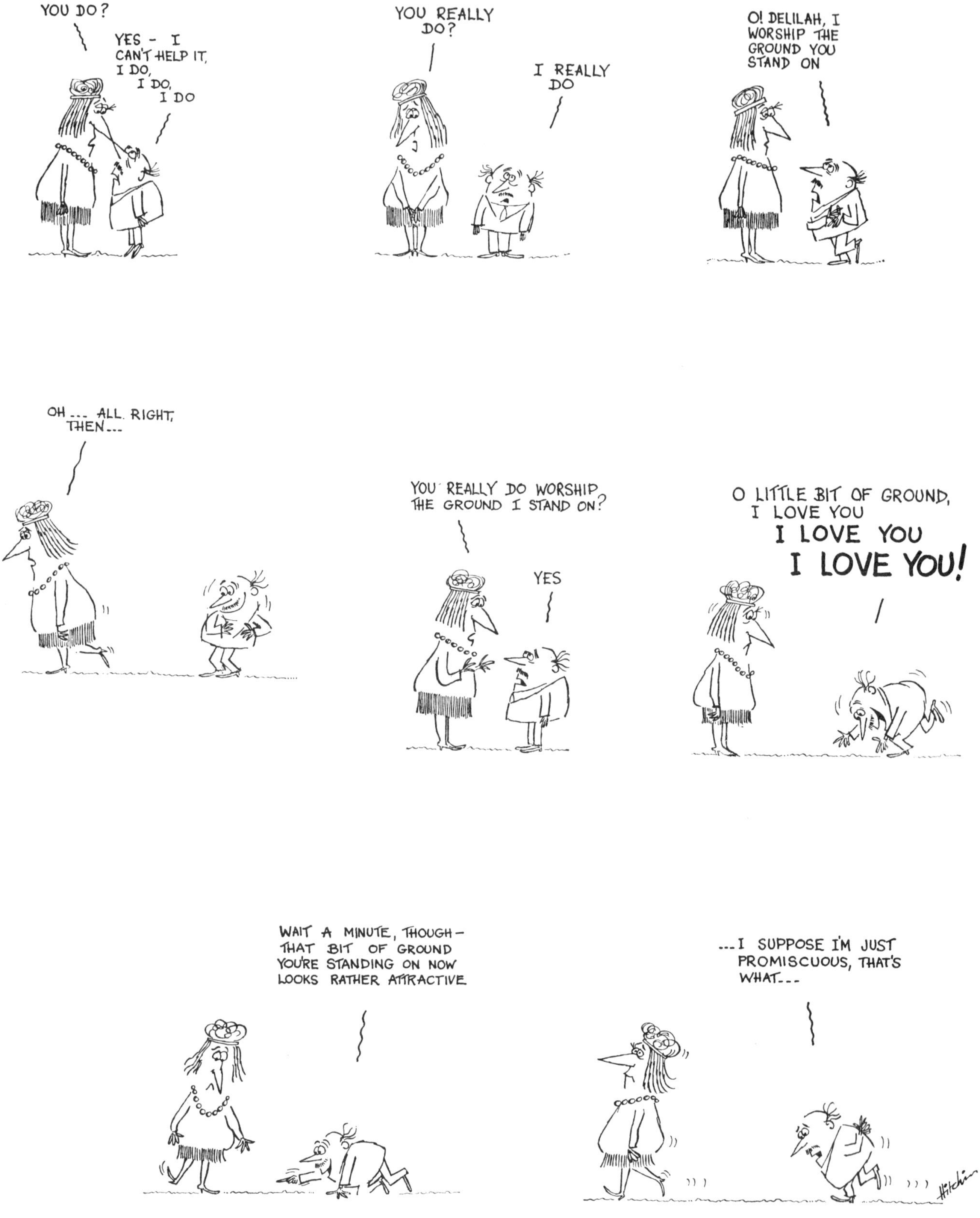
YOU DO?
YES - I CAN'T HELP IT, I DO, I DO, I DO
YOU REALLY DO?
I REALLY DO
O! DELILAH, I WORSHIP THE GROUND YOU STAND ON
OH ... ALL RIGHT, THEN ...
YOU REALLY DO WORSHIP THE GROUND I STAND ON?
YES
O LITTLE BIT OF GROUND, I LOVE YOU
I LOVE YOU
I LOVE YOU!
WAIT A MINUTE, THOUGH - THAT BIT OF GROUND YOU'RE STANDING ON NOW LOOKS RATHER ATTRACTIVE
... I SUPPOSE I'M JUST PROMISCUOUS, THAT'S WHAT ...
Hitchins

ARNOLD WILES

Arnold Wiles was born in Southampton in 1926 and has had no art training. With his brother, who is equally enthusiastic about the subject, he ran a fishing magazine for five years, and he has written a guidebook to sea fishing. He has four books of cartoons in print. He is married, with three children.

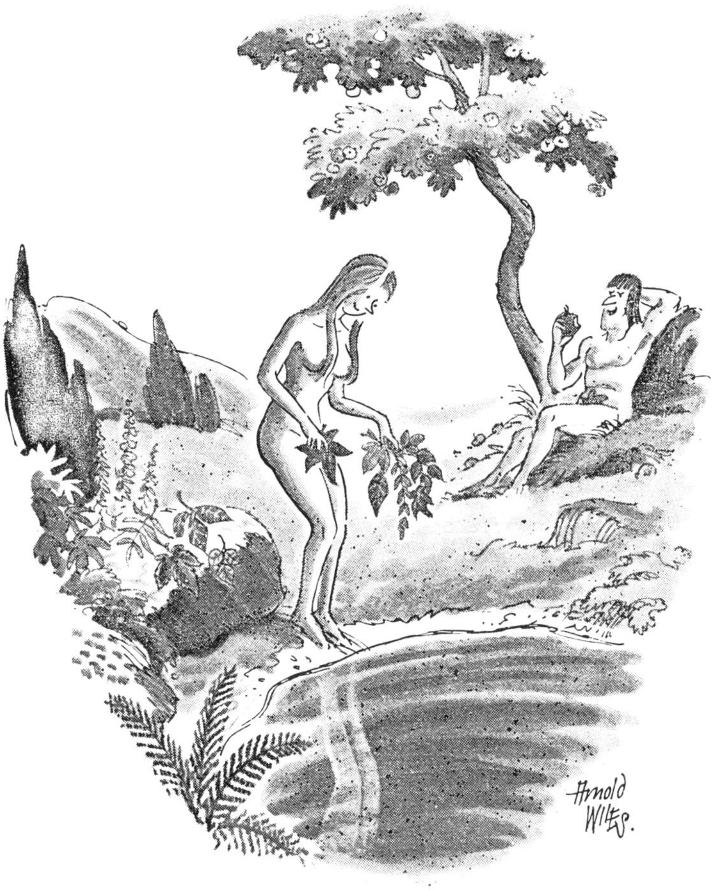
Arnold
Wiles.

"I like it—it looks sexy."

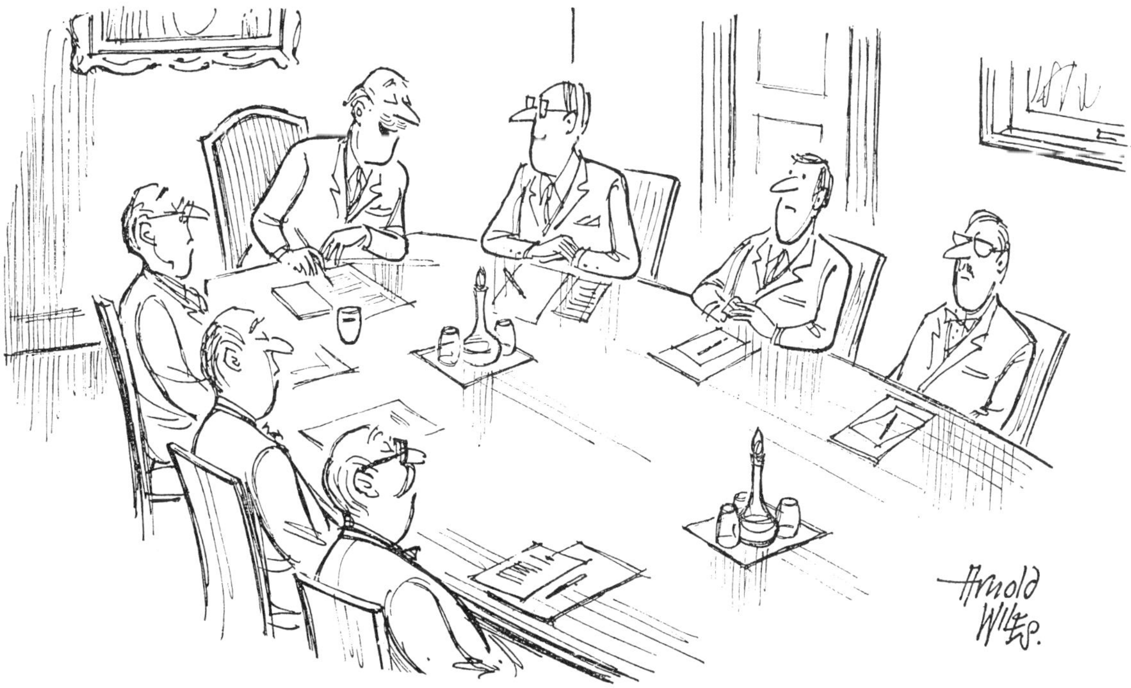
Arnold
Wiles.

*"I like that streak of independence in Perkins.
That slight hesitation before he agreed with me."*

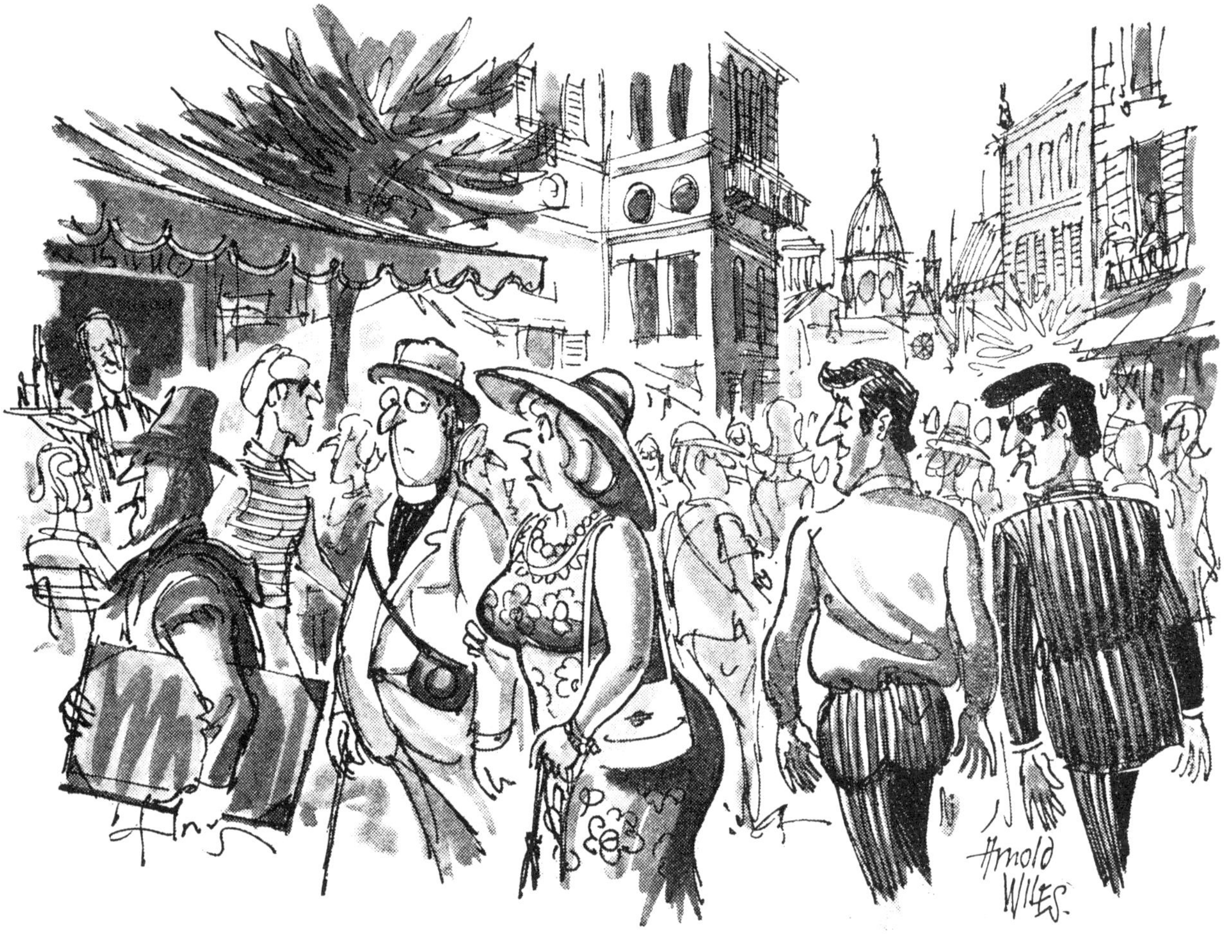
Arnold
WILES

"Turn the other cheek? In Rome?"

Hitching Post

"Stop! That looks like one of ours!"

"Pretend not to notice them . . ."

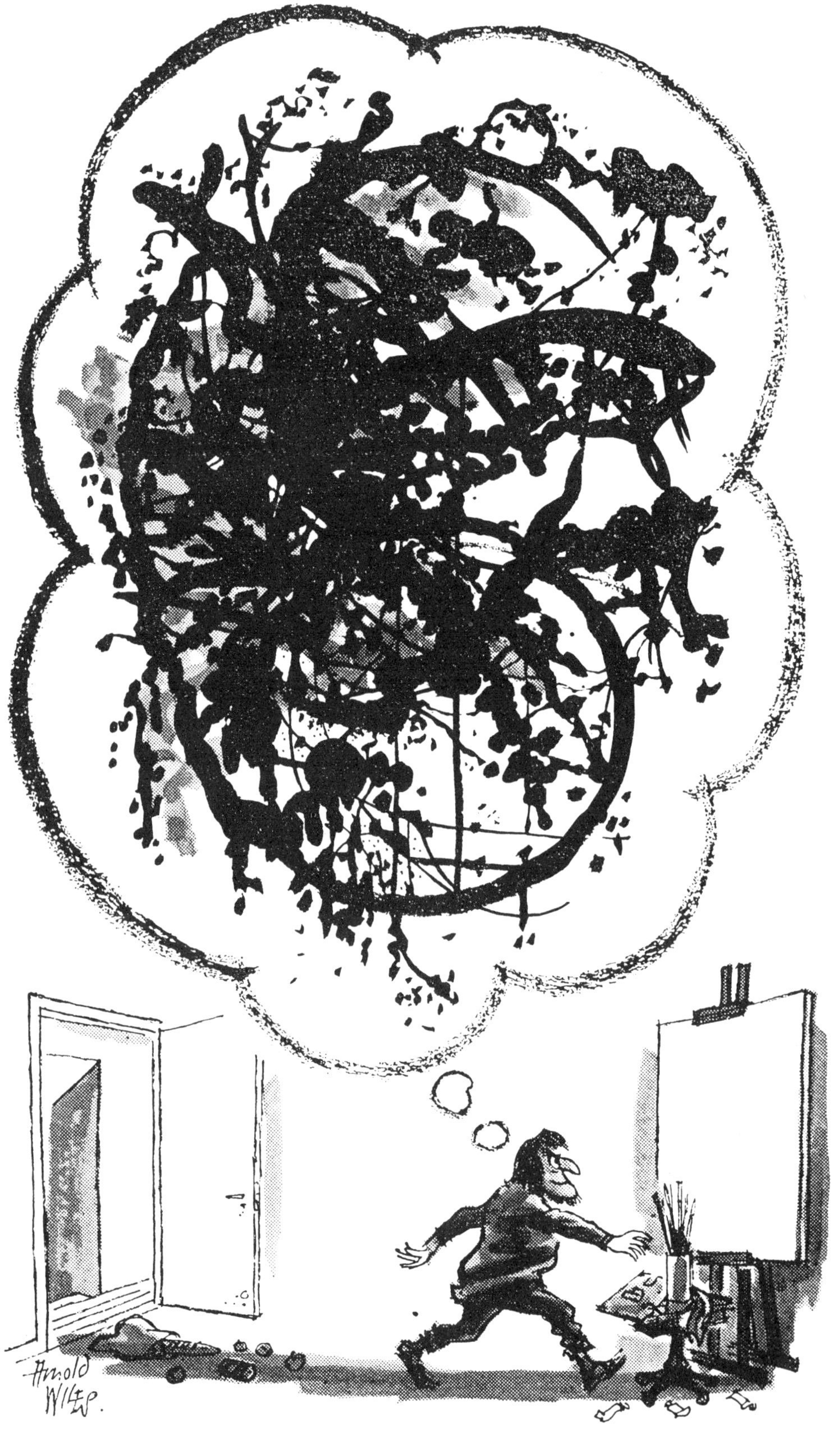
Arnold
WILES.

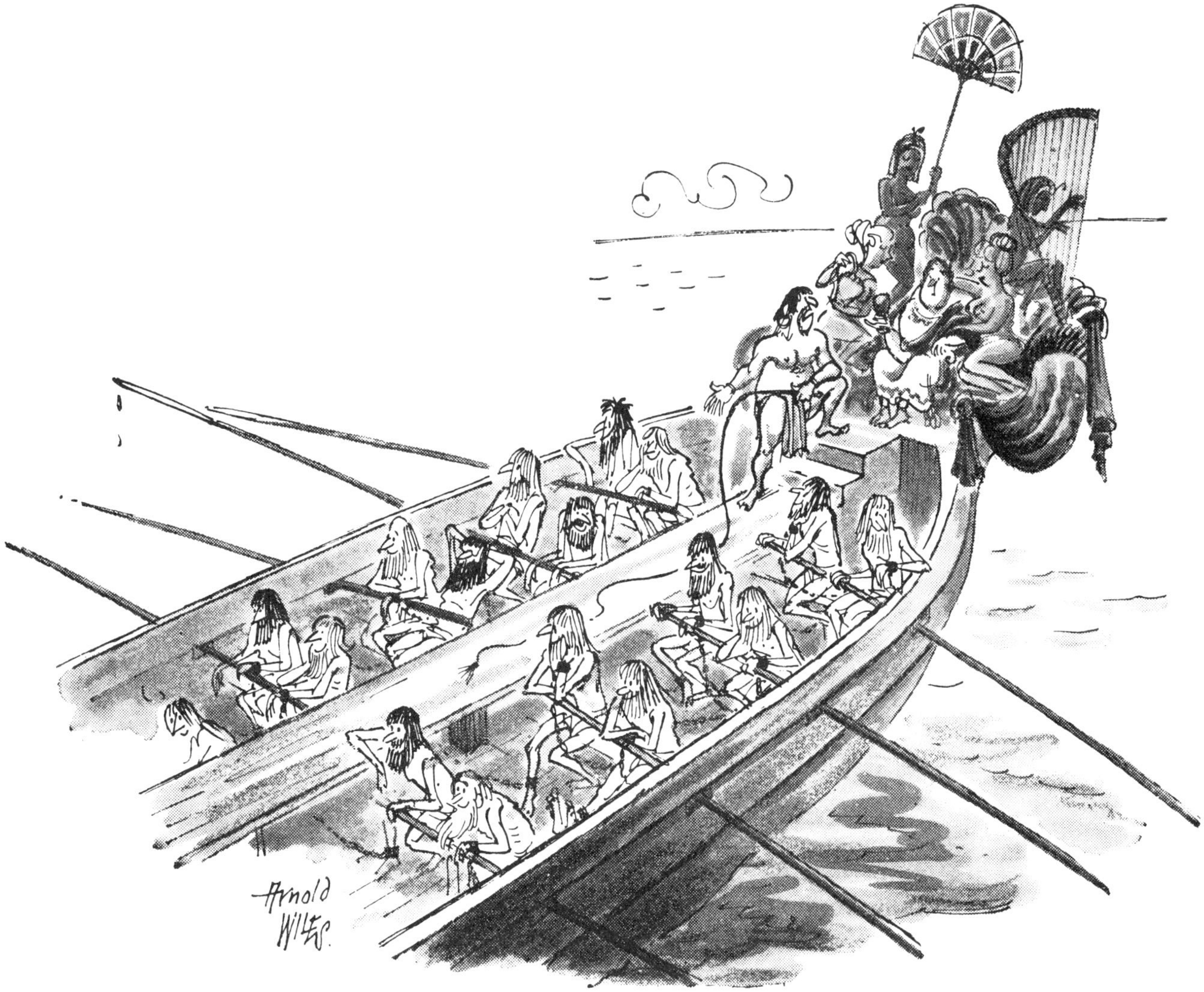
Arnold WILES.

"How can you expect to get anywhere with a boatload of sado-masochist flagellants?"

HECTOR BREEZE

Hector Breeze was born in London in 1928. He studied at a technical college and became a draftsman with the Civil Service, attending art classes at evening school. He sold his first cartoon in 1957 and has since made his living as a free lance.

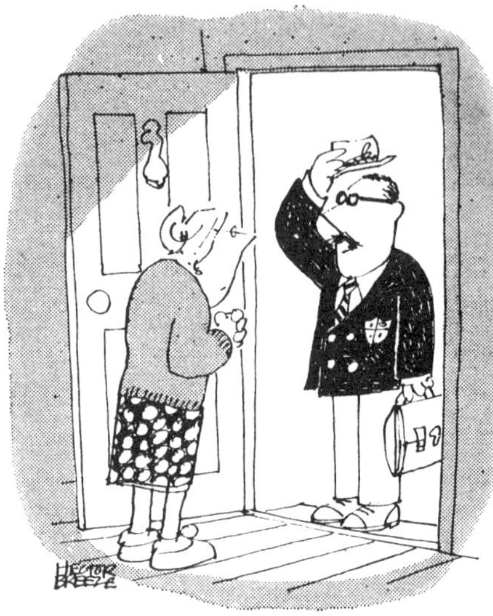

"Good afternoon. I'm a confidence trickster and I've come to swindle you out of your life savings . . ."

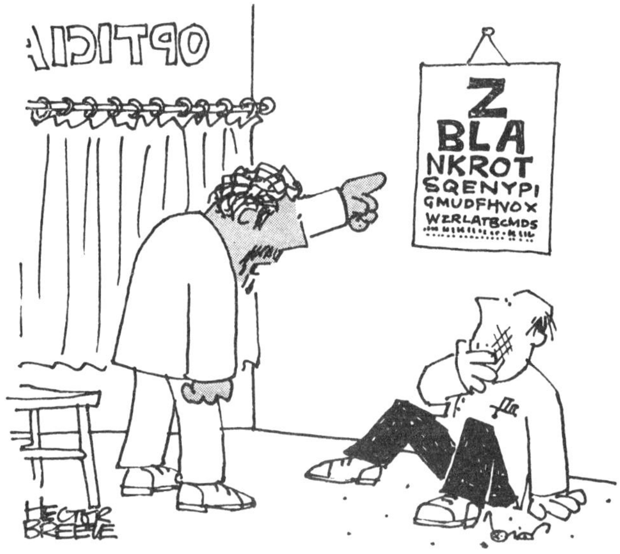
Z
BLA
NKROT
SQENYPI

"Don't try to kid me you can't speak Golubrian!"

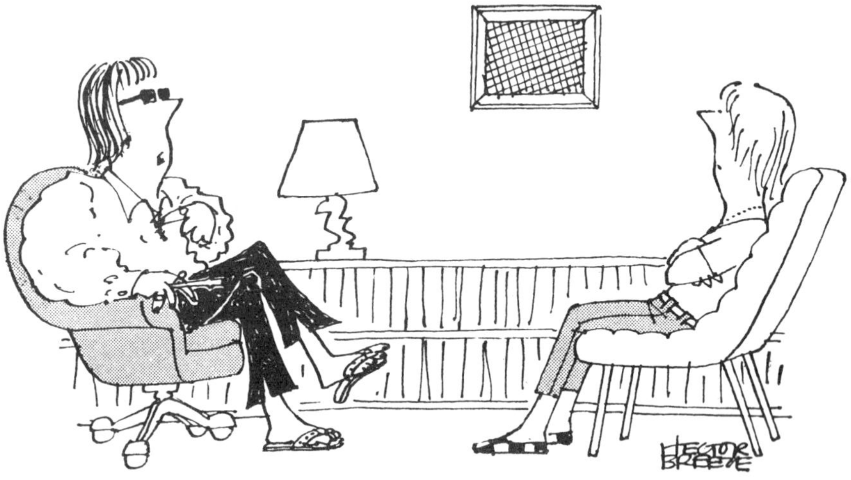

"I keep forgetting—is it you that's Hilary and me that's Evelyn?"

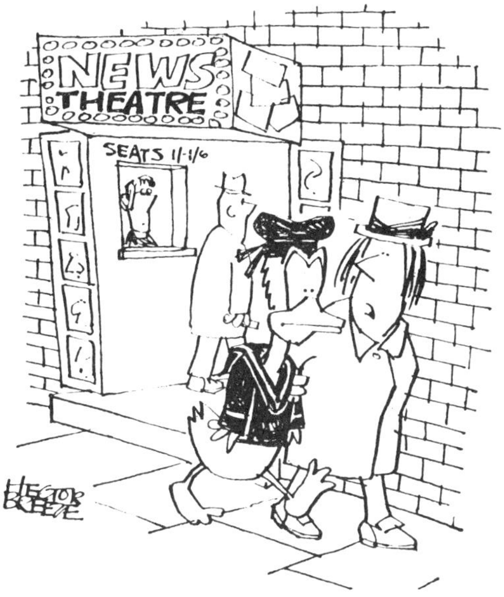
NEWS
THEATRE
SEATS 1/-1/6
HECTOR BREEZE

"Do you always have to identify yourself with the hero, Arthur?"

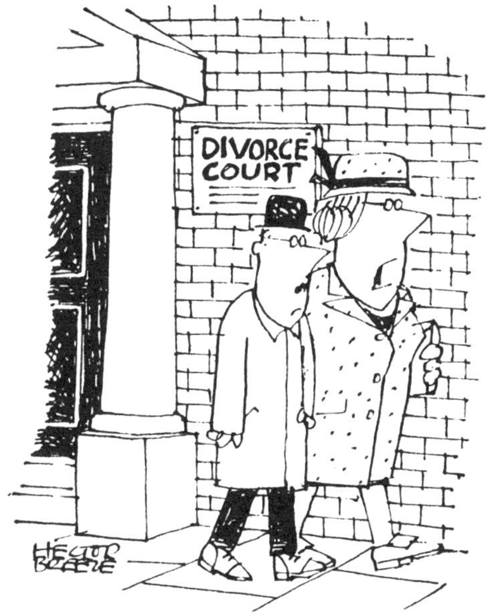
DIVORCE COURT
HECTOR BREEZE

"Then you just sat there and let him talk us into a reconciliation!"

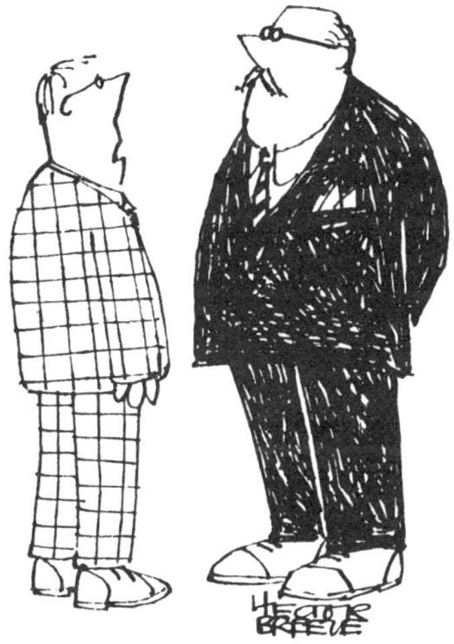
HECTOR BREEZE

"You're a kind of father-figure to me, Dad."

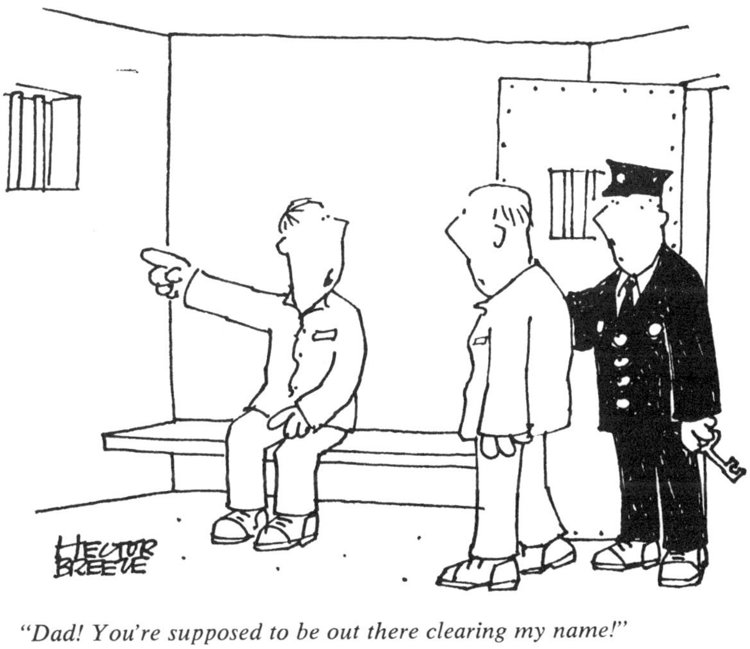
HECTOR BREEZE

"Dad! You're supposed to be out there clearing my name!"

McKEE

David McKee was born in 1935 in South Devon. He attended Plymouth College of Art and Hornsey Art College, and his main work has been illustrating children's picture books. He lives in Putney with his wife and three children.

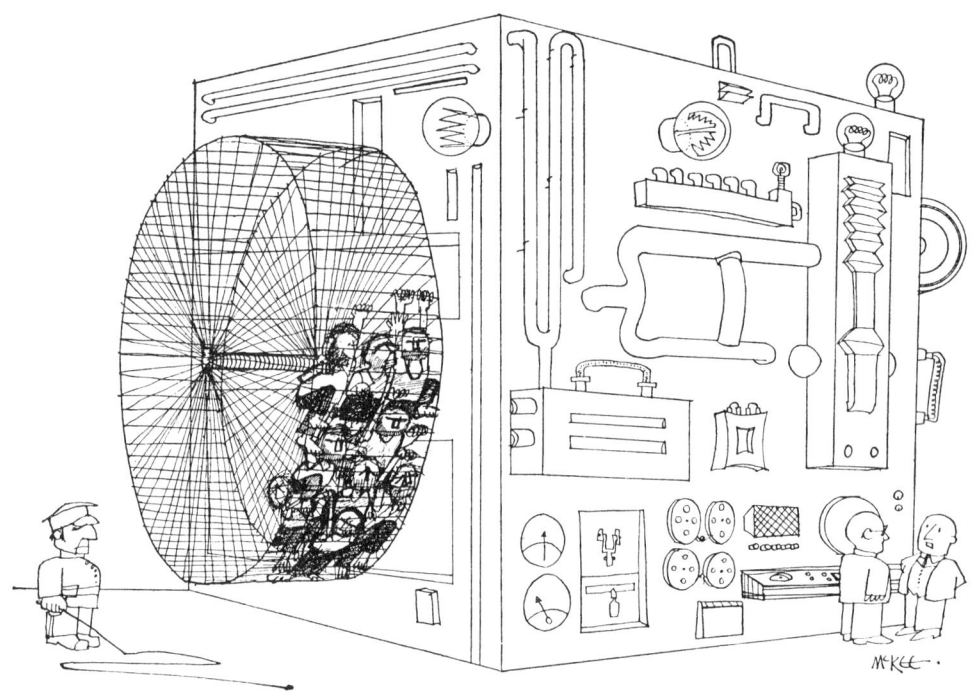

"What happened to the men it replaced?"

"I wondered what would follow the craze for uniforms."

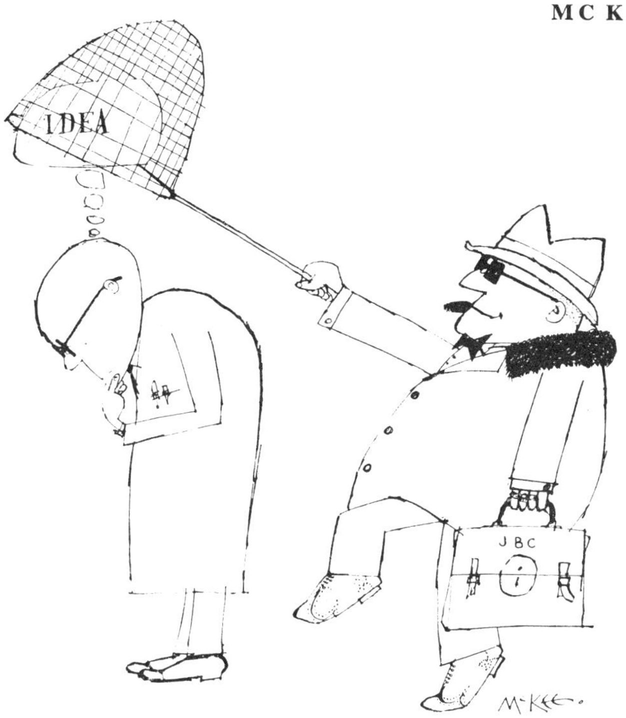
IDEA
J B C
McKee

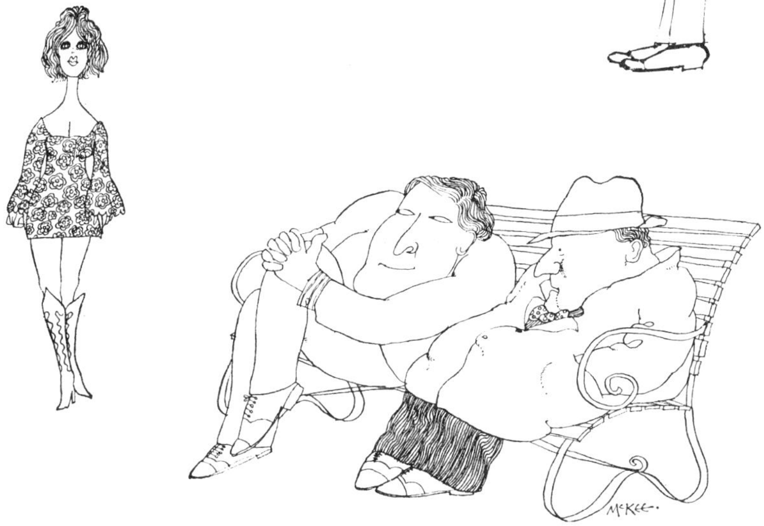
McKee

"It's the ankles I miss."

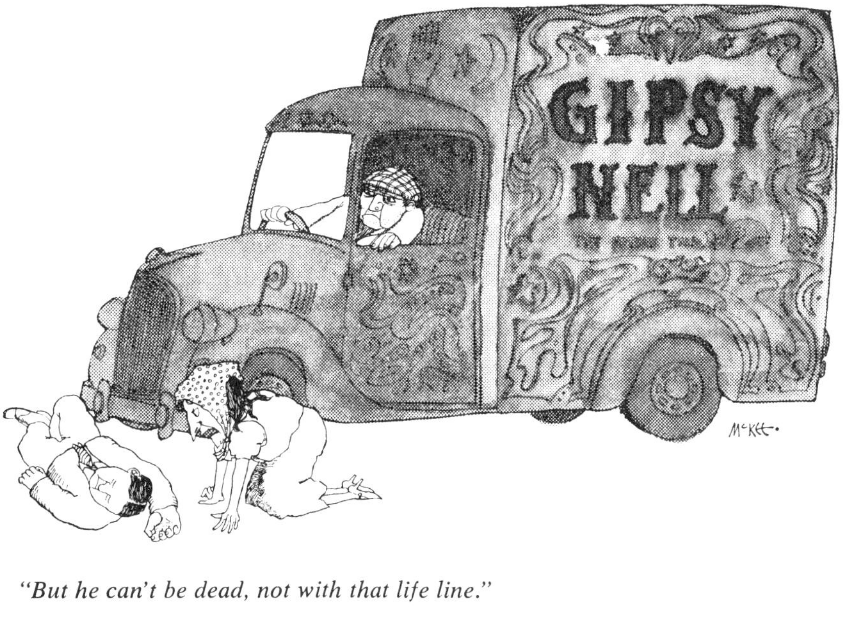
GIPSY
NELL
McKee

"But he can't be dead, not with that life line."

MAHOOD

Kenneth Mahood was born in Belfast, Northern Ireland, in 1930. He worked as an apprentice lithographer from 1945 to 1949 and was the assistant art editor of *Punch* from 1960 to 1965. He is married and lives in Surrey.

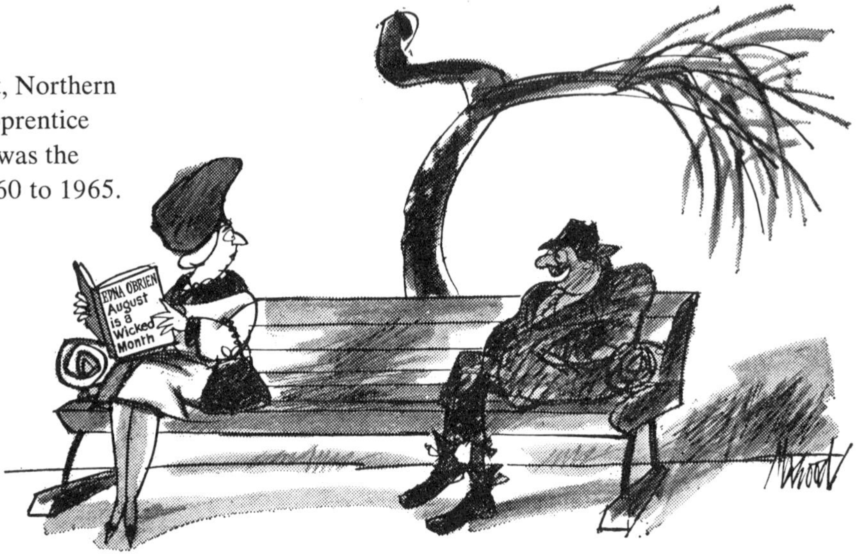
EDNA OBRIEN
August is a Wicked Month

"I'm a very good listener if you'd care to read aloud."

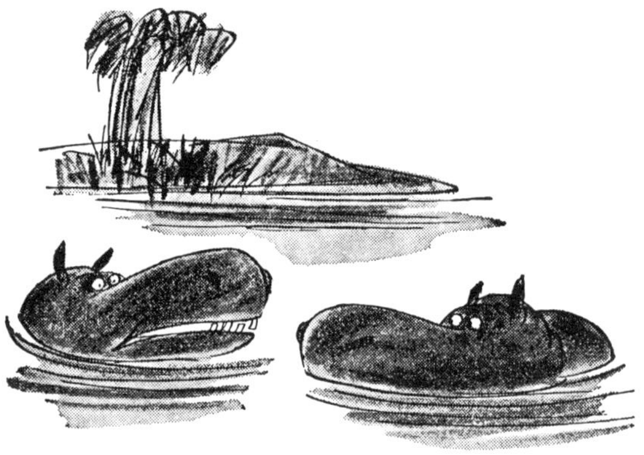

"I think I've developed a slow puncture."

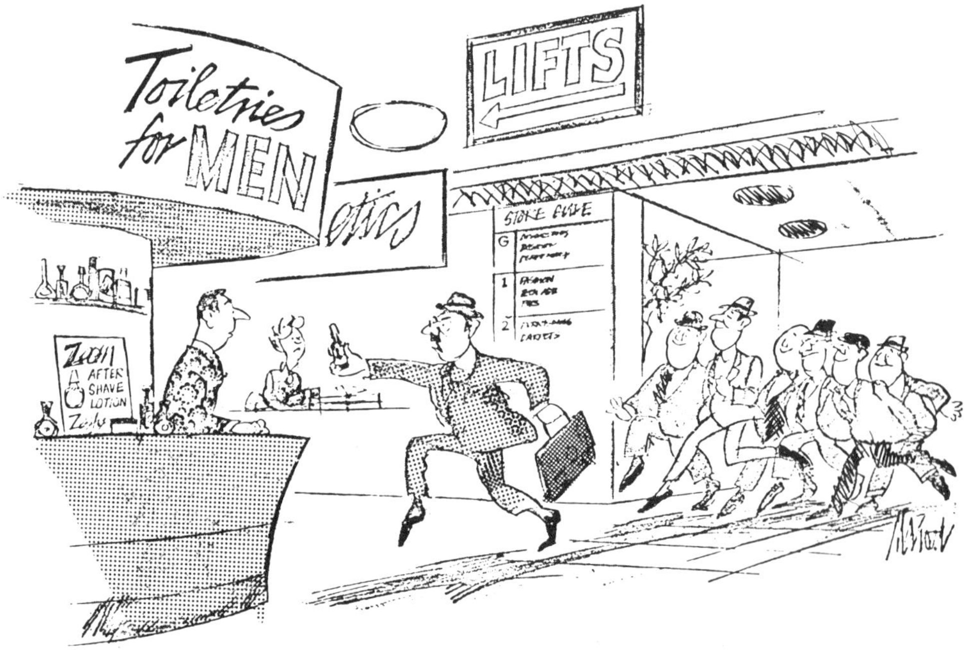
Toiletries for MEN
LIFTS
AFTER SHAVE LOTION

"I want to make a complaint."

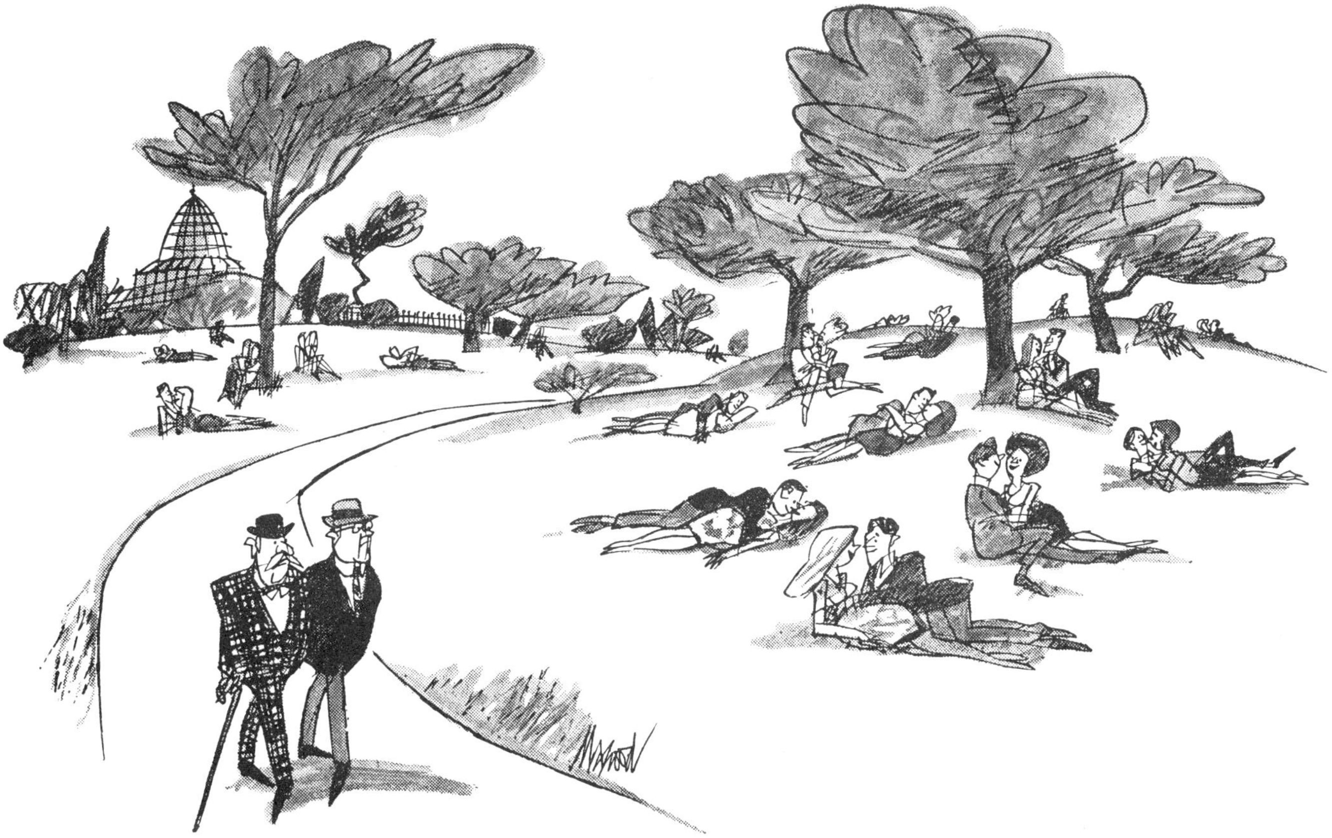

"I never cease to be amazed at the conformity of the young."

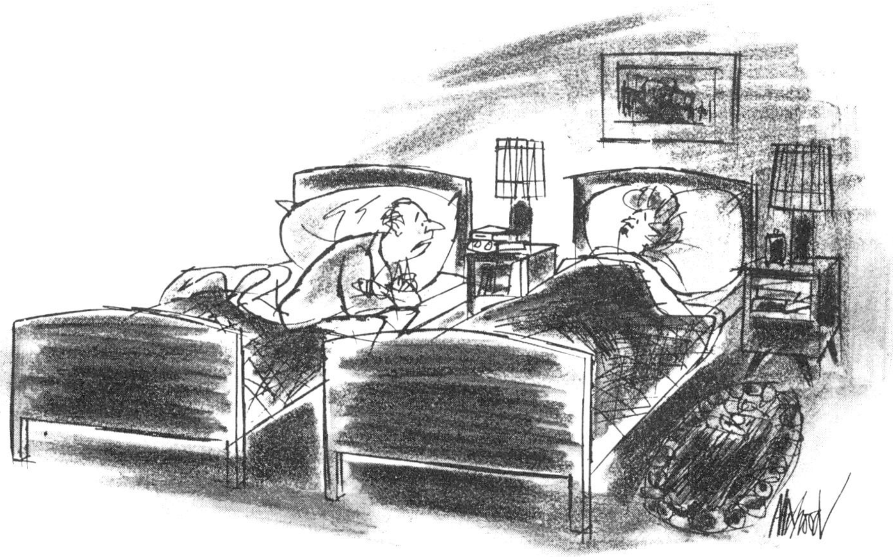

"It's not that I have a suspicious mind, Lilian, but I can't help wondering why you haven't asked me to give up smoking."

RAYMONDE

Roy Raymonde was born in Lincolnshire in 1929. He had a scholarship to the National School of Art and served two years in the army in Malaya. He has been a free-lance cartoonist and illustrator for the past ten years and has a regular feature in the *Sunday Telegraph.*

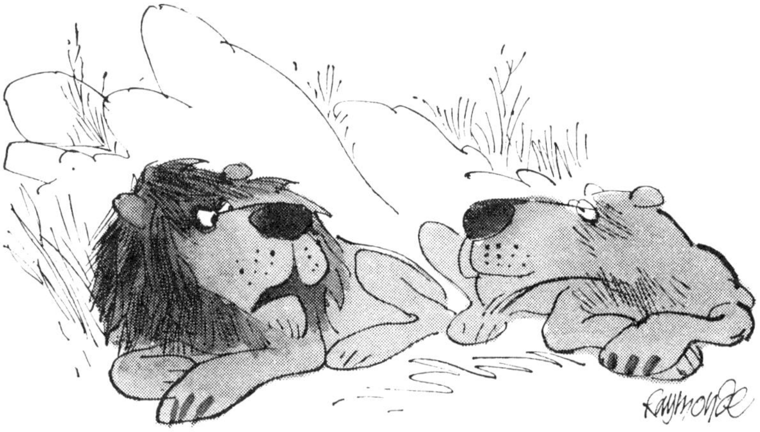

"I wasn't growling—I was humming."

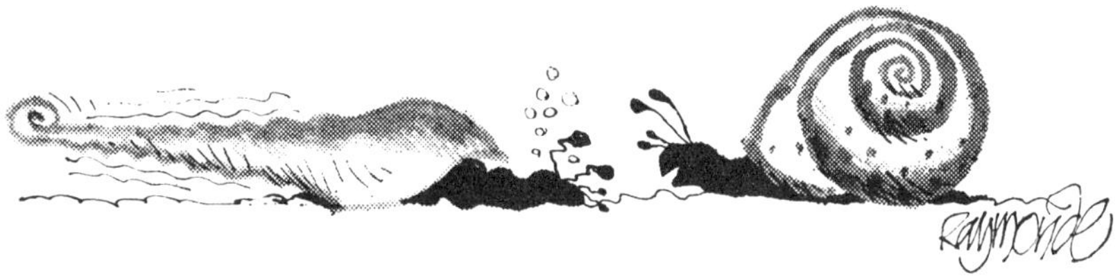

"Bless you!"

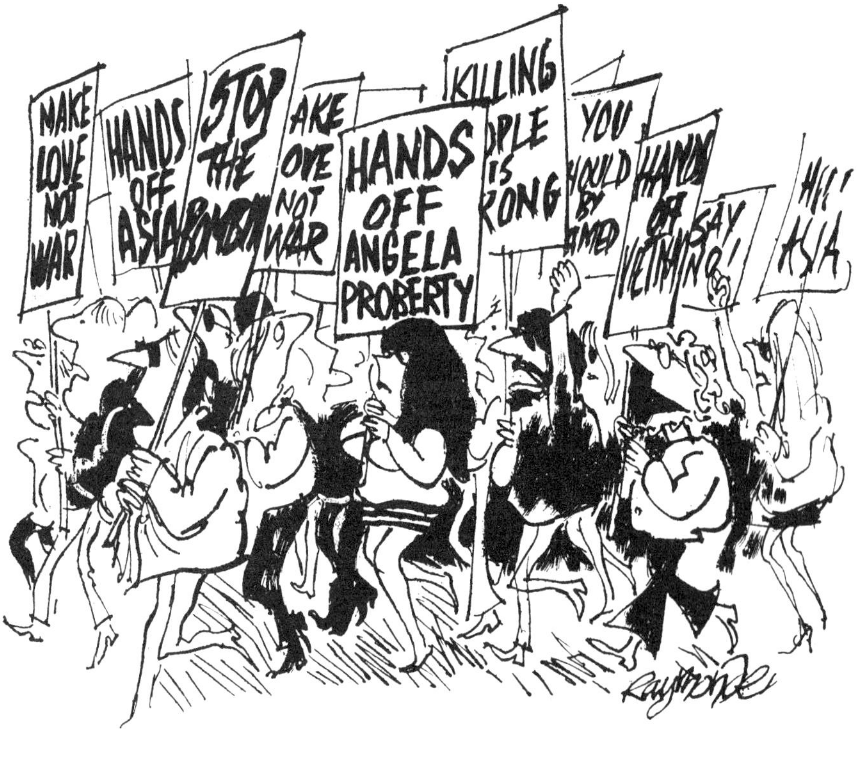
MAKE LOVE NOT WAR
HANDS OFF ANGELA PROBERTY

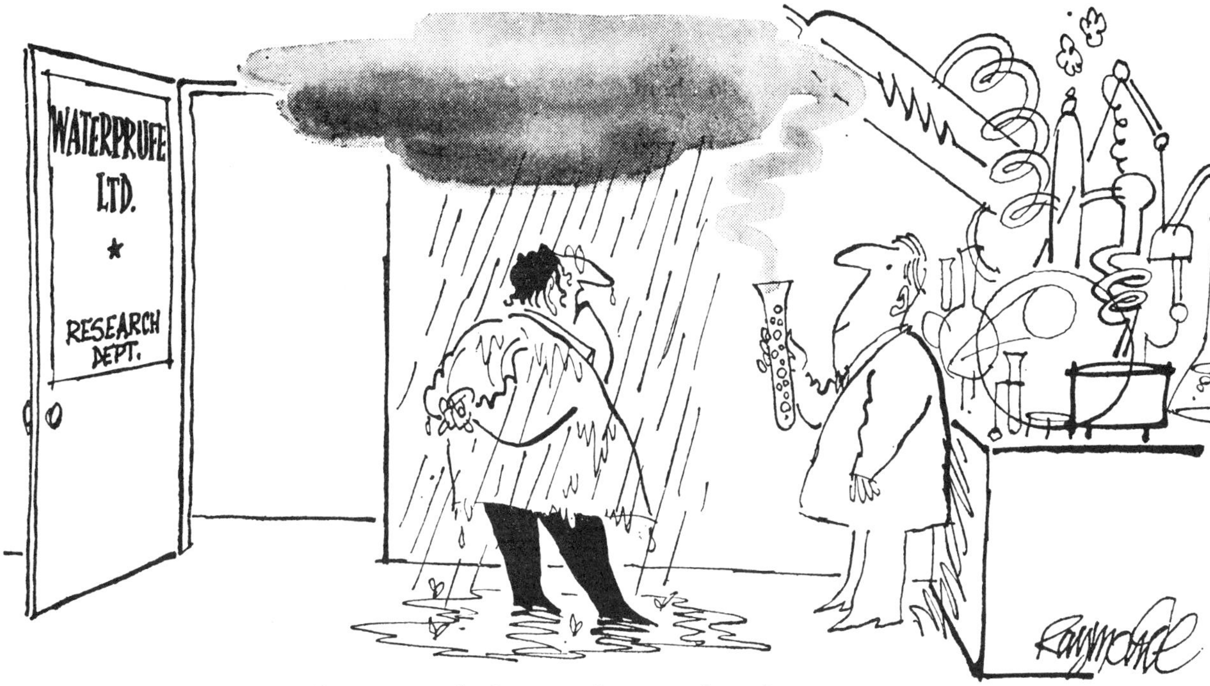
WATERPRUFE LTD.
★
RESEARCH DEPT.

"Simpson—I think you ought to run through your calculations again."

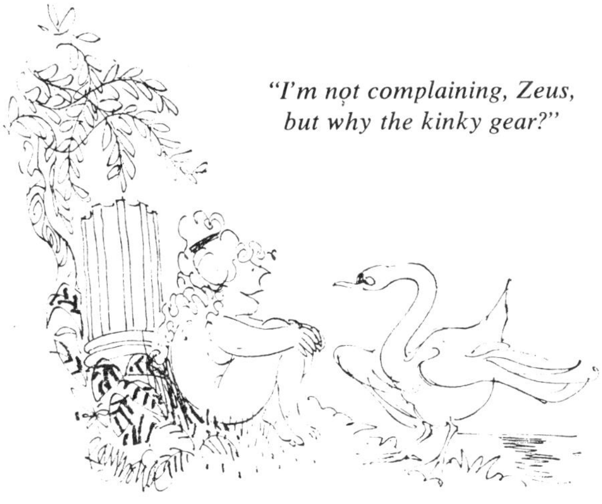

"I'm not complaining, Zeus, but why the kinky gear?"

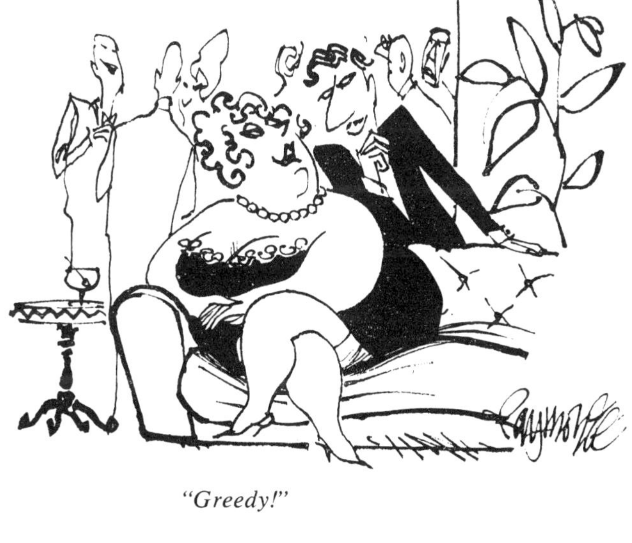

"Greedy!"

W. SCULLY

W. Scully was born in Derbyshire, briefly attended the Nottingham School of Art, and became a free-lance cartoonist in the mid 1930s. He is married and lives in Derbyshire.

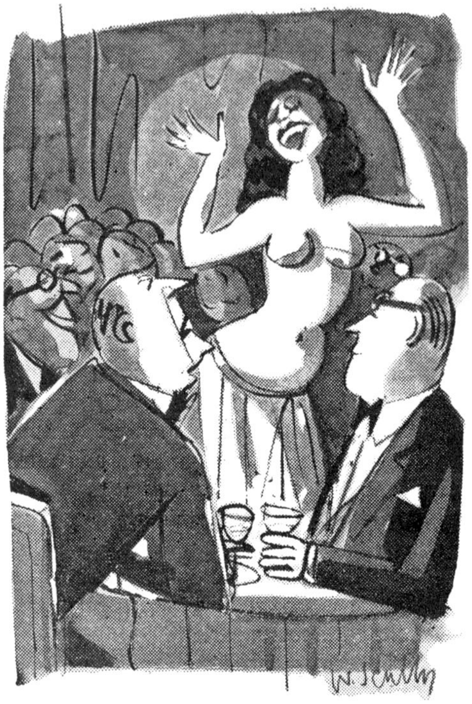

"That reminds me. Where's that dammed waiter got to with the food?"

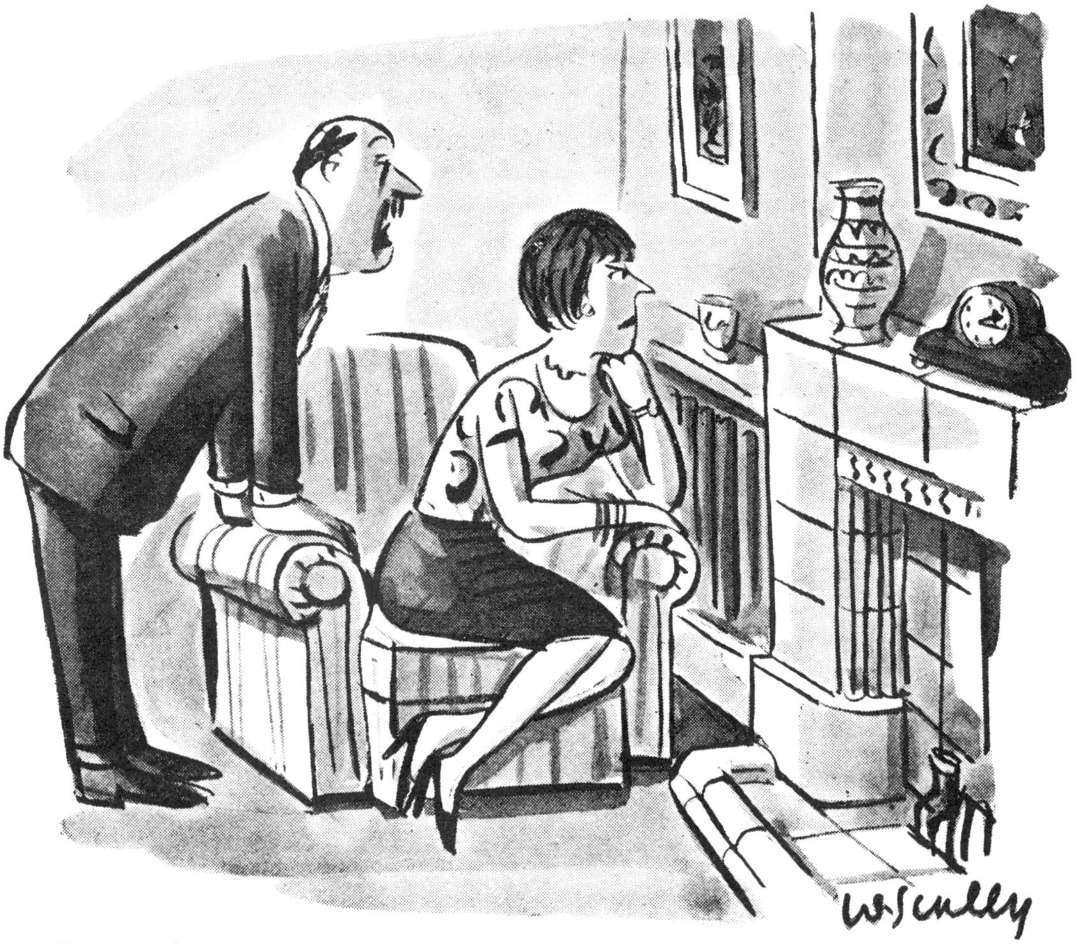
W. Scully

"Is it something I've done? Is it something I've not done? Is it something I've said? Is it something I haven't said, or is it the way I didn't say it?"

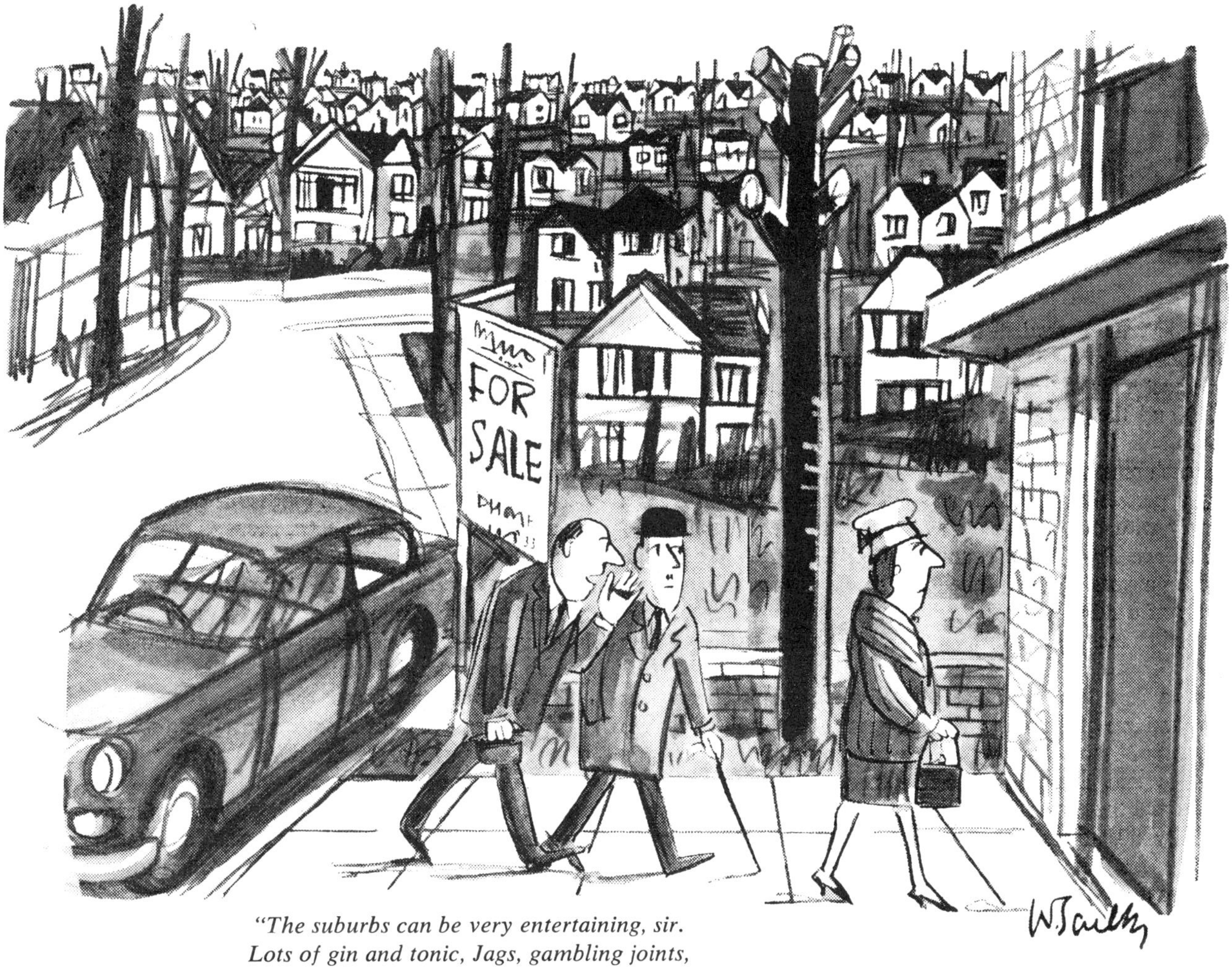
FOR
SALE
W. Scully

"The suburbs can be very entertaining, sir. Lots of gin and tonic, Jags, gambling joints, striptease clubs, and wife-swopping."

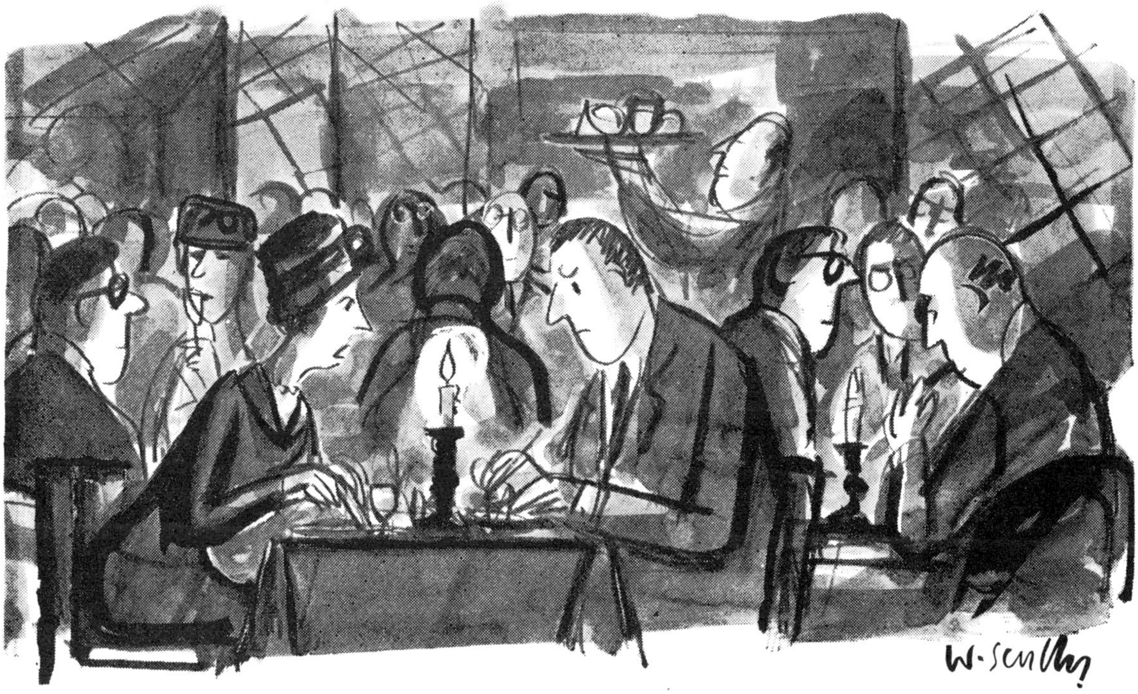
W. Scully

"It doesn't taste too bad—I wonder what it looks like."

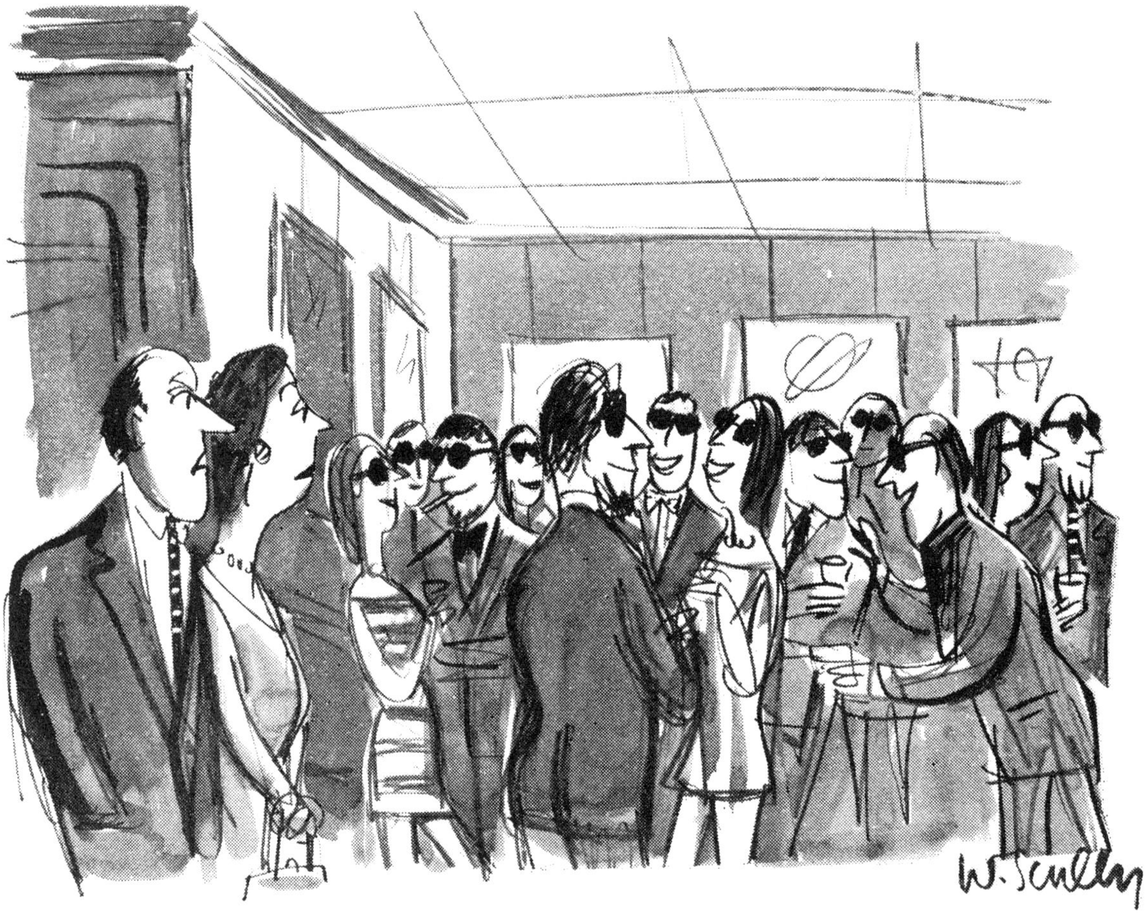
W. Scully

"I didn't notice anything on the invitation about dark glasses."

"Well, what a coincidence! I was just going to tell you you'll have to."

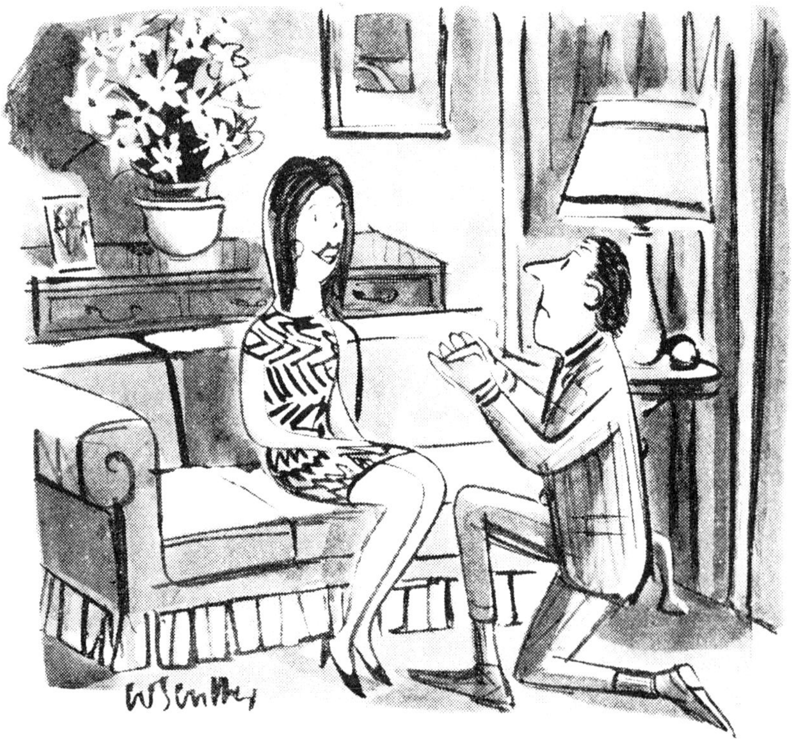
W. Scully

HEATH

Michael Heath was born in London in 1935. He trained at the Brighton College of Art and has worked with Rank Screen Services doing story boards for cartoon commercials. He is married and lives in Sussex.

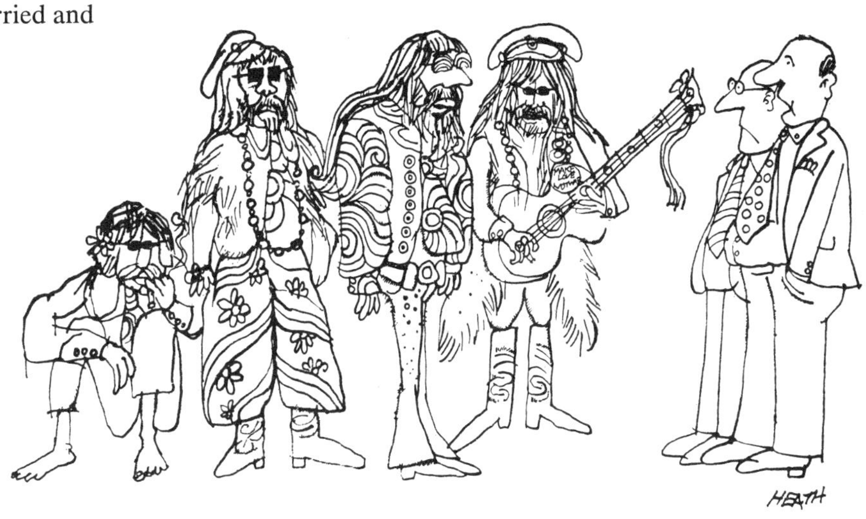
HEATH

"I've got a son in there somewhere."

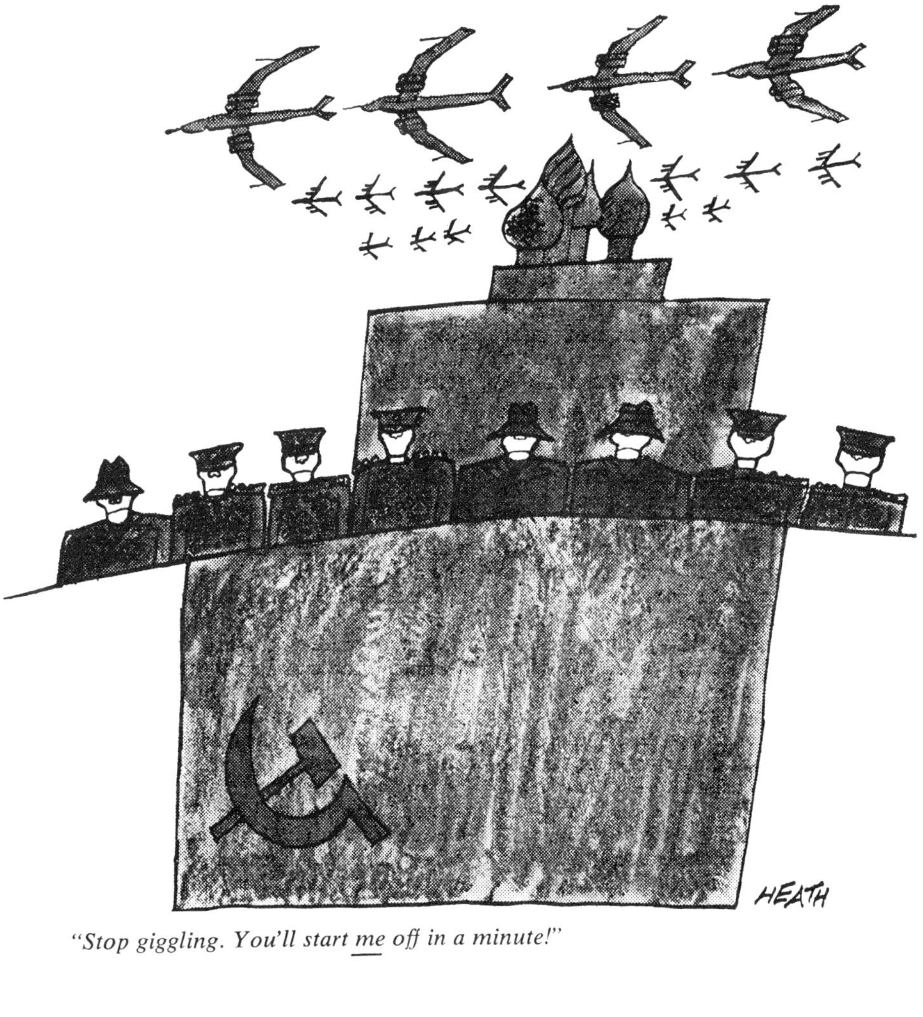
HEATH

"Stop giggling. You'll start me off in a minute!"

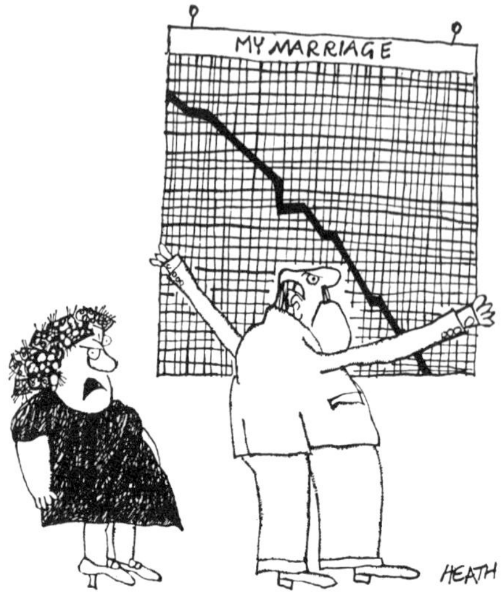
MY MARRIAGE
HEATH

"Must you put that up in the bedroom!"

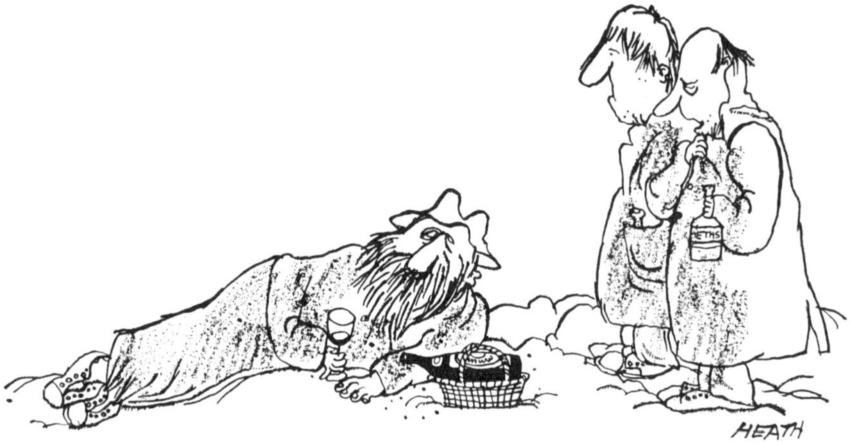
HEATH

"He may be a drunk, but he's still got class."

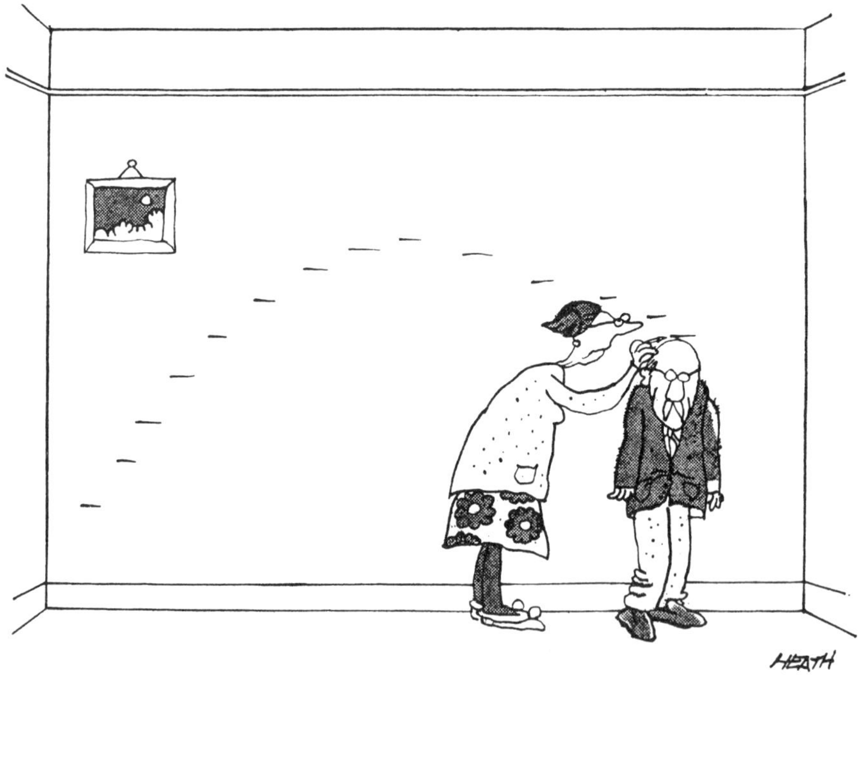
HEATH

Chaises Langues

"All you youngsters think about nowadays is your figures."

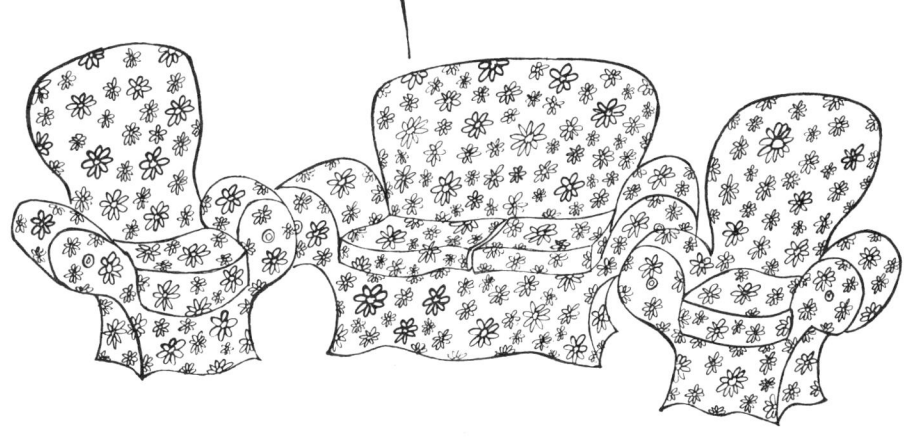

"As a family we must always stick together."

"I'm C. of E. actually."

"What I like about you is that you are so uncomplicated."

"The place is full of foreigners!"

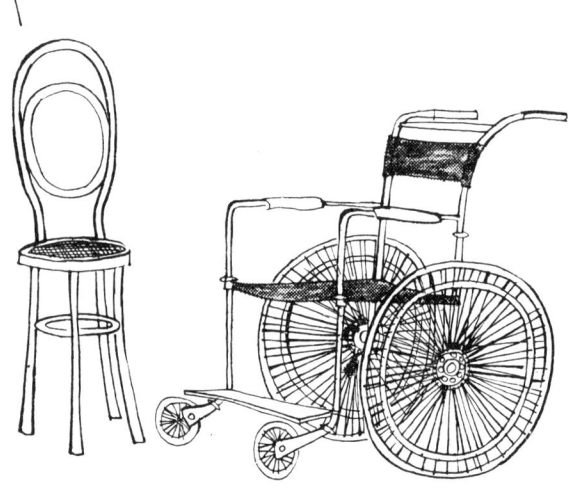

"It's all right for you— you've seen life."

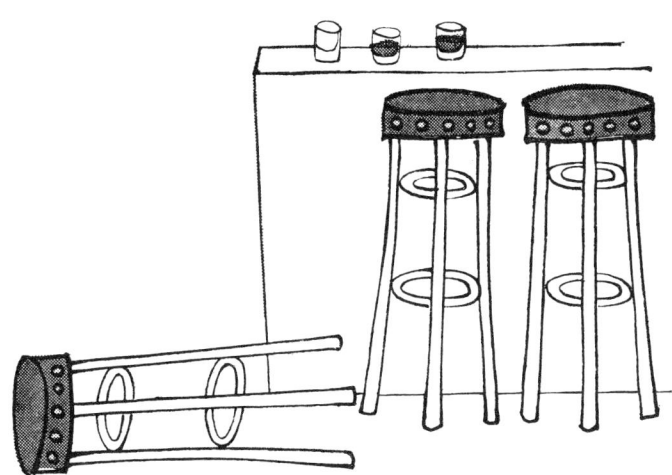

"Some of us can take it, some of us can't."

"I'm sorry, I'm not very good at conversation."

"She's making a very successful comeback."

SMILBY

Smilby is Francis Smith, born in Rugby in 1927. He attended Camberwell Art School. He lives in Sussex with his wife and two children.

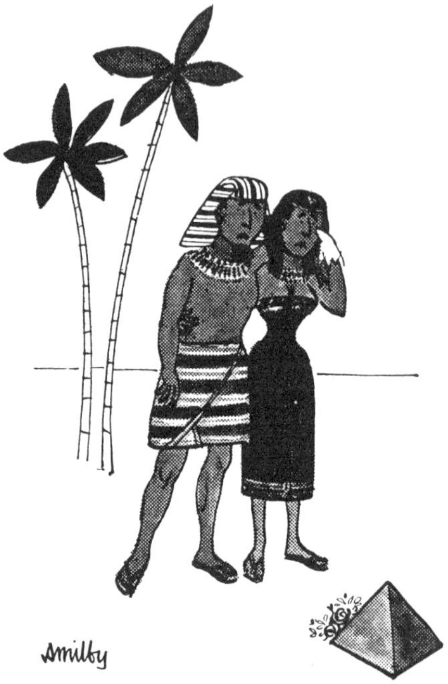
Smilby

"He was a fine dog."

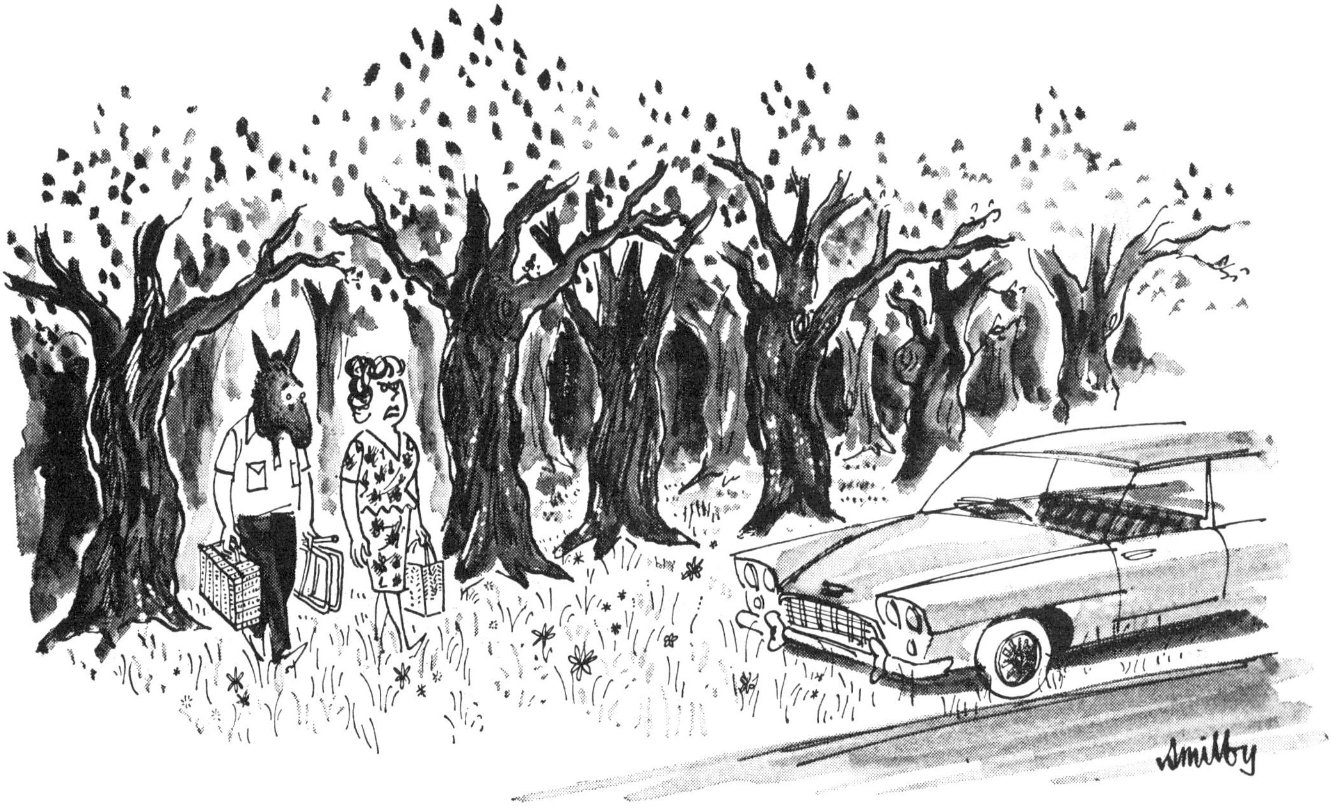
Smilby

"Next time, I'll choose the place we picnic."

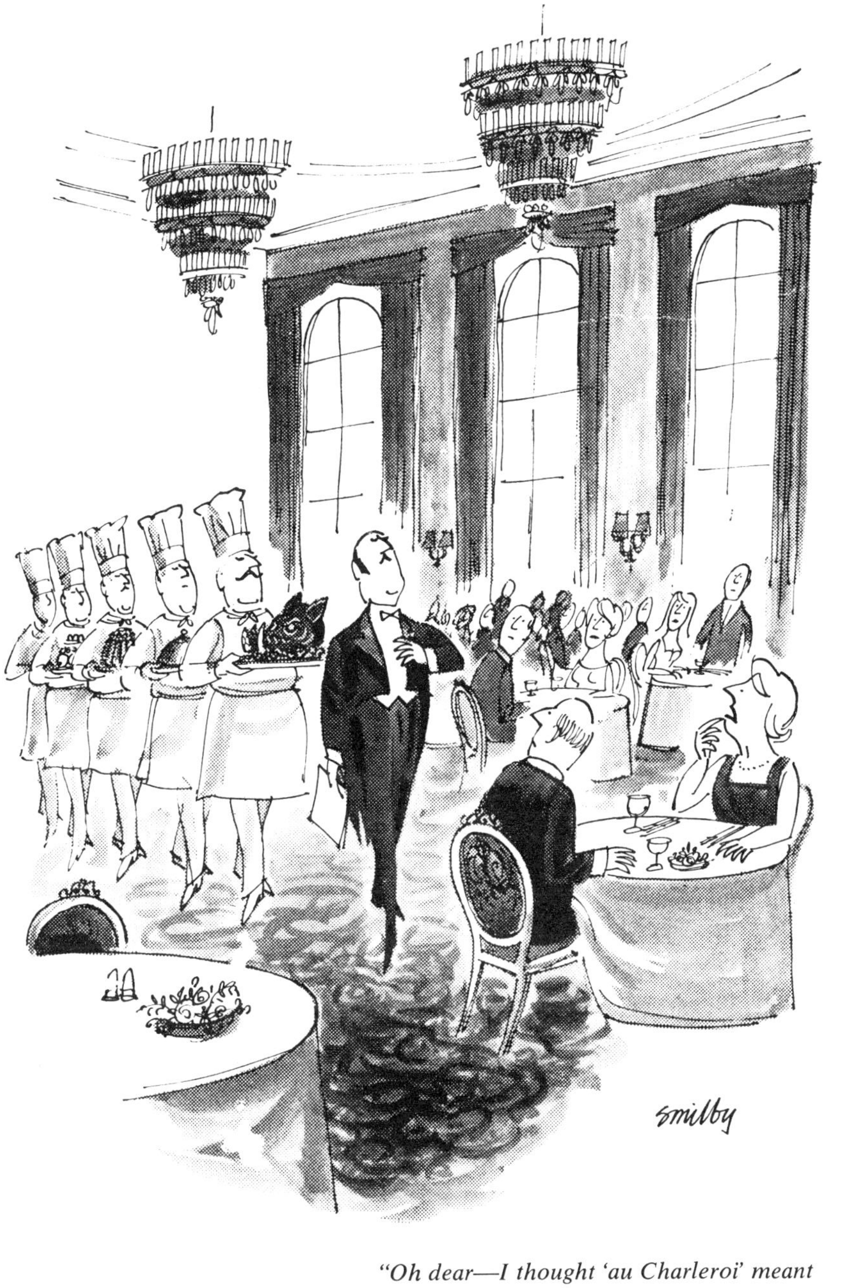
smilby

"Oh dear—I thought 'au Charleroi' meant garnished with carrots."

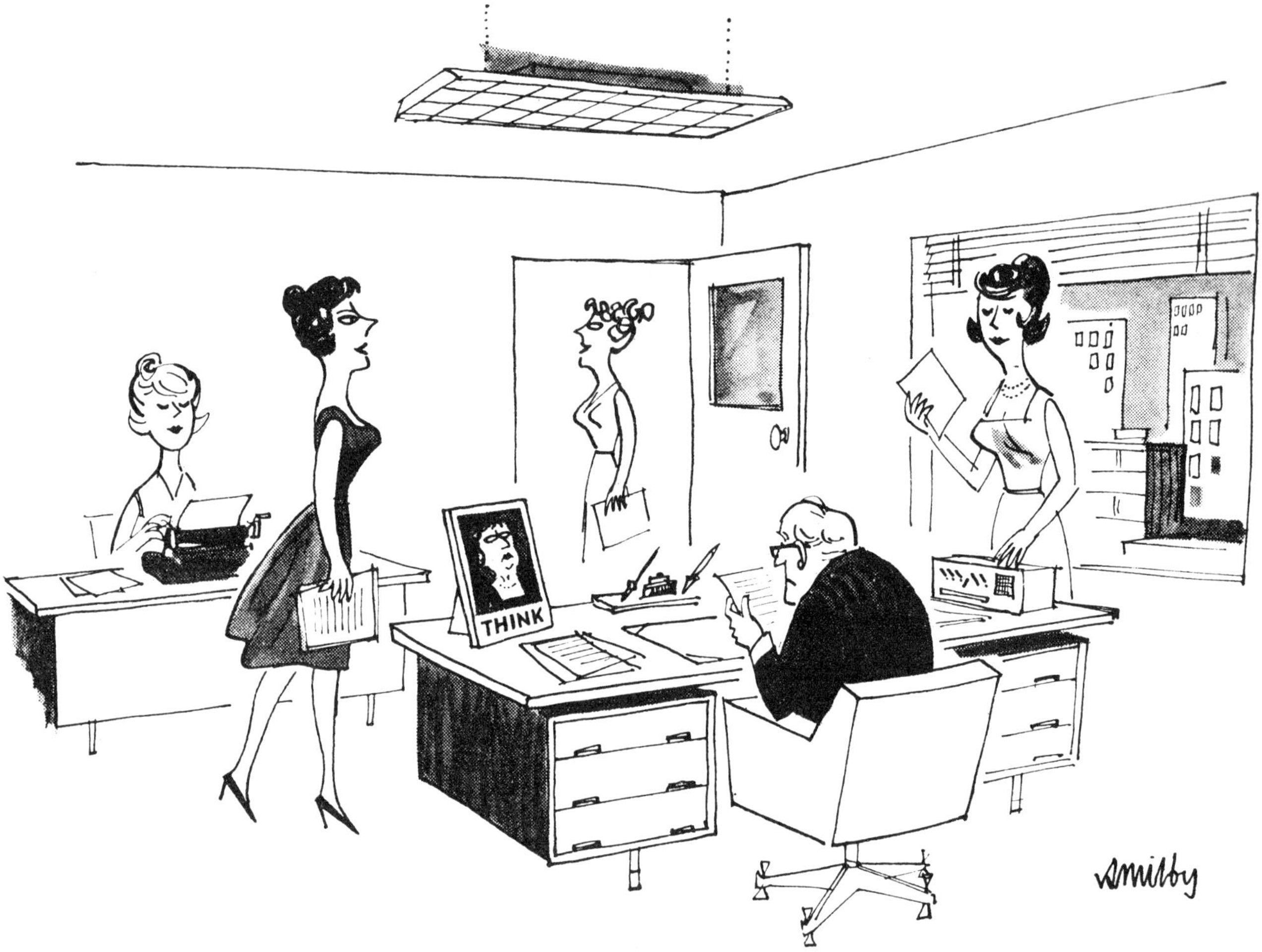
THINK
smilby

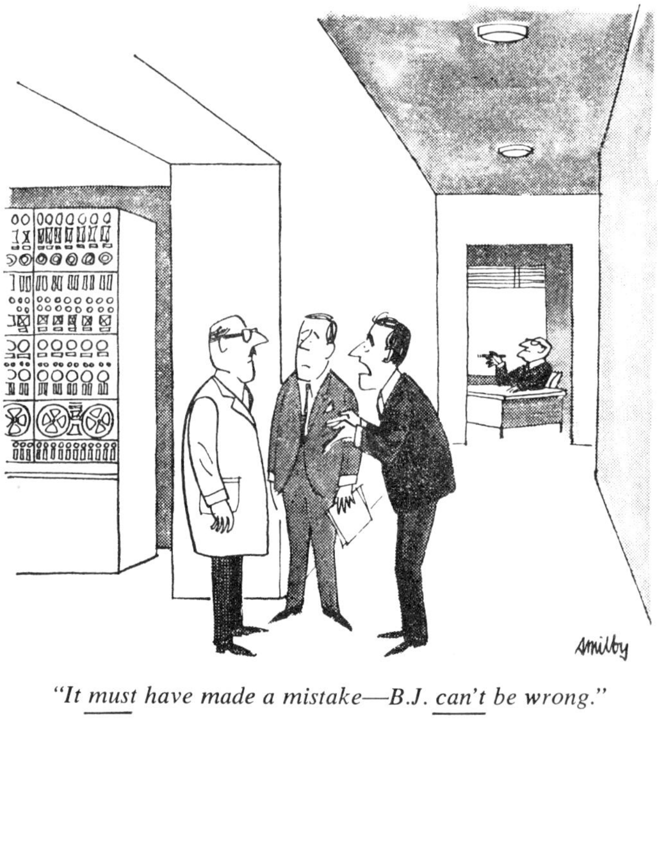
smilby

"It must have made a mistake—B.J. can't be wrong."

ANTON

Anton is the pen name of Antonia Yeoman, born in Melbourne, Australia, in 1913. She has been a leading *Punch* cartoonist for thirty years and lives with her husband in Dulwich Village.

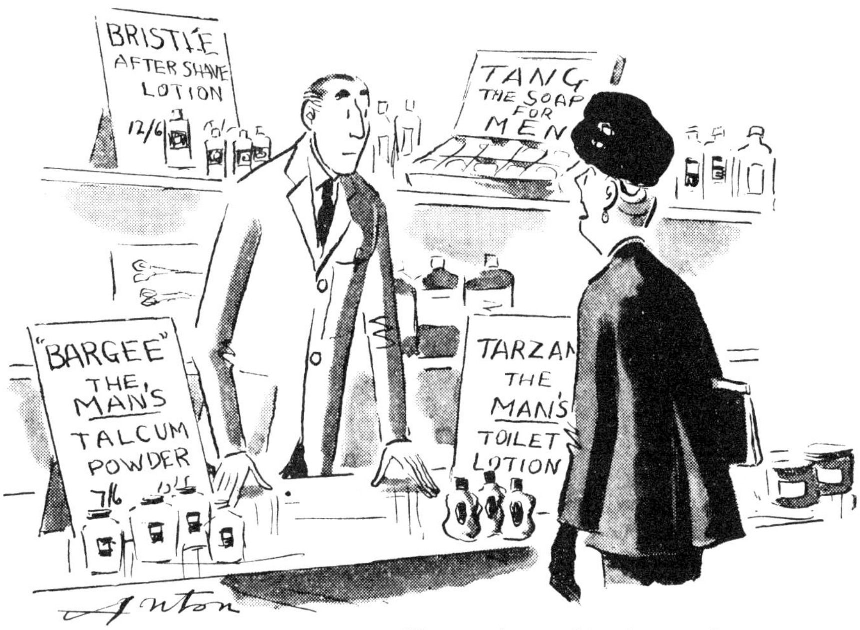
BRISTLE AFTER SHAVE LOTION
12/6
TANG THE SOAP FOR MEN
"BARGEE" THE MAN'S TALCUM POWDER
7/6
TARZAN THE MAN'S TOILET LOTION
Anton

"I wanted something for a rather more feminine type of man."

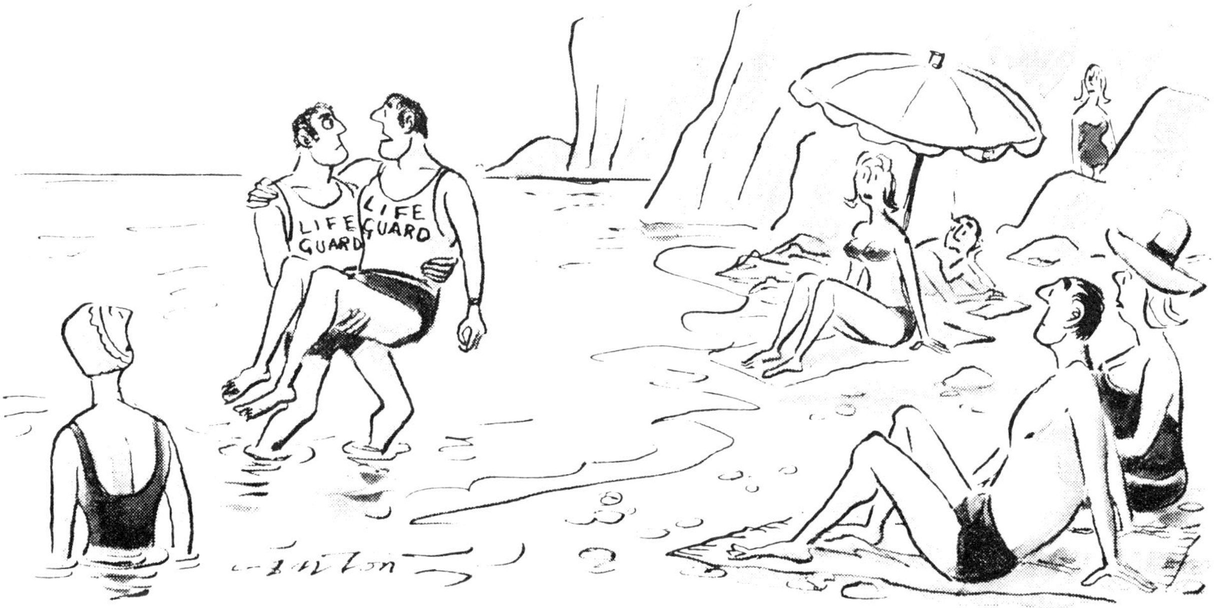
LIFE GUARD
LIFE GUARD
Anton

"You and I know I've just cut my foot, but do they?"

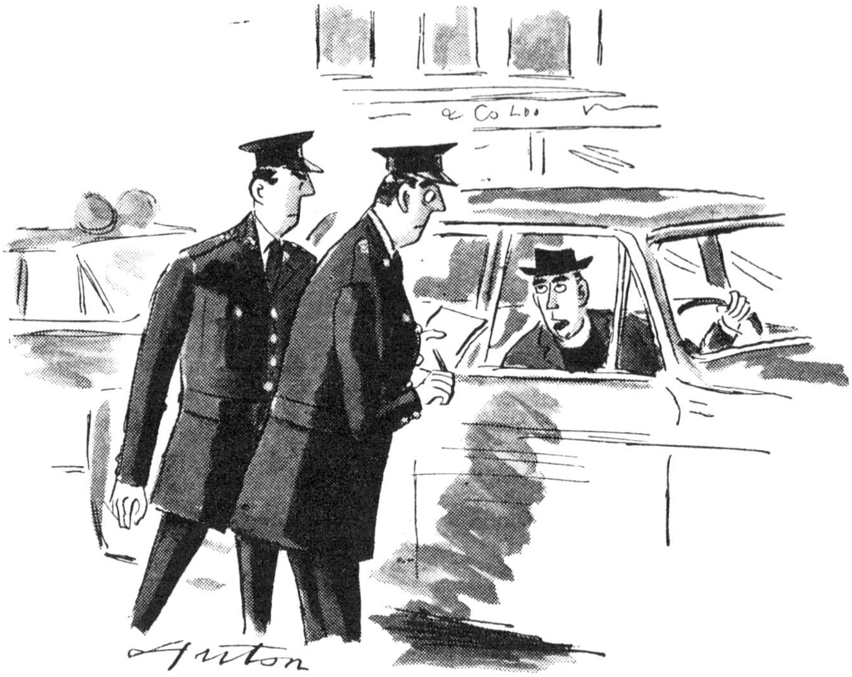

"It is only your word against ours."

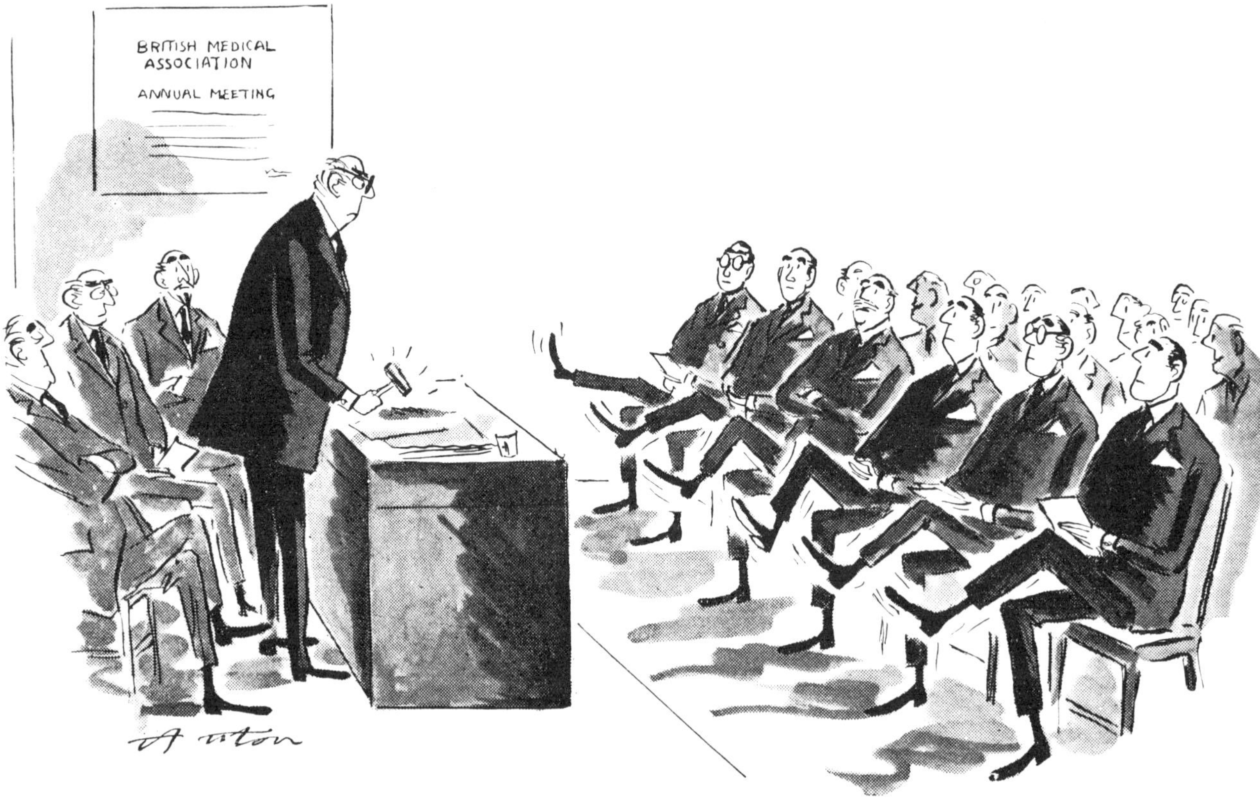
BRITISH MEDICAL ASSOCIATION
ANNUAL MEETING

S. McMURTRY

Stan McMurtry was born in 1936. He attended Birmingham College of Art and for nine years produced cartoon commercials. He is the daily topical cartoonist for the *Daily Sketch* and lives in Berkshire.

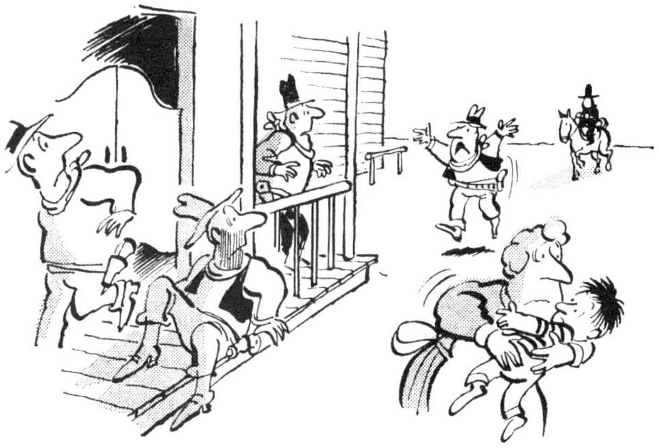

"Keep clear folks! Jed Dilligan's just hit town."

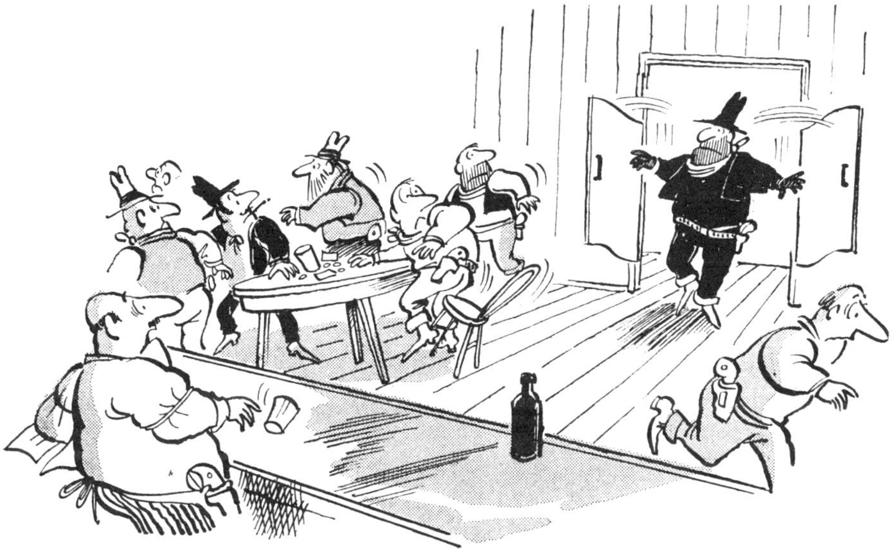

"Jed Dilligan! I thought you'd been run outa town . . .

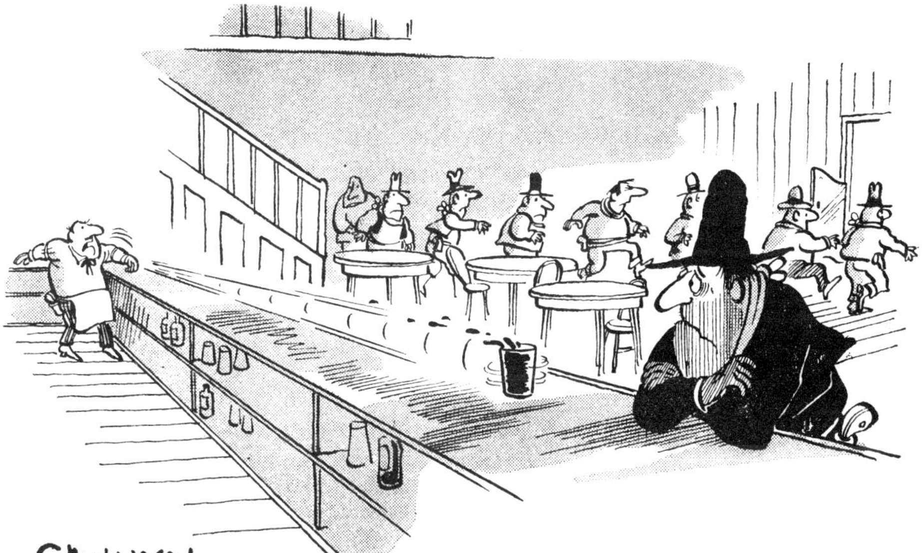
S.McMURTRY.

. . . Yuh lousy creep! When yuh goin' to do somethin' about personal freshness?"

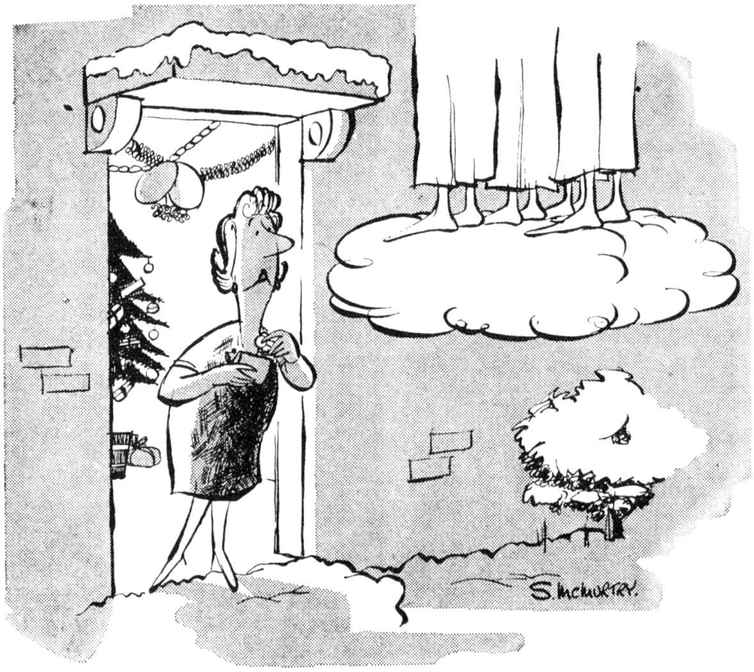
S. McMURTRY.

"Well, that was about the nicest rendering of 'Hark the Herald Angels Sing' I ever—"

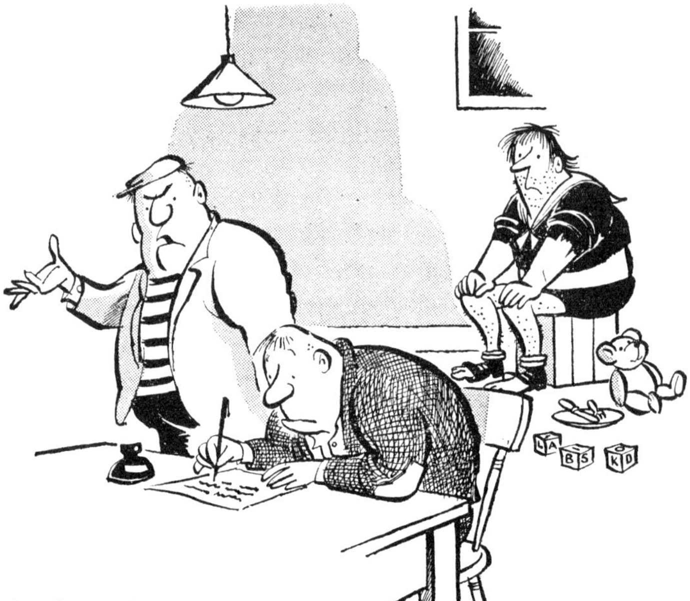
S. McMURTRY.

". . . and our patience is exhausted. If you don't pay the ransom this year . . ."

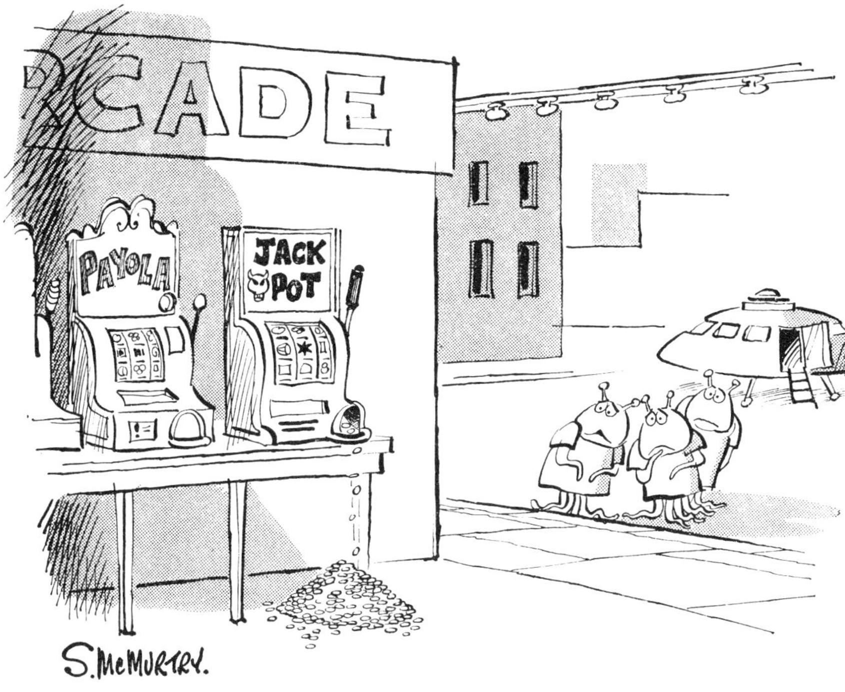
CADE
PAYOLA
JACK POT
S. McMURTRY.

"I just shook his hand and he was sick."

"Well, gentlemen . . . Shall we join the ladies?"

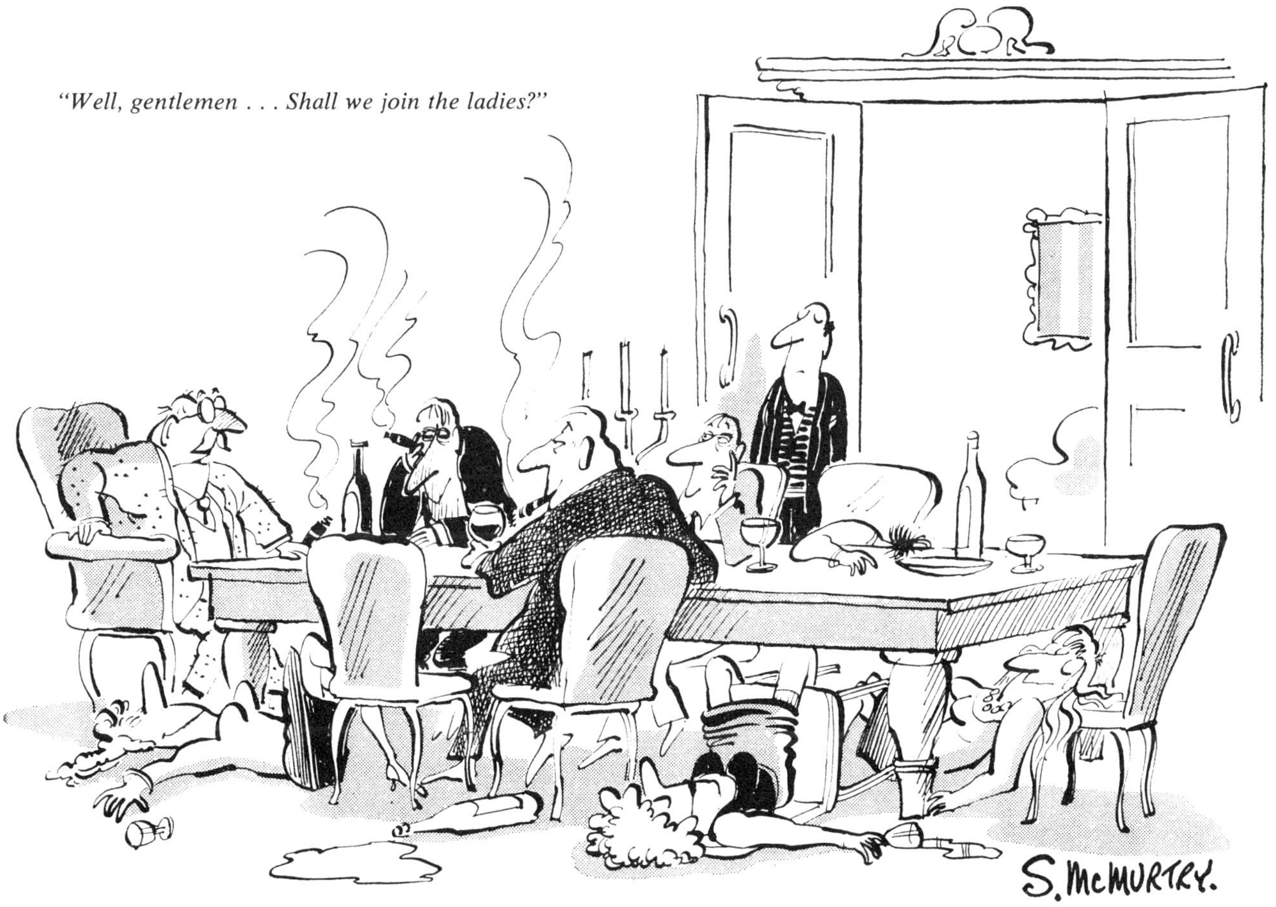
S. McMURTRY.

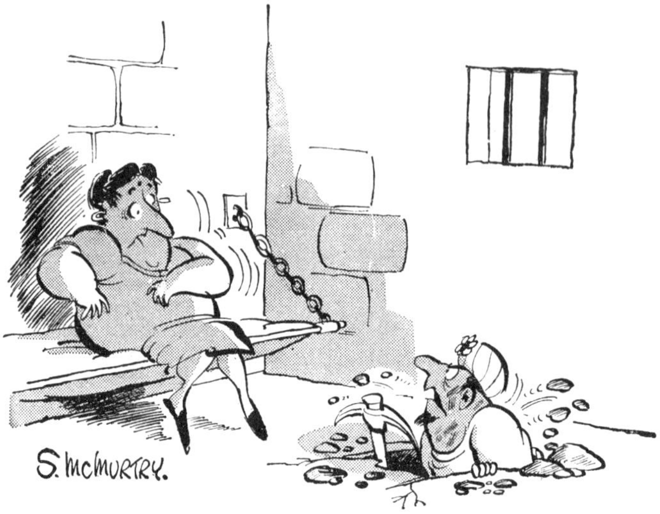
S. McMURTRY.

"I divorce thee . . . I divorce thee . . . I divorce thee."

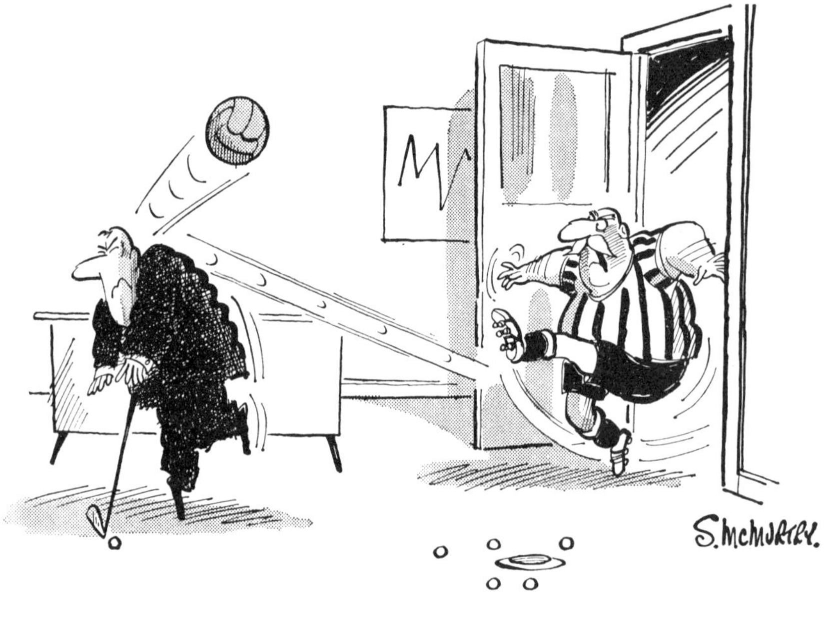
S. McMURTRY.

"Get on with your work, Gregston!"

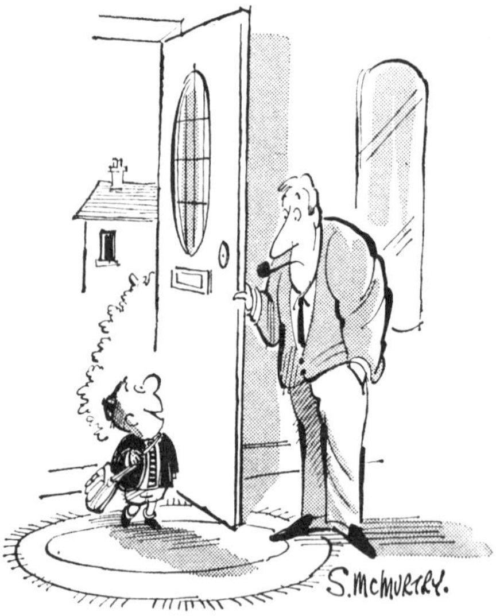
S. McMURTRY.

"We had Oscar Wilde today, sweetie."

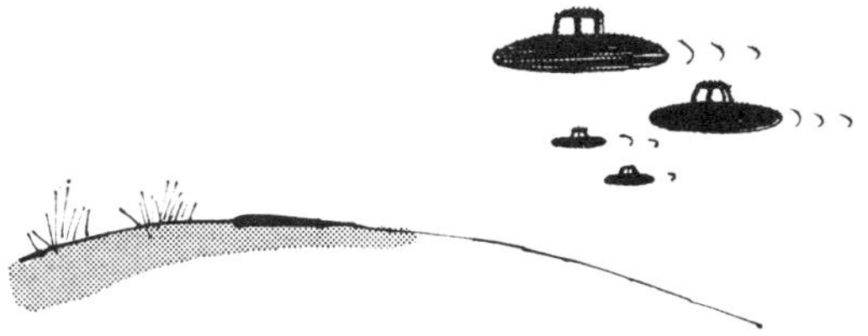

"Over there . . . desolate scrubland, an ideal spot for our first base . . .

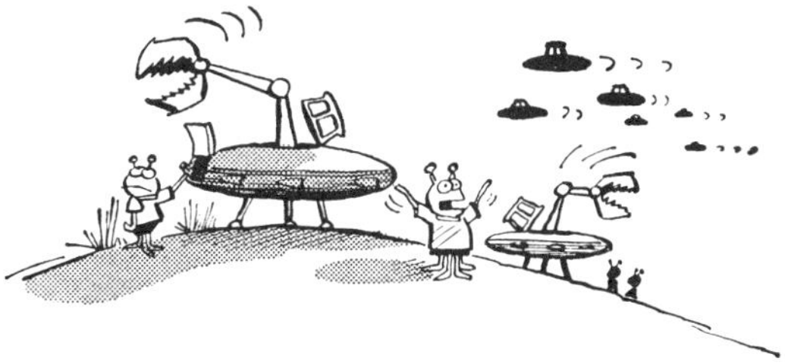

. . . I name this place 'Nubolaxy.' From here our great people will commence operations to take over the primitive earth creatures . . . start digging . . ."

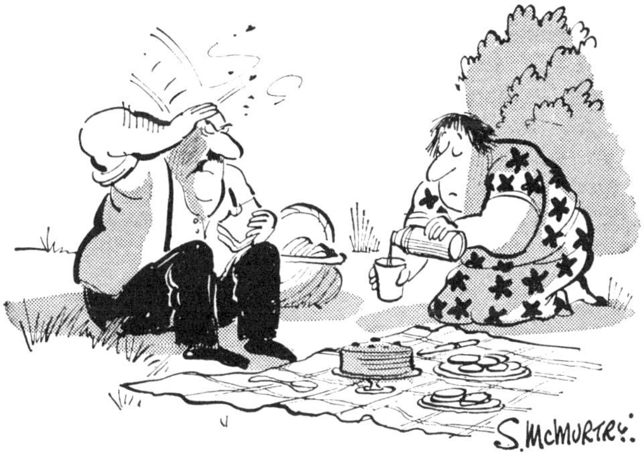
S. McMURTRY

"Damned midges!"